D0777184

LIGHT BLUE REIGN

ALSO BY ART CHANSKY

*The Dean's List: A Celebration of
Tar Heel Basketball and Dean Smith*

*Dean's Domain: The Inside Story of Dean
Smith and His College Basketball Empire*

*Blue Blood: Duke-Carolina: Inside the
Most Storied Rivalry in College Hoops*

LIGHT BLUE REIGN

How a City Slicker, a Quiet Kansan, and
a Mountain Man Built College Basketball's
Longest-Lasting Dynasty

ART CHANSKY

FOREWORD BY
DEAN SMITH

INTRODUCTION BY
RICK BREWER

Thomas Dunne Books
St. Martin's Press ≈ New York

THOMAS DUNNE BOOKS.
An imprint of St. Martin's Press.

LIGHT BLUE REIGN. Copyright © 2009 by Art Chansky. Foreword copyright ©
2009 by Dean Smith. Introduction copyright © 2009 by Rick Brewer. All rights
reserved. Printed in the United States of America. For information, address St.
Martin's Press, 175 Fifth Avenue, New York, N.Y. 10010.

www.thomasdunnebooks.com
www.stmartins.com

Library of Congress Cataloging-in-Publication Data

Chansky, Art.
    Light blue reign / Art Chansky. — 1st ed.
        p. cm.
    Includes bibliographical references and index.
    ISBN 978-0-312-38408-1
  1. University of North Carolina at Chapel Hill—Basketball—History.
  2. North Carolina Tar Heels (Basketball team)—History.   I. Title.
    GV885.43.U54C43 2009
    796.323'6309756565—dc22
                                                    2009020033

First Edition: November 2009

10 9 8 7 6 5 4 3 2 1

To All Those Who Have
Loved Carolina Basketball

CONTENTS

ACKNOWLEDGMENTS

Thank You!

FOREMOST, to my two primary editors. Alfred Hamilton, a great friend and long-time colleague, is a master wordsmith. Owen Davis, my *Daily Tar Heel* compatriot from the good old days, has edited Mitch Albom's books in Detroit and, thankfully, this one, too.

Dan Satter, who is too bright to call my protégé, fit in his editing around his new job and baby in Boston.

Thanks to Rick Brewer, UNC sports information director emeritus, who knows more about Carolina athletics than any three men, for the introduction that sets up this improbable story of sports supremacy.

My gratitude goes to the family and friends of Frank McGuire, who supplemented my own personal accounts and reportage with more stories and anecdotes about the great man who began Tar Heel Basketball as we know it.

ACKNOWLEDGMENTS

Thank you, Dean Smith, for not only writing the sweet foreword capsulizing your unparalleled Hall of Fame career, but for
your frankness and friendship over the years. Coach, I love the
wall of "family" photos in your new office!

Sincere thanks to Roy Williams, our newest coach for the ages,
for his absolute candor and faith that I would make it come out
the right way. If it's possible after all of his success, ol' Roy keeps
getting better, and that's not good news for the ABC crowd!

Thanks, always, to Larry Brown, who is so helpful and granted
interviews that are used in these pages when they were supposed to
go into a book on his charismatic career. That one's coming later,
Coach, after you get the Bobcats over the top!

The insights of Woody Durham, "the Voice," and Steve Kirschner and Matt Bowers are always appreciated. As are those from
scribes Al Featherston, Ron Green Jr., Ron Green Sr., Eddy Lan-
dreth, Lenox Rawlings, Ron Morris, Barry Jacobs, Curry Kirkpatrick, and Caulton Tudor, through their clippings and comments.

Thanks to Robert Crawford, the Carolina insider who is the
only photographer asked when there is only one invitation, and to
Katherine Morton, who still presides over the historic photos of her
father, Hugh, whom we all miss so much. To Keith Longiotti at the
Carolina Collection, for his patience to let me look in the stacks
through a hundred pictures even though we had room for only a
few.

Thanks to Ron Smith, the full-time minister and part-time his-
torian, who will publish the ultimate Carolina basketball book
some day soon, for his notes and quotes. To Bob Fulton, who co-
authored two books about Frank McGuire filled with good stuff.

To the numerous former players and coaches and managers
I've known through the years, who told me stories when I asked,
and some before I ever got to the question. Eddie Fogler and Jim

Delany are at the top of that list, and Rich Gersten and Bob Gersten are not far behind.

As he did with *Blue Blood,* which HBO used extensively for its documentary on the Carolina-Duke rivalry, Pete Wolverton at St. Martin's Press put this book together expertly. His highly organized assistant, Liz Byrne, kept the gentle deadline reminders coming.

Thanks to Gary Sobba, the best boss a guy like me could have and one of the most capable marketers and administrators in all of college athletics. To Casandra, Brian, Seth, Mike, and Missy, who seem to understand my schedule even when I don't.

Rob McNaughton, whose dad is among those keeping me sane on golf-course Sundays, did some editing at the beginning and the end. Even Carolina sophomore Ryan Watts told me what he thought I should know about the Tar Heels when asked. His mother and my wife, Jan, is always willing to listen, read, or research, even though she is the busiest person I know. Hurley, of *Blue Blood* fame, has been gone for a few years, but Nellie now sits on my lap while I'm editing and eventually dozing.

All of them, plus Carolina basketball, make it a life well spent in Chapel Hill.

THE TEN "WHAT-IF'S" OF CAROLINA BASKETBALL

1. What if Frankie McGuire had not been born with cerebral palsy?

2. What if Everett Case had not turned down Lennie Rosenbluth in 1952?

3. What if Rosenbluth had been called for charging at the end of the 1957 ACC tournament semifinals against Wake Forest?

4. What if Pete Brennan had not saved the 1957 national semifinal with his last-second basket against Michigan State?

5. What if Joe Quigg had missed those last two free throws against Kansas the next night?

6. What if Dean Smith had taken the assistant coaching job at Kansas, and not UNC, in 1958?

7. What if Smith had not convinced Larry Brown and Billy Cunningham to stay at Carolina after Frank McGuire left?

8. What if Larry Miller had gone to Duke and Charlie Scott had gone to Davidson?

9. What if Phil Ford had followed David Thompson to N.C. State?

10. What if Roy Williams had said "No" in 2003?

FOREWORD

I feel so lucky to have coached at Carolina for thirty-nine years, including my first three seasons with Coach Frank McGuire.

I feel lucky to have recruited and known so many great young men, some of whom were better basketball players than others, but almost all of whom were outstanding individuals from great families. I don't dare name a single player (or manager) because I would not want to leave any of them out.

I can name all of my assistant coaches, beginning with Bill Guthridge, who was the best lieutenant a head coach could have for thirty years. He proved he would have succeeded in any of those head coaching jobs he was offered through the years by taking two of our teams to the Final Four in the three seasons he followed me.

My first assistant coach was Ken Rosemond, who played for Coach McGuire and went on to take over at the University of

Georgia. Then came Larry Brown, a former player and one of the great coaches in the history of the game, and another dear friend, John Lotz.

We had a strong staff when Eddie Fogler and, later, Roy Williams joined Bill and me in practices, out recruiting, and on the bench. Some of Carolina's greatest players were in school during this period, and of course we managed to win a national championship with them in 1982.

Both Eddie and Roy were having their own successful head-coaching careers when we won our second NCAA title in 1993 with three more very capable assistants joining Bill: Phil Ford, Dave Hanners, and Pat Sullivan. All of them are currently coaching in the NBA, which proves how good they were then and are now. Randy Weil, another assistant, became a college head coach.

I also feel lucky to have had such a great support staff: secretaries from Betsy Terrell, to Linda Woods, Kay Thomas, Angela Lee, and Ruth Kirkendall. Our office could not have run as smoothly without them. When Coach McGuire left in 1961, I kept trainer John Lacey on, and that was one of my best moves! After John retired, Marc Davis took over and stayed for more than thirty years. I also had only two equipment managers in my time, Sarge Keller and Ken Crowder.

I worked for five athletic directors—Chuck Erickson, Homer Rice, Bill Cobey, John Swofford and, briefly, for Dick Baddour—before I retired. They all had confidence that we would run a program with integrity while graduating our players. Fortunately, we made enough money to give some back to the athletic department to help support our Olympic sports teams.

Of course, I have to mention the man who gave me the job in the first place: Chancellor William Aycock, maybe my oldest living friend in Chapel Hill.

Recently, I wrote a book with Professor Gerry Bell called *The Carolina Way*, and while there are other ways of doing things, I believe ours is the best way. We take care of our own people first, help them accomplish their life goals, and always work as a team.

Coach McGuire taught us all how to build a team that recruited good people from good families, and we helped them along their way. I will always consider myself a teacher first, and one who was lucky to have worked for the University of North Carolina and lived in Chapel Hill for all these years.

—**Coach Dean Smith**

INTRODUCTION

Unlikely Dynasty

BASKETBALL has a long history of success at North Carolina, but not until the mid-1950s did many people know it. As at most schools, particularly in the South, it was simply not the favorite sport on campus. From its beginning in 1911, basketball trailed football and baseball in popularity.

Some thought that might actually change after the 1946 season. The Tar Heels were 30-5 and reached the NCAA championship game before losing to powerful Oklahoma A&M (now called Oklahoma State). Four starters were scheduled to return, including All-Americans John "Hook" Dillon and Jim Jordan. Meanwhile, the football team had struggled during World War II, going 20-24-3 from 1941 through 1945.

But any thought that basketball would emerge as the biggest sport on campus changed in the fall of '46. World War II had just ended and the GI Bill allowed an influx of students to UNC. Many of these were older men who had played football on service teams. Carl Snavely, who had been hired to rebuild the program, found himself with a wealth of talent. The most important player in this group was freshman Charlie Justice, who had been the most famous prep star in the South at Asheville High School. Justice became the key figure in the greatest era in Carolina football history, leading the Tar Heels to three major bowl games in four years.

The 1946 basketball season quickly became a memory. The Tar Heels won fifty-nine games the next three seasons, but were overshadowed by what was happening on the football field. It is unlikely that basketball would have become the favorite sport on campus anyway. Even during the 1946 season, attendance at basketball games was irregular. Woollen Gym might be filled one night and half-empty a week later. That pattern was especially evident during World War II, when the student body was regularly changing. But inconsistent attendance was nothing new. That had been the case since the game was first played at UNC in 1911.

Despite basketball's early success, there was no reason to think that Carolina would become the most dominating school in the sport, as it has been for the last fifty years. The game just was not that important in the first half of the twentieth century.

Football was a much more exciting sport. The nature of the game dictated that there was always action, even in low-scoring games. Baseball was the oldest sport on the Carolina campus, and it was played as early as 1876 and supported by a solid fan base.

There was little interest in even organizing a university-sponsored basketball team. Few students at Carolina had played or even seen the sport in high school. Basketball in North Carolina first became popular at YMCAs in Durham and Charlotte.

After that, a group of students from Charlotte approached the UNC administration about beginning an official team in Chapel Hill. Fortunately, Marvin Ritch, who later became a prominent attorney in the state, argued the case. The University agreed to form a team in 1911.

Nat Cartmell, the Carolina track coach, was selected to be the head coach. He had played the game occasionally while in school at Penn. That experience was enough to get him the job. The team practiced and played in Bynum Hall, a multi-purpose facility. Cartmell had to plan his use of the building around physical education classes and even social events such as parties and dances, which was an indication of how basketball was regarded in its early seasons.

The game did not catch on quickly for several reasons. Most students knew little about it. Football and baseball were played outdoors in generally comfortable weather, whereas watching basketball meant sitting or standing in a gym as cold as the winter weather outside. Also, as a new sport, the quality of play was not very good. Games were slow and methodical. Carolina failed to score 20 points eleven times in its first three seasons. Only once in the school's first eleven seasons did the Tar Heels even average 35 points a game.

Scheduling, too, was haphazard at best. Games occasionally had to be canceled for one reason or another. Other games were sometimes added if competition became available. Some colleges had only club teams. Carolina often filled out its schedule with games against various city or YMCA teams. These teams were more imposing than college competition. The players were older and more experienced. For example, the Durham YMCA was one of the best teams in the state, and Hanes Hosiery in Winston-Salem sponsored one of the strongest club teams in the area.

Intercollegiate competition was always the first choice in choosing opponents. Games against other schools were likely to attract the most attention of students. Attendance was limited by Bynum Hall, which could hold only a few hundred spectators. Most fans watched games from an elevated track above the court. However, the small capacity was rarely a problem in the early seasons. Games sometimes drew 100 or fewer fans. No one in those days could have imagined the size of today's arenas or the ways that Carolina fans desperately seek tickets.

One of the problems for several years was lack of coaching continuity. Cartmell had the job for four seasons, the longest that anyone served as head coach in the sport's first sixteen years at Carolina. In that period, the Tar Heels had seven head coaches. There were also two seasons when the team played without a coach. Athletic director Bob Fetzer handled the team's arrangements and schedule in 1922 and 1923. Then he and his brother Bill, neither of whom had much knowledge of the sport by self-admission, simply traveled with the team. The players organized practices and made game decisions.

Carolina finished 7-4 in its first season in 1911. Three of the next four years resulted in losing records. The Tar Heels simply did not have the talent or the fundamental skills to compete against most of their opponents. What little interest that curiosity had generated in the new sport began to disappear as the team struggled. Carolina finally began to have real success in 1918 with a 9-3 record.

There would be a 7-9 season in 1920, but then there was only one losing record again until after World War II. The highlight of 1920 was a split of two games with Trinity, which eventually was renamed Duke. Although Trinity had begun playing basketball in

1905, a football dispute in 1894 had halted all athletic competition between Trinity and UNC until these games in 1920.

High schools in the state finally started playing basketball, and more talented players were arriving on campus. Guard Billy Carmichael was the first of a group of players from Durham who began a run of tremendous success in the 1920s. The record was just 12-8 in 1921, but that was deceiving. The team went on an extended road trip at midseason. Nine games were played in ten days, but Carolina did manage to win three of the nine.

Lengthy road trips to the Northeast became a part of the annual schedule. This often meant living on a train for eight or nine days and playing almost every night. The first western swing came in 1929, when the season opened with games at Butler, Ohio State, Louisville, Kentucky, and Tennessee on successive nights.

The Southern Conference was formed in 1921, and Carolina established itself as the top basketball power in the Southeast. The league originally had thirteen members, but at one time it grew to twenty-three. Several schools dropped out in 1933 to form the Southeastern Conference. Because of the Southern Conference's size, a post-season tournament was used to determine the conference champion. In the twenty-five years from the league's first season to the Tar Heels' 1946 NCAA championship game, Carolina won more of those titles and also finished first in the regular-season standings more often than any other school.

The Tar Heels won four of the league's first five tournaments. These championships created the first real interest in basketball in Chapel Hill. Billy Carmichael and his younger brother Cartwright were the stars of the 1922 team that swept the first title. Carolina finished with a 15-6 record, including five victories on consecutive days to win the conference tournament in Atlanta. Cartwright scored 18 points in the finals against Mercer. The record improved to 15-1 in 1923, but the loss came in the Southern Conference tournament to Mississippi.

This success prompted Fetzer to find a coach, and he gave the job to Norman Shepard. Not only did the players get a coach again, they moved into a new arena. The Indoor Athletic Center, or The Tin Can as it soon was called, opened as a replacement for Bynum Hall. The building had a regulation-size court and improved seating, but it was colder than Bynum because its sides were made out of tin. Although the building had been planned for years, it was soon clear that a better facility would have to be built.

Shepard inherited a veteran team along with newcomer Jack Cobb, a 6'2" sophomore from Durham. Cobb immediately became the team's top player. In his career, he would average almost 15 points, which was an extremely high figure in those days.

The 1924 team finished 26-0. The Helms Foundation named both Carmichael and Cobb as All-Americans. Only six opponents came within nine points of the Tar Heels all season, and Carolina swept its Southern Conference tournament games by an average of 14 points. Helms later retroactively selected Carolina as the 1924 national champion.

Despite the 26-0 record, Shepard resigned and entered private business. Monk McDonald, who had been a four-year starter, agreed to take the job for one year before entering medical school. The Tar Heels were 20-5, and they again won the conference championship. This was the team that writers called the "White Phantoms" for the way the players apparently glided by the opposition.

Harlan Sanborn replaced McDonald, but another coaching change seemed to be no problem for the players, who compiled another 20-5 record and again rolled through the 1926 Southern Conference tournament, thus giving Carolina four tournament championships in five years and an overall record during that time of 96-17. Helms named Cobb the national player of the year in his senior season.

Even with all the success and the growing excitement that it generated, basketball still could not match the interest of football or baseball at Carolina. Boxing also usually drew larger crowds after it became an intercollegiate sport in 1926. Cobb, Carmichael, and McDonald were the only players well known on campus. McDonald was a four-sport star who was most recognized for his football career. Other than these three, the big sports figures in the 1920s were football players Gus McPherson, Red Whisnant, Herman McIver, Grady Pritchard, Pierce Matthews, and Bill Blount; baseball stars Manly Llewellyn, Lefty Wilson, Rabbitt Bonner, and Casey Morris; and boxer Add Warren.

An example of basketball's status can be found in the *Yackety Yack*, the school yearbook. In the section devoted to athletics, basketball was listed last among all sports throughout the 1920s.

Across the state, most people probably would have had trouble even naming one college basketball player—quite different from today, when some fans can recite the starting lineup for every team in the Atlantic Coast Conference (ACC).

That unfamiliarity meant basketball had not attained any national status. The most popular sports were major league baseball, college football, and professional boxing. The 1920s belonged to Babe Ruth, Red Grange, and Jack Dempsey. The World Series and the heavyweight championship fights featuring Dempsey vs. Luis Firpo and Dempsey vs. Gene Tunney were the decade's biggest stories. Newspaper accounts recorded attendance at the Dempsey-Tunney fights as more than 120,000 in Philadelphia in 1926 and more than 150,000 in Chicago the following year. More fans may have combined to witness those two bouts than the number of fans who saw all of the basketball games at most colleges for two decades.

Players like Grange and Ernie Nevers, the growth of the Rose Bowl, and the emergence of Notre Dame as a national power had brought college football into greater prominence. Basketball remained a local and regional sport. There were several different football All-American teams, but only the Helms Foundation chose one in basketball.

In the fall of 1926, James Ashmore took on the unenviable task of trying to continue Carolina's run of success in basketball. He was in charge for five seasons, the longest coaching tenure at Carolina until Tom Scott after World War II. Ashmore actually had been hired as the baseball coach, but when Sanborn left after one year, Ashmore also was assigned the basketball job. His teams went 80-37, but they never reached the tournament finals. Bunn Hearn then expressed interest in the baseball position, and Ashmore lost both jobs.

George Shepard was chosen as the next basketball coach. He led the Tar Heels to Southern Conference championships in 1935 and 1936 and to the only two UNC titles of the decade. Carolina consistently had good teams, but the dominance that had existed in the 1920s was over. Some of the outstanding players on the 1930s teams were Wilmer Hines, Virgil Weathers, "Snooks" Aitken, Jack Glace, Ramsey Potts, Earl Ruth, and Jim McCachren.

In the 1930s, the growing campus was filled with star athletes and teams. Carolina won two football and three baseball titles in the 1930s. The tennis teams, which had been among the most popular and successful in Chapel Hill since the turn of the century, won seven conference titles. The cross country, indoor track, and outdoor track teams won six championships each.

Athletes from these teams generally were better known than

the basketball players. Although Hines and Potts were two of the school's best basketball players in the 1930s, they were more famous for tennis. George Stirnweiss, who also was a premier football player, was one of the best baseball players in school history. Burgess Whitehead, Jim Mallory, John Peacock, and John Humphries were among the other baseball players who were as well-known as their basketball counterparts. The biggest stars still came from football—George Barclay, Steve Maronic, Don Jackson, Crowell Little, Paul Severin, and the most popular athlete on campus, Andy Bershak.

In the 1935 basketball season, Carolina returned three starters—McCachren, Aitken, and Glace—from a team that had gone 18-4 the previous year. The 6'4" Glace had little experience when he came to Chapel Hill, but by his senior year he had developed into a solid player and gave the Tar Heels an inside presence they had lacked since the mid-1920s. The team opened the season with an eleven-game winning streak and then won its last nine, finishing 23-2 and sweeping the Southern Conference tournament in Raleigh.

Shepard then resigned because of bad health. Walter Skidmore, the freshman coach, was named as his replacement. Carolina was so loaded with talent in 1936 that a 21-4 record was almost disappointing. However, the Tar Heels swept their second straight league tournament. McCachren, Potts, Ruth, and Pete Mullis formed the team's nucleus. The most important addition was Bershak. He had just won all-conference honors in football and would be an All-American the following year. He immediately became the team's top rebounder and defensive player.

Still, basketball was not recognized as a major national sport. Two things, though, happened in 1938 that began to increase basketball's popularity and help its status across the country. The rule calling for a jump ball after every score was changed, and opposing teams were instead given possession. Speeding the pace of the game eventually led to more scoring.

In addition, the first National Invitational Tournament was played at Madison Square Garden, and the inclusion of Colorado and Oklahoma A&M made it a truly national event. The NCAA tournament then began the following year. College football had attained a national following from post-season bowls and intersectional games. Now basketball had the opportunity for a similar stage. Before those tournaments could begin to gain great prominence, however, World War II slowed the growth of all sports.

Carolina's decade ended in disappointing fashion with a 10-11 record in 1939. The highlight of the year was a move out of the Tin Can and into Woollen Gym. The Durham newspaper reported "only a small crowd turned out" for the home opener against Atlantic Christian. Attendance at games continued to fluctuate, and it would do so until the 1950s.

Students and fans who stayed away missed some great performances by one of the most unusual players in school history. George Glamack was a 6'6" center who was named national player of the year in both 1940 and 1941. He averaged 17.6 points as a junior and 20.6 the following year. He was the biggest scoring threat in the South even though he barely could see.

His eyesight was so poor that he struggled to find the basket even while standing directly beneath it. It took hard work for him to become a premier player, but he was up to the challenge. He found spots on the floor where he felt comfortable, and he practiced hook shots from those every day. He developed such accuracy that he was almost unstoppable.

Glamack helped Carolina improve to 23-3 in 1940 and win the Southern Conference tournament. The record slipped to 19-9 the following year despite an even better season by Glamack. Woollen Gym was less than half filled in February when he scored 45 points against Clemson, a Southern Conference scoring record. After going 14-1 in the league, the Tar Heels were upset in the conference tournament. Carolina was still chosen to compete for a spot in the NCAA tournament, but the team played one of its worst games of the season and lost to Pittsburgh, 26-20.

By the following season, World War II had changed the face of college sports as many athletes joined the armed forces. Team rosters were so depleted that freshmen were made eligible for varsity play. Football was hit hardest in Chapel Hill because the team needed a larger number of players. The basketball team, however, continued to post winning records.

The military had set up training bases on some campuses, including Carolina. Servicemen were allowed to participate in college sports where they were stationed, and some of them became prominent players.

Bill Lange had replaced Skidmore as head coach after the losing season of 1939. Lange resigned after a 17-10 finish in 1944, and he became athletic director at Kenyon. Ben Carnevale, who was working with the Navy's V-12 program on campus, was allowed to take the head coaching job. The team was filled with new faces. Freshman John "Hook" Dillon quickly became a regular. Jim Jordan, Bob Paxton, and Manny Alvarez were among the servicemen who played major roles as the Tar Heels went 22-6 and won the conference tournament. Carolina was invited to play in both the NCAA tournament and the NIT. Since military personnel could not travel, the Tar Heels had to turn down those invitations.

Four starters returned in 1946, and they made up an imposing front line. Jordan and Paxton were 6'3" and Dillon was 6'2". Dillon played bigger than that with a hook shot that taller men had trouble defending.

More help came in February when Horace "Bones" McKinney was discharged from the Army. McKinney had played at N.C. State before the war, but relaxed wartime rules allowed him to transfer to Carolina. His presence gave Carnevale the flexibility to do more things on offense and defense than any previous coach in school history.

Despite such an exciting team, game attendance was inconsistent. There were hopes that attendance would increase after the 30-5 record and the runner-up finish in the NCAA tournament. That's when Justice and the returning servicemen helped turn around the football program.

However, the basketball team had other problems. Since World War II had ended, the Navy was no longer paying Carnevale. He also had been getting a salary from the athletic department and he asked that it be increased to make up for his military pay. When the university refused, Carnevale resigned and became head coach at the U.S. Naval Academy.

Student enrollment increased dramatically after World War II, and basketball game attendance began to grow. However, it still was not consistent. There was more interest, but it was not at the same level as football. That was not the case at N.C. State, where Everett Case had been hired to make the Wolfpack into a national power. In fact, Tom Scott, who had replaced Carnevale, never won a game against State during his six years in Chapel Hill.

When the Justice Era ended in 1949, Carolina's football fortunes began to slide. More attention was finally turned to basketball, although no one had thought much about what could be accomplished in that sport. For the first time since 1912 and 1913, the Tar Heels suffered back-to-back losing seasons in 1951 and 1952.

These resulted in ninth- and eleventh-place finishes in the Southern Conference. Scott resigned, and the university turned to a New Yorker named Frank McGuire to rebuild the basketball program.

In McGuire, the school hired a man who not only did that, but also helped to create the passion that exists today. Fans were about to discover what big-time college basketball could really be. No one could imagine what they were about to see over the next half century and beyond.

—Rick Brewer

PROLOGUE

One for the Ages

THE chartered jet carrying the 2009 national champions broke through the clouds on its approach to Raleigh-Durham Airport and entered a wide expanse of Carolina blue sky. The team, coaches, support staff, and university administrators aboard were finally home after six days of sun, cold, and snow in Detroit and the NCAA Final Four.

Their approach was smooth—not aborted twice, which had happened fifty-two years before when North Carolina's first national championship team returned from Kansas City on an Eastern Airlines propjet. That plane almost did not land because an estimated 5,000 fans had broken through whatever security they had in those days and swarmed near the runway.

This time, the North Carolina Tar Heels were greeted by the

high-tech stuff of the twenty-first century, or at least the 1990s. Cameras replaced people for the moment.

ABC-TV's Chopper 11 hovered in the airspace above the terminal, waiting for the team and travel party to board three buses for the thirty-minute trip back to Chapel Hill. The TV helicopter would trace every mile of the ride down Interstate 40 and their victory lap as the buses snaked through the UNC campus.

The lower level of the Dean Smith Center had filled with about 12,000 people of all ages, thanks to the afternoon schedule and public school vacation, which allowed excited Tar Heels fans from seven months to seventy years old a chance to welcome their latest hoop heroes. Inside the light blue arena, four large video screens were showing live coverage of the buses, which were accompanied by police escorts fore and aft as they traveled the last mile up Manning Drive.

The biggest roar from the crowd came when the three tiny white rectangles on the screen turned down Skipper Bowles Drive and parked behind the huge octagon, where North Carolina had won fourteen games on the way to first place in the ACC and another No. 1 seed in the NCAA tournament. In the arena, the four fascia scoreboards had been lit up with the final score: UNC 89, Michigan State 72. Adjacent electronic signs read: *2009 NATIONAL CHAMPIONS*.

Finally, the buses emptied out, heightening the anticipation of the fans inside, and video cameras now scanned the crowd. The cameras panned up to the five national championship banners hanging from the rafters, and then they focused on the empty space next to 2005, which would be filled in a few months.

The crowd cheered impatiently.

How long would it take the team to walk the few hundred feet through the tunnel and climb up on the stage where twenty-four chairs had been arranged in a perfect oval?

At the other end of the court stood a media platform with a phalanx of cameras ready to record the moment. On the wooden playing floor in between, which was covered by a blue tarp, students moved toward the stage while behind them in the open areas children cavorted with their parents and cheerleaders-to-be cartwheeled the time away.

The portion of the UNC pep band that had not made the bus trip to Detroit set up in a corner of Section 105 and readied to sub for the regulars, who were still on the road *from* the Final Four. The band blurted out the Tar Heels' fight song and "Rah, Rah, Carolina." People waiting at three open concession stands in the concourse scurried back inside when they heard Woody Durham, Voice of the Tar Heels, bellow: "Isn't this great!"

Durham said he told the players on the plane ride that they had had a pretty good party the night before on the court at Ford Field and afterward in the hotel. However, that was nothing compared to what was going on at home. Then he walked off the stage.

Some cheered while others conjured up their ultimate fantasy: to be at courtside when the Tar Heels won it all and then, a moment later, to be among the Chapel Hill fans who flooded Franklin Street.

Durham returned a few minutes later with a small table that he set down right in front. "We have something to bring out and we need a place to put it," he said. At long last, he introduced the traveling party one by one. The Tar Heels, all looking weary, wore coats and ties—not the blue blazers and gray slacks of the McGuire era, but classy by modern standards.

Some of the players carried camcorders pointed at the crowd.

3

Bobby Frasor cradled the ball from the national championship game. Danny Green cracked everybody up when he said, "But did you see *how* we won it," and then he got provoked into doing his jersey-pulling Jump Around dance. Girls in the front row held up "Marry Me" signs as the last player was called: Tyler Hansbrough walked out to the biggest roar of all.

Finally, Roy Williams arrived holding the national championship trophy, which was draped by one of the nets that had been stripped about fourteen hours earlier. He put it down on the table. "It doesn't get any better than this," UNC's favorite son said to cheers, "winning a national championship for *our* alma mater. These guys took me on one fantastic ride."

Williams looked up at the video boards as Carolina's own version of "One Shining Moment" played: Tar Heel highlights only, which Williams watched with misty eyes.

Standing only 5'10", Williams had grown into a coaching giant over the weekend, winning his second NCAA tournament title in five years and, perhaps more important, returning Carolina basketball to its greatest heights of the past. After enduring a painful transition from the Dean Smith years, the program seemed all the way back in every measurable manner—with the same spirit of the soul that a Tar Heel fan could finally *feel* again.

Joining Smith and eleven other elite coaches who had won at least two NCAA titles, Williams was positioned to match those who had won three (Bobby Knight and Mike Krzyzewski) and four (Adolph Rupp).

On the home front, which was as important to many UNC grads, his Tar Heels had reclaimed the superiority that Duke enjoyed for much of the last twelve years since Smith retired with a 26-14 record against Krzyzewski-coached teams. Leading a program that still owned the most victories, NBA graduates and TV exposure in the 55-year history of the ACC, Williams' two national championships and three Final Fours had come since the last time Duke was there in 2004.

He was in the prime of his life and career, coaching at America's most famous basketball school and using a fast-paced pro playing style that maximized his inherent recruiting advantages. Who wouldn't want to play for this guy? His fifth Final Four team in the last eight seasons had the perfect blend: a point guard who led an explosive fast break and scored enough to become ACC player of the year, wing shooters who had the green light to fire away, and post men who started every offensive set by looking to score themselves.

But this season was far from how easy it seemed at the end, when Carolina fulfilled its long-time mantra of playing hard, playing smart, and playing together at the highest level.

The 2009 Tar Heels made every coach's dream come true—reaching this peak performance at exactly the right time. They did it by repairing a defense that, only weeks before, couldn't stop dribble penetration or shut down a hot outside shooter. On offense, they shared the ball so expertly that they appeared impossible to stop.

The coach sought such perfection all season and was rewarded with the most dominant NCAA tournament performance in his school's storied history, leaving absolutely no doubt about which was the best team in the country. Even so, Williams had fought through what he called "one of my hardest years in coaching."

The Tar Heels began in the polls as even more of a favorite for the national championship than Barack Obama—who had scrimmaged with them during his campaign—was in the presidential race. TV talking heads said they could be the *first undefeated team* since Indiana in 1976.

5

Then, one by one, injuries reduced Williams' deepest roster ever to a number of question marks. Marcus Ginyard's off-season ankle surgery was not healing. Hansbrough began the season sidelined by a potential stress fracture. Promising freshman center Tyler Zeller suffered a broken wrist in the second game, leaving Williams momentarily with only two post men, junior Deon Thompson and freshman Ed Davis.

Among Williams' biggest fears was that Hansbrough would not be healthy enough to reach the records he could surely break after returning for his senior season. The workhorse of few words from Poplar Bluff, Missouri, had become the standard for staying in school when he refused to leave after a third straight season when he was unanimous All-ACC and consensus All-American, and he had won almost every national player of the year award given out.

Hansbrough hated to do it, but he sat out some practices, and he sat out three starts at the season's onset before returning to score 50 points in the last two games of the Maui Classic. Those who were looking for parallel universes noted that the 2005 national champions had spent Thanksgiving week on what Hawaiians call the Valley Isle, carving up three unranked opponents by a total of 63 points. Four years later, the Tar Heels devoured three foes by 89 points. A matured Ty Lawson won the Maui MVP award with 22 points and 11 assists, his only double-double of the entire season, against eighth-ranked Notre Dame.

The ultra-disciplined Hansbrough sat out a fourth game for safety's sake and then returned with a vengeance for the ACC–Big Ten Challenge in Detroit. He had 25 points and 11 rebounds in only 27 minutes as Carolina trounced tired and dinged-up Michigan State 98-63 on the experimental raised floor in the middle of Ford Field. The dress rehearsal for the Final Four drew a crowd of 25,267, but Motown hoped to have three times as many people there four months later. The Heels went home with Hansbrough only 34 points away from Phil Ford's thirty-one-year-old career scoring record at UNC.

Williams orchestrated the timing of the occasion by taking Tyler out of the Saturday evening game against Oral Roberts after he had scored 26 points and led Carolina in a 100-84 victory. Thus, the big moment would come in the first half against underrated Evansville the following Thursday on ESPN's primary national network. Ford, an assistant to Carolina icon Larry Brown with the Charlotte NBA franchise, could be in attendance because the Bobcats were off that night.

Contrary to mentor Dean Smith, who rarely acknowledged individual achievements with ceremony, Williams wanted to halt the game on Hansbrough's record-breaking point, acknowledge the legendary Ford (who would be seated at courtside), and let the 22,000 fans and national TV audience participate. Hansbrough deserved such recognition, and it wouldn't hurt recruiting, either.

Still, Williams was worried he might have gone overboard. He nixed the scripted celebration and hurried Hansbrough through the whole gig: Here's the ball, go hug Phil, listen to the announcer, wave to the crowd, and let's get on with the game!

"He hijacked the ceremony to make sure we'd get it done quickly," veteran sports information director Steve Kirschner said, laughing. "He wanted it for Tyler and it was good for recruiting, but he did not want to seem inconsiderate to everyone else."

Williams' next decision along the way was whether to play Ginyard, whose ankle still bothered him three months after the operation. Bad for the team, Williams thought, but maybe good for Green, the sixth man who was talented enough to be invited to NBA tryout camps the previous spring even though he had started exactly one game in his college career. So, as a senior, Green gave up his sideline dance before tip-off and headed for what later amounted to stardom.

Ginyard tried to play two games in late December but could not push off the ankle well enough to drive with the ball or guard his man. He had only one more game, against Boston College, before losing his chance for a medical redshirt and to come back fully healed the following season. Williams shut him down until the ankle healed properly, then left the decision of whether to return to Ginyard and his family.

Carolina spent New Year's Eve in Reno, playing Nevada, nailing down its thirteenth straight victory just as 2009 rang in back on the East Coast. Williams enjoyed it quietly with a few friends and his family, having shot some lucky craps the night before at Lake Tahoe. He had done the same thing prior to beating Brigham Young in Las Vegas the season before, and he thought about doing it in Detroit the previous month. Williams was only inclined to gamble through superstition. As long as he kept rolling the dice and his team won, he would continue. His old high school coach had taught him how to shoot craps, he had seen Dean Smith do it during his coaching career and, though he did not know for sure, figured Frank McGuire knew his way around a casino.

The 2009 Tar Heels won their first thirteen games easily, all by double digits. Too easily, it turned out.

Without a healthy Ginyard, their defensive stopper, they were lit up in January by Boston College's Tyrese Rice for the second straight season and then by Wake Forest sophomore Jeff Teague. Those scoring guards shredded Carolina's defense for a combined 59 points with their penetration and perimeter skills.

The team that pundits said couldn't be beat had lost twice right out of the ACC gate, the Tar Heels' worst league start in twelve years. Williams had to counter the sniping and criticism that ensued with reminders that his first Final Four team at Kansas had also been 0-2 in the old Big Eight, and the 1997 UNC team that started 0-3 in the ACC had also reached the Final Four.

He claimed too many bewildered fans "abandoned ship." Maybe so, but it nonetheless appeared that Carolina wasn't playing as hard on the defensive end and, indeed, seemed less lovable than it had been in November and December. Fans dreaming of a national championship now wondered whether this team could even get back to the Final Four.

Another winning streak began, only not as smoothly; Ty Lawson's buzzer beater rescued the Tar Heels at Florida State and his five three-pointers did the same at Miami. That win, in which the Hurricanes' Jack McClinton hung 35 points on the Tar Heels, was Williams' 165th coaching victory at Carolina and pushed him past Frank McGuire into second place.

Meanwhile, Lawson's emergence as perhaps the most valuable player in the ACC came none too soon. Running mate Wayne Ellington was shooting far worse from the field and three-point line in his first seventeen games than he had in 2008. After three years of scouting Hansbrough, interior defenses were openly hacking away at him and shoving him off his sweet spots on the low blocks.

The same day Ginyard decided to sit out the rest of the season, reserve forward Will Graves got suspended for violating a university policy that nails a lot of North Carolina students. What was once the deepest team in the ACC and the country was down to eight healthy regulars, and it forced Williams to give freshman Justin Watts and senior bench-warmer Michael Copeland more minutes than he had anticipated.

Despite ten straight victories that sent the Tar Heels into first place in the ACC, including their fourth consecutive win at Cameron Indoor Stadium, Williams remained frustrated with their defense. They allowed non-contender N.C. State to shoot 54 percent and keep the game much closer than it should have been. Afterward, the media peppered ol' Roy on why he had stubbornly stayed with his man-to-man all season and not trapped more, switched more, or pressed more.

He had set up this confrontation himself, saying that not switching keeps players from being lazy and he coaches to "get your butt through the screens" at the top of the key. By not practicing changing defenses, he admitted the Tar Heels were not very good at it when they tried.

Having three times explained that "we're frickin' bad at it," he accidentally dropped the f-bomb in his next answer. He apologized repeatedly for the remainder of the press conference and immediately called his athletic director and chancellor to apologize. They thanked him for his sincerity, and Williams watched his language for the rest of the season.

He was still furious after the Tar Heels flubbed away a 16-point lead at Maryland, which halted the winning streak at ten and left Duke only one game back in the ACC race. They let the Terrapins rally by shooting quickly and poorly when they should have milked the clock, a surprising lack of poise this late in the season.

Carolina came back with its biggest ACC blowout, a 30-pointer over last-place Georgia Tech in which Hansbrough went 8-for-8 from the foul line and, appropriately, set the all-time NCAA record for most free throws made.

The Tar Heels were ready for their—and Hansbrough's—home finale against Duke until Lawson slammed his big toe into a basket support two days before the game and limped out of practice on crutches. Once the news hit the message boards and Internet, the tale of Ty's toe had fans fretting that the Heels would lose to the Blue Devils, wind up tied for first in the ACC, and leave their NCAA seeding resting on Lawson's lameness.

After taking a pain-killing shot, and getting fitted for an oversize shoe and steel plate to protect the toe, Lawson somehow made three key plays in the final minutes and finished with 13 points, 9 assists, and 8 rebounds in a tense, 8-point victory over Duke. Carolina wrapped up the regular-season title and Lawson ACC player of the year honors. He later won the Bob Cousy Award as the nation's best college point guard and joined Hansbrough on several All-America teams.

Even though a No. 1 seed in the NCAA tournament seemed assured, the story of Ty's toe did not end there. The next day, his foot was so swollen and painful that Williams thought he might have lost his indispensable point guard for the entire postseason.

Lawson sat out the ACC tournament in Atlanta, and Williams wrote "Find a Way" on the white board in the locker room before Friday's quarterfinals against Virginia Tech. The Tar Heels survived the Hokies in the last minute for the second straight season, but without their motor they could not muster enough offense the next day against Florida State when Hansbrough passed Sam Perkins as UNC's all-time leading rebounder. Despite losing, they had begun building defensive intensity that would carry over to the NCAA tournament.

After Duke defeated Florida State for the ACC tournament title, Carolina drew the expected No. 1 seed in the NCAA South Regional, the Tar Heels' third top seed in a row and a record thirteenth since the NCAA started seeding teams in 1979.

President Obama stuck with them to win the national championship, although he hedged his bet if Lawson did not return. After filling out his own bracket on ESPN, Obama told the Tar Heels on national television, "I went with you last year, and you let me down. Don't embarrass me in front of the nation."

Several coaches around the country poked fun at the new president, saying he should be more concerned with the slumping economy than with the NCAA tournament.

Lawson suited up for the first-round game against sixteenth-seeded Radford, but he was scratched from the lineup after he and Williams talked during warm-ups. The only drama was how long it took Hansbrough to surpass Duke's J. J. Redick as the ACC's all-time scoring leader. Hansbrough earned a long, loud ovation from the Greensboro Coliseum crowd when he did it with a pair of free throws in the first half.

Carolina won by 43 points, extending Williams' NCAA record to twenty consecutive seasons with at least one tournament victory. Dean Smith is second with seventeen straight.

After Lawson returned against LSU, scoring 21 points in the second half, Obama's bracket (and all the others that had UNC on the last line) looked promising. The game was on, but the favorite's role added to the pressure and increased the burden of having bombed out so badly against Kansas in the 2008 Final Four.

If Williams had failed to use his timeouts judiciously in San Antonio, it was not going to happen again on the drive toward Detroit. He called them early in the second half against LSU and again in the regional final against Oklahoma to stem runs by both opponents.

Against LSU, he found himself screaming in the huddle to remind his players that their defensive lapses might well send them home. The Tar Heels erased their only second-half deficit of the entire tournament and ran away from the Tigers, 84-70. UNC reached thirty wins for the third straight season, adding to what was already the best three-year record in school history of 97-14.

After Carolina played nearly perfect offense and blew out Gonzaga in the Sweet Sixteen at Memphis, the supposedly stubborn Williams turned to a rare double-team strategy to contain Oklahoma All-American Blake Griffin and leave the game in the hands of the outmanned Sooner guards. Lawson, Ellington, and Green outscored them, 46-24, in the 12-point victory.

Four straight wins by double figures continued Carolina's assault on the NCAA tournament record book and secured Williams' third Final Four trip in his six seasons at UNC—and the school's NCAA record eighteenth in its ninety-ninth year of basketball. The Tar Heels then closed off the lane to deny Villanova's penetration in the national semifinals at Ford Field in Detroit, defeating the Wildcats soundly to reach the national championship game and soften memories of the Kansas catastrophe.

The last obstacle proved to be widespread sentiment in support of Michigan State after the Spartans surprisingly ran away from UConn in the first semifinal. Coach Tom Izzo had adopted the city's 22 percent unemployment and the state's suffering economy as his causes, saying he hoped his team could be an inspiration for all of Michigan.

"We have a cause, too, and it's to win the national championship, period, the end," Williams said. But it didn't exactly end there. He went a little further, as he is wont to do when the cameras and recorders are running. "If you told me that if Michigan State wins, it's gonna satisfy the nation's economy, then I'd say, hell, let's stay poor for a little while longer."

That, obviously, was a joke, but some saw it as insensitivity by the Carolina coach. Unintentional insult is one thing. Abject foolishness is another.

CBS analysts Seth Davis and Greg Anthony *both* predicted Michigan State to win. Weren't these guys supposed to be experts?

One upset pick was good theater, for sure, but both men picking the Spartans stretched their credibility.

Top-ranked since preseason, Carolina had already blown out the same team on the same court in December. The Tar Heels had compiled the biggest NCAA tournament total point differential in thirteen years as five previous opponents tried to run with the best-running team in college basketball. Izzo himself suggested his Spartans would be the sixth.

"Detroit, defense, and destiny" were the reasons for an upset given by Davis, a Duke graduate. He should have known that, while most of Motown favored Michigan State, a hostile atmosphere was really more helpful to the Tar Heels. The fans were too far away from the floor to be much of a factor, but Roy Williams used Frank McGuire's old "us against the world" motivation to keep his team focused on getting off to a great start.

"Remember what happened last year," he harped all weekend. "I *love* playing on the road," he had said Sunday; his latest Carolina team had played twenty-two true away games and won twenty of them.

As for the defense Davis mentioned, it belonged to the team wearing white and not green. The old coaching adage that good offense beats good defense made the high-scoring Heels a solid favorite anyway. Michigan State's only hope was to get the Tar Heels into a physical showdown from the start, and that did not happen.

Ridiculed and reminded throughout the season of its offense-only rap, Carolina capped two weeks of lock-down "D." The Tar Heels' suffocating defense made the championship game boring for most people not pulling for them. Their unselfish offense was vintage Roy Williams.

Lawson and Ellington seized the perimeter and made the Big Ten player of the year (Kalin Lucas) and defensive player of the year (Travis Walton) look like they couldn't cut it in the ACC. Lawson's seven steals in the first half tied a Final Four record (his eighth in the second half broke it). Ellington's 17 points catapulted Carolina to an NCAA title game high of 55 in the first half and a 21-point lead at the break.

A quote from Jean Nidetch, founder of the famous Weight Watchers diet, best sums up Seth Davis' third premise: "It's choice—not chance—that determines your destiny." By choosing to play at the highest level, the Tar Heels gave Michigan State no chance to avenge the earlier loss at Ford Field. The Spartans wore the look of defeat long before the ho-hum second half. The game began to feel like one of those December nights at the Smith Center when the Tar Heels were winning big and fans started texting each other.

The eventual 17-point victory was so one-sided that lots of viewers switched over to "Dancing with the Stars" and tanked the TV ratings. The players on the bench, hidden by the elevated court, actually talked about what they might do after the game. The coaches cracked smiles in the closing minutes, rarely seen on the Carolina sideline.

Williams enjoyed another Sean May–like bear hug, this time with Hansbrough, whose entire demeanor seemed to slip into another place as he realized his dream was actually going to happen. He let everything out, looking and sounding as awkward as he sometimes did throughout his spectacular four years at UNC. But the big blond star didn't care and told the media so afterward.

"Write anything you want now, because we have the championship," he said to the microphones in his face, half smiling and wearing the whole net that he and his teammates had just cut down.

The Lennie Rosenbluth and Phil Ford of his era, whose retired No. 50 would join theirs in the Dean Dome rafters, Hansbrough and the senior class had won a school-record 124 games. They accomplished the only goal left, as he and his teammates atoned for the one big embarrassment in their college careers. The loss to Kansas had stuck in all of their craws like bad garlic. "We wanted to redeem ourselves," offered Ellington, the Final Four Most Outstanding Player, who finally found his stroke and looked like he would never miss a shot during the last ten games of the season. "We learned from our past experience that it was important to come out strong," added Lawson, who made 15 free throws while Michigan State fouled and fouled in frustration.

This championship game was dramatically different from UNC's previous four, which were grinding pressure-cookers. Never had Carolina performed like this with the NCAA title on the line, playing a first half so commanding that the second was all but an afterthought.

In their previous sixteen Final Fours from the McGuire era on, the Tar Heels had won close championship games (1957, 1982, 1993, 2005), lost with disappointing performances (1977, 1981), or gotten wiped out (by UCLA in 1968). Even more often, they had fallen with a thud after sorry semifinals (1967, 1969, 1972, 1991, 1995, 1997, and 1998). They had knocked down some walls, but they had never blown them away like they did on April 6 in Detroit.

In becoming the first NCAA tournament team to win all six games by 12 points or more, the Tar Heels were dominant up to and through the final game of the season, clearly the best team in the country. No doubts remained at the end. This might have been Carolina's proudest moment, and a Dean Smith disciple got it done—the one-time assistant who had now won fifty-five NCAA tournament games in twenty-one seasons and climbed to within ten victories of Smith's sixty-five in his thirty-six years.

"Roy Williams and Dean Smith don't fit in the same sentence," Williams insisted. "I'm not being humble. I really believe that."

16

———

Carolina's newest national champs filed off the stage and huddled briefly with their coaches in the home team's tunnel before dispersing into the April evening, and resuming lives that had been changed forever. They would be back in that tunnel ten, twenty-five years from then to be so feted.

It was there that the 1957 and 1982 Tar Heels had lined up during the first half of the home game against Wake Forest on February 10, 2007, for the most moving halftime tribute in Carolina athletic history. Williams had put the incredible reunion together.

Here were the players who had started it all with a fabled run to an undefeated season and the 1957 NCAA championship and, as if ordained, the team that twenty-five years later won it all for a coach who built basketball at North Carolina into an elite sport. The late Frank McGuire had been gone for thirteen years, but Dean Smith, aging gracefully, lined up with the other Tar Heel heroes.

The day was bigger than the game, a 104-67 blowout of Wake Forest. And it was even bigger than the American idols who were part of the 1982 national championship team—a freshman named Jordan, a role player that season and later the best-known athlete of his generation; a sweet, sensational sophomore named Sam, who will always be remembered for his wingspan and wider smile; and a junior named James—Big Game James—the heart and soul of Dean Smith's first national champions.

The day was biggest for the ten living members of the 1957 team and the deceased coach who came from New York to put basketball on the map in North Carolina and at its state university. Finally, and long overdue, a banner was hoisted among the others and the jerseys in the rafters, commemorated Frank McGuire and his perfect Tar Heels.

Without McGuire, none of this would have been there—Dean Smith down on the floor, the man known worldwide as Michael, who kissed his old coach on the head at the end of the ceremony, and the 22,000-seat stadium in which everyone stood at halftime while the current Carolina coach and his players were in the locker room.

Basketball would have survived at the university without them—but not as well, not as successfully, and, surely, without the regular rejoicing across the Tar Heel state. The players, both stars and reserves and certainly the coaches, would have been different without McGuire's lead. Had he not left New York and St. John's for Chapel Hill, Carolina basketball might look more like something at Clemson or Maryland, and there might not be such a legend of basketball on Tobacco Road.

"I don't think Coach McGuire gets enough credit for starting everything down here," said Lennie Rosenbluth, the 1957 national player of the year. "And I don't think we get enough credit. Basketball was absolutely nothing at Carolina before McGuire came."

Without McGuire, Dean Smith might have coached at Kansas, and Roy Williams might be a successful high school coach in the mountains of North Carolina. Football at Carolina still might be bigger than basketball, which it was when McGuire arrived. The future stars who grew up in the state might have chosen other paths, such as baseball for Phil Ford, football for James Worthy, and a career in the Air Force that late-blooming Michael Jordan considered at one point. Certainly, basketball in the Atlantic Coast Conference, influenced by Carolina more than any other member school, would not have become the national phenomenon it has been for the last forty years.

Instead, McGuire forged the first link in the chain. Good decisions by a university, along with some very good luck, kept the chain from breaking, as it has in most similar circumstances, both college and pro. The result has been the longest running sports success story in American history—known far and wide as North Carolina Basketball.

Although UCLA boasts the greatest college *dynasty* from 1964 to 1975, it lasted no longer than Hall of Fame coach John Wooden's tenure. Red Auerbach and Bill Russell led the Boston Celtics to eleven world championships from 1957 to 1969, but the Celtics later suffered through eleven losing records in fourteen seasons before winning the 2008 NBA title, their first in twenty-two years. Oklahoma football won thirty-one and forty-seven consecutive games, plus seven national championships, but the dominant eras of coaches Bud Wilkinson, Barry Switzer, and Bob Stoops were each separated by ten seasons, and often mediocre ones. The Green Bay Packers, Dallas Cowboys, and Pittsburgh Steelers all had long periods of dominance in the NFL, but none of those teams were among the league's best for more than twenty years at a stretch.

Even the New York Yankees' superiority did not last fifty years. From 1919 through 1964, they finished lower than third in the American League only twice and won twenty of their twenty-six World Series crowns. But then came eleven straight seasons without a pennant or division title and later a twelve-year run without any sort of championship.

North Carolina's longest lapses in basketball greatness came from 1962 through 1966 and from 2002 through 2004, both during coaching transitions. In the last fifty-four seasons, the Tar Heels have never gone more than five without a conference championship of some kind and top 10 national ranking, and no more than three seasons in the last forty-three.

No team in any sport has been *that good for that long.*

The 2007 tribute to the two championship teams was all about that amazing longevity. There they were, Carolina basketball blood brothers reaching across fifty years, being honored by 22,000 people who had heard about them, read about them, and, in some lucky cases, *seen* all of them create this historic legacy.

Williams and his team had to miss the halftime ceremony, but in the closing seconds against Wake Forest, the head coach walked down the bench toward Section 119, where the honorees were all sitting. He looked up at them and began applauding, and his players stood and clapped along with him.

That evening, the 2007 Tar Heels were seated front and center at a private dinner at the Alumni Center on campus. Williams wanted them to all be aware and more appreciative than they might have been if left to their own adolescent devices.

"Don't be cool," he told them, which meant no headsets, no texting, and no nodding heads during the speeches. "We're a family," he reminded them. Listen to what these retired Tar Heels say and try to relate it to your own careers. Imagine being their age because all of you will be some day, we hope with your own championship to honor.

Williams learned much of this from Smith, who used fewer words and imparted this tradition to his players more by example. Smith began each practice with a thought of the day, usually unrelated to basketball and stemming from an upbringing of education as well as athletics. He took them to faraway places, housed them in five-star hotels, and emphasized that the game of life was more important, but let's play hard and try to win, anyway. "He was teaching us how to be coaches, businessmen, how to be successful, if we were listening," said Chuck Duckett, the head manager in 1982. Smith respected his players as citizens first, athletes second.

Early in his tenure, Smith spoke to John Wooden about the self-expression his UCLA stars sought during the late 1960s and the

Vietnam War years. Wooden had two All-American centers who were especially headstrong—Lew Alcindor (later Kareem Abdul-Jabbar), who sympathized with black power figures in his native New York City, and Bill Walton, a peace activist in the off-season. Walton wore a beard and headband when he marched and demonstrated in Westwood, but he had to trim his hair and shave once practice started. Eventually, Smith struck the same balance as Wooden between his players' human rights and their responsibility to their team and university.

Smith never stopped teaching, trying to make his players better. He held individual meetings after the last game and gave out personalized practice plans for the off-season, following that up with letters during the summer. Even Jordan received a written regimen after he had been national player of the year as a sophomore in 1983.

Jordan was told to "shoot the same way" from different distances on the floor, refine his foul line routine, and play point guard in pickup games—the last counsel more for his pro basketball career than for his junior season at UNC. In asking Jordan to "visualize cutting down the nets in Seattle" (site of the 1984 Final Four), Smith obviously knew that Jordan's junior year would be his last in college. Smith was preparing him for his basketball life in the NBA.

Jordan credits his parents for the desire that drove him and Smith in expanding his natural ability, making him the greatest all-around player ever known. During the reunion game in 2007, UNC ramped up security so Jordan could not be approached by fans, but on the court and later that night, he was just one of the guys, the freshman who had dreamt the night before of hitting the winning shot in the national championship game, then closed his eyes when he let it go with 17 seconds left against Georgetown.

"The memories I have with the '82 team can never be replaced; it was like no other team I ever played on," said Jordan, who went on to lead the Chicago Bulls to six NBA titles.

Still, the most moving memories of the weekend came from the 1957 Tar Heels, who were almost all in their seventies. One of their starters, Bob Cunningham, had passed away in the previous year, and they seemed to know this was likely their last time together for such a ceremony in Chapel Hill.

"It's mind-boggling that people still remember us after fifty years," Rosenbluth said. "We played for Coach McGuire, but it was Dean Smith and now Coach Williams who have kept everything going."

Jimmy Black, the only senior starter in 1982, was asked by Williams to speak on behalf of his team at the dinner Saturday night. He was reluctant at first because he wanted others to have their chance.

"I spoke from the heart," Black said. "It was emotional because it wasn't just the players, coaches, and managers who were there, but also the secretaries, support group, and a few special fans who followed us all season. That was the beauty of it for me."

Black said he had no clue that his skip pass to Jordan on the left wing on the Monday night of March 29, 1982, would be part of history. He said they were just kids, playing the game they had played all of their lives and doing what their coaches had taught them.

"It never entered my mind what it would mean for the school and the basketball program," he said. "We were happy for Coach Smith, so everyone would stop talking about him not winning the big one."

After the game, Black and Smith shared a long, memorable moment in front of the bench. "He said, 'I love you, Jimmy,' and I said, 'I love you, Coach.' Where in the world can a black kid from the Bronx and a Caucasian male from the Midwest hug each other and say that? Except in sports."

Black said he and his teammates had begun to develop the passion for each other and their unforgettable season during the past twenty-five years, similar to what they witnessed among the 1957 team. "I hope all of us are around for our fiftieth reunion," he said. "It will mean even more to our group than it does now because we'll still be here and, hopefully, telling our grandkids about it by then."

At the end of the ceremony on the court a few hours earlier, Black had led his teammates over to their 1957 counterparts. They took turns hugging each other. Jordan wrapped his arms around Tommy Kearns, the point guard who had jumped center against Wilt Chamberlain. Perkins embraced Pete Brennan, the smooth forward who saved the 1957 semifinal game against Michigan State with a last-second basket. Worthy shook hands with big Joe Quigg, the center who hit the two winning free throws in the third overtime against Kansas.

"They all thanked us," Rosenbluth recalled of the final moment under the Frank McGuire banner. "They said that without you, none of us would be here."

1

Beginnings

THREE men were born a thousand miles and thirty-seven years apart, into three different regions, refinements, and family resources. They were as uncommon as a city slicker, a quiet Kansan, and a poor mountain man could be. Yet they shared some values that, innately, made them similar.

Their overlapping story began early in the twentieth century in a place called Hell's Kitchen, or close to it, where a ten-story tenement provided refuge from the streets of New York.

The Greenwich House was the tallest building in the neighborhood and was a testament to the burgeoning population in lower Manhattan. A settlement house for mostly Irish and Italian immigrants, it also served as a de facto community center because its playground attracted children from all over the neighborhood melting pot.

On this particular spring day in 1926, youngsters played basketball on the asphalt, dribbling and shooting a soft, leather ball into a metal rim that hung from a dilapidated wooden backboard. After a scrum under the basket, the game stopped and the fighting started. Lots of pushing, shoving, and swinging until a tall black man with long slender fingers ran toward the boys and pulled one of them out by his shock of red hair.

"I didn't show you how to use that punching bag for basketball games," the man said to the boy. "It was for protection, not to settle arguments in the yard."

The boy, tall and lithe, with an angular jaw and dimpled chin, nodded and went back to the game, knowing a little more about when to fight and when to back off.

Born on November 13, 1913, Frank McGuire grew up fatherless in Greenwich Village, the youngest of thirteen children, and had to figure it out for himself. He had only two older brothers and one, sickly Robbie, lived barely into his thirties. His other brother, William, died in his forties after working for two New York newspapers. McGuire's ten sisters spanned almost twenty years in age; the last (and second-youngest child), Anne Evelyn, died in 2008 at ninety-six. The traits of toughness, roguish charm, and loyalty that characterized McGuire's life, some of which he passed on to his protégés, were more a matter of survival than anything else on the streets of New York City. Perhaps because McGuire was a "narrowback"—an Irishman born in America—and the son of an Anglo mother, he felt a kinship to all backgrounds, races, and religions.

Robert McGuire, a strapping traffic cop and one-time amateur boxer, had died in 1915 when the infected needle of rabies serum he took after being gnawed by a bulldog gave him fatal yellow jaundice. That tied two-year-old Francis Joseph McGuire to the hip of his mother, Anna, whose monthly police pension of $25 and the daily wages of her older children working down at the waterfront somehow supported the family.

Despite the hardship, Anna McGuire still liked to browse through Macy's and Gimbels. Although she was unable to buy anything, she exposed Frank to fancy clothes. He also had those twelve older siblings to look up to when they left the house and came back with stories of where they had been and what they had done. He listened and learned, eventually embodying both the independent and nurturing natures of them all.

McGuire, the street urchin, knew there was more to life than his two-story brownstone on West 11th between Bleecker and Fourth Avenue, where his brothers and sisters slept three or four to a bedroom before they were old enough to go off on their own. Young Frank spent hours out of the house, too, just never far from home.

The Irish-Italian neighborhood was rough, but nothing like Hell's Kitchen, his father's old beat, thirty blocks north. The worst prank Frank and his chums pulled off was stealing sweet potatoes from the corner store to roast them in the street fires the bigger boys built to stay warm in the winter.

"I grew up on the sidewalks of New York City," McGuire told *Sports Illustrated* in 1957, "and you had to get along with all kinds of people. You had to get along with them or fight them. We did considerable getting along and considerable fighting."

The local policemen, many of whom knew Robert McGuire and looked after Frank, were the real-life role models and, in McGuire's case, the father figures. For most of his early childhood, McGuire figured he would follow his father and become a flatfoot. It wasn't glamorous, but the cops cared about people, watching over them and never seeming to want anything in return.

The rich and famous—like heavyweight boxing champion Gene Tunney and Tammany Hall boss Carmine DeSapio, both raised just down the street—were the preferred idols, living dreams unattainable for most kids who read the headlines on the newsstands about screwball pitcher Carl Hubbell of the New York Giants, big Babe Ruth of the Yankees, and Notre Dame coach Knute Rockne, who had revolutionized college football with the forward pass and the famous Four Horsemen.

McGuire's circle was mostly Irish and Italian with a few Jews. His best friends remained so for life, including Jack LaRocca and Joe Powell (whose son played on one of McGuire's teams); Danny Patrissy, who went on to own restaurants in Little Italy; and Harry Gotkin, whose family stayed entangled with McGuire's coaching career. He also chummed with a kid named Jimmy Cannon, who went on to be a legendary sports columnist in New York.

Another one of his good friends, Bill O'Brien, became New York police commissioner and gave McGuire what he always called a "passport" in the city whenever he returned to visit and recruit. McGuire kept a lifelong fascination with the New York City police and knew more about how the department worked than many of the cops. His heritage and contacts made McGuire comfortable among both "kings and commoners."

African-Americans were unwelcome in McGuire's neighborhood and could not get any work at the waterfront when the longshoremen hired extras at what then was the world's largest port. But teenaged Frank was intrigued by Jack Johnson, a black boxing champion who married a white woman, and influenced by a tall, black cartoonist for the local *Amsterdam News* named Ted Carroll, a director of the Greenwich House who became his first mentor.

Years later, those early curiosities forged a color-blind coach, who had black players on his teams at St. John's and then lobbied the UNC administration to let him recruit what might have been the school's first minority player, Philadelphia schoolboy sensation Wilt Chamberlain. But Chamberlain could not gain admittance to UNC, instead going to Kansas. Their paths would cross again to form another lifelong friendship.

Long before he pulled young Frank out of that playground fight, Ted Carroll's race balanced McGuire's exposure to all-white, Catholic grade school St. Veronica, where thanks to Carroll's tutoring he made the football, basketball, and baseball teams. On weekends, McGuire spent hours playing ball at Greenwich House (where he took his first shower bath) and his mother let Carroll take him to the Polo Grounds for Giants games and to see basketball and boxing at the original Madison Square Garden. The Garden made such an impression on McGuire that he considered it a sacred shrine for the rest of his life.

About that time, Carroll began training his young friend on the punching bag, telling him he could use that skill some day. McGuire had to be a street fighter, for sure, but he also talked his way out of a lot of jams. He developed the silver tongue that eventually charmed mothers and fathers and churned up opponents and referees while rarely having to raise his voice. At home, he was very much a momma's boy, helping Anna chop wood by candlelight during the Great Depression and learning, above all, that family came first. She was proud of her baby boy, but knew neither the range of talent he had nor the network of friends and acquaintances he was making. In fact, he was already forming some longtime bonds with people who turned out to be the fathers and uncles of his future players.

After he graduated from St. Veronica, Anna wanted Frank to extend his parochial school education at Xavier High. Xavier was an all-male military school of a thousand students run by Jesuit priests, and McGuire not only attended Mass daily but also wore a uniform and drilled every afternoon after Latin class. This sort of regimen became part of McGuire's fabric, too, and seemed to conflict with what was later a flashy lifestyle.

Al McGuire (no relation), a former player who became a famed coaching contemporary, said that people would see McGuire walk into the hotel at 8:00 A.M. and assume he was returning from a night on the town when in fact he had attended an early morning Mass. Those days at Xavier instilled a deep sense of faith in Frank McGuire.

The private school required tuition, which was tough following the stock market crash of 1929, but Anna McGuire and her children (including Frank, who worked weekends on the docks) scraped up the money to keep him at Xavier and continue shaping his life.

Every time McGuire later strutted regally onto the basketball court as the St. John's head coach, his family credited his stride and posture to those afternoons of marching maneuvers. Late into his life, even as arthritis racked his body, McGuire stood up straight and had the gait of royalty. It was as much a part of his appearance as the expensive silk suits he had tailored in his native New York.

But his days at Xavier gave McGuire as much substance as style. He found out that people differed in backgrounds and thus their opinions, and that it did not necessarily make them wrong.

"One of the big things we learned was that we should respect everybody," McGuire recalled years later, "and I have tried to carry that philosophy with me throughout my life."

McGuire became a three-sport athlete at Xavier, a right end on the football team, what was then called "lead" guard in basketball, and a pitcher in baseball. Despite the widespread popularity of the fall and spring sports, McGuire's preference was a basketball game that bore little resemblance to the one he later coached to unprecedented heights. The rules at the time held that a center jump followed every made basket. He figured if his team had the tallest player or best athletes, it could control the game by keeping the ball on their end of the court, thereby increasing their chances to score and win the next center jump.

The meticulous way his St. John's and Carolina teams would protect the ball came from those early days when little contact was allowed and the team ahead went to the line on every foul. This made the lead paramount in basketball of the late 1920s. Players perfected the underhand free throw to capitalize on these situations. Whether his teams played fast or slow through the years, they always treated the ball like gold and made more free throws than their opponent. This was the game he learned to love as an all-city guard at Xavier, a game played below the rim with little of today's physical mayhem.

The Xavier coach in all three sports was Marty O'Malley, an Irish charmer but a stern disciplinarian from the streets of Boston who had attended Holy Cross College. More than a father figure, O'Malley was McGuire's next mentor, turning him on to coaching and guiding his life perhaps more than any other individual.

That O'Malley insisted on discipline, proper dress, and decorum, while coaching his teams to be tough competitors, gave McGuire the blueprint for his own career. Never knowing his father growing up, McGuire could have become an uncaring, win-at-all-cost coach, but instead he counseled players throughout his life and treated them like sons. O'Malley became a friend forever, was there in 1977 when McGuire entered the Naismith Hall of Fame, and actually outlived his protégé, well into his nineties.

McGuire flourished at Xavier as one of the school's hall of fame athletes, and he captained all three sports as a senior. He developed a standstill two-handed set shot, but what he loved most was when the other team had the ball and he could steal it or get the rebound. At 6', he was hardly the biggest player, but he was atypically aggressive, earning the nickname "Elbows" from his teammates, which was no surprise to anyone who watched McGuire's college teams play years later.

Basketball remained far behind in popularity when McGuire graduated from high school in 1931. Only the year before, the rules changed to allow an opponent to take the ball out of bounds following made free throws. Critics who claimed the game had grown stale were unsatisfied until the jump ball after every field goal was scrapped before the 1937–1938 season.

McGuire was actually better known for the other two sports. During a sterling senior year at Xavier, he had attracted attention from the football coaches at Georgetown and from several minor league scouts for the Brooklyn Dodgers. However, he was paying the most attention to the charismatic basketball coach at St. John's named Buck Freeman.

On February 28, 1931, about the time McGuire decided to turn down Georgetown for St. John's, a baby boy was born to Alfred and Vesta Edwards Smith in Emporia, an east Kansas railroad town. Dean Edwards Smith was the youngest of two children, baby brother to sister Joan, and the son of dedicated teachers, devout church-going Baptists, and fiercely loyal family members.

The Smiths lived in a stucco house they built for $3,600 on tree-lined Washington Street in a town of about twelve thousand residents, many of whom were connected by the two teachers colleges where they worked and studied. Education in Emporia somewhat insulated an already frugal family from the Great Depression, which was ravaging nearby farmers and faraway cities.

Alfred Smith coached football, basketball, and track at Emporia High, and Vesta began her own teaching career with English classes at the high school. She eventually became a superintendent at the county level. Together, they earned nearly $5,000 a year, which was far above the average household income of a devastated nation that had reached a 25 percent unemployment rate before embattled President Herbert Hoover lost his office to Democrat Franklin Delano Roosevelt in 1932.

When Dean Smith was three years old, his father fielded the first integrated basketball team in Kansas scholastic history. However, midway through what looked to be a championship season, he was asked to cut black forward Paul Terry, the team's sixth man. The Eastern Kansas Athletic Conference threatened to throw Emporia out of the league, and when confronted, Alfred Smith gave Principal Rice Brown two choices. "They drop us and we'll find other schools to play," Smith told Brown, "or I'll quit and you can have someone else put Terry off the team."

One upcoming opponent, where Emporia was scheduled to play the next week, sent a Western Union telegram warning Alfred Smith to "leave the Negro boy at home or don't come." Not only did Paul Terry make the trip to Chanute, Kansas, he helped Emporia win a tough game against a team starring Ralph Miller, who went on to glory as a player at Kansas and a Hall of Fame coaching career at Wichita State, Iowa, and Oregon State.

"Afterward, I learned the situation Coach Smith was in," Terry told an Emporia *Gazette* reporter years later. "Young people don't think of things like that, but I understand now that he put his job on the line by having me on his basketball team. My being on the team meant there was going to be one white boy who didn't make it."

At the state tournament level, however, Alfred Smith had no choice but to leave Paul Terry at home or his entire team would be disqualified. Emporia won the 1934 state championship with Terry still listed on the roster, but it wasn't exactly the same as if he had been there. Terry went on to Kansas State Teachers College and played on all-black intramural teams. He remained in Emporia, married, and raised eight children, all of whom were accepted to college, with three playing Division I college basketball. He lived in the same house and ran a successful dry-cleaning business until he retired in his early eighties.

Dean Smith heard about Paul Terry as he grew up and, later, watched his father take further action against racial injustice. Once, as a grade-schooler traveling with his dad to a tournament in Lawrence, Smith and the Emporia team stomped out of the Jay-hawk Hotel because the restaurant refused to serve their next black player, Chick Taylor, one of several African-Americans Alfred Smith was to coach in all three sports. These were lessons that later put Dean Smith, the Midwesterner, on the same page with McGuire, the city slicker, with regard to integrating their basket-ball teams.

Smith's father was a gentle man but a consistent disciplinarian. He suspended four starters for a big game against Plainview for breaking curfew by attending a dance the night before the game. Son Dean was essentially the players' mascot, sitting on their laps on the way to games and never telling his father when they smoked. He did not understand the suspension, but he learned another lesson when the eligible players banded together and pulled off a one-point victory over Plainview.

"I think it was the most animated I ever saw my father over a game," Smith wrote in his autobiography, *A Coach's Life.* In their coaching careers, both father and son believed that a good team—be it theirs or their opponent's—was most dangerous at the game after losing one of its star players.

Alfred and Vesta Smith were Republicans, as were most people in rural Kansas of the day, but Republicans of the time were often liberals, and the Smiths' leanings were unmistakable. Besides his stand on integration, Alfred became close friends with William Allen White, outspoken editor of the Emporia *Gazette*, who gave the new president and his New Deal their due when he wrote of FDR: "How do you account for him? Was I just fooled before the election or has he developed?" The values of open-mindedness, interest in politics, and emphasis on education were so strong in Emporia that someone nicknamed the town the "Athens of Kansas."

Smith developed such natural curiosity that his mother called him Christopher Columbus because he was inquisitive as a small child and later always wanted to explore—once crawling down a manhole to see how the sewer system worked, and another time climbing the tower at the teachers college. Combining his environments of family, faith, and sports, Smith and a grade-school girlfriend once walked to the local florist pretending they were the Emporia basketball star and head cheerleader planning a church wedding.

When young Dean's grandparents grew too old to live alone, the Smiths opened their two-bedroom, one-bath house to Vesta's mother (while Grandpa Edwards moved in with Vesta's brother four hours away). Grandma stayed with Joan while Dean went out to the sleeping porch, an early lesson to the children about sacrificing for the family. They spent many Saturdays driving back and forth so the grandparents could visit each other.

Each Sunday, the family attended services at the First Baptist Church, where Vesta played the organ and Alfred was a deacon. They also went back on Wednesday evenings. Vesta always set the table the night before she went to bed and meticulously prepared a big Sunday lunch of pot roast, potatoes, and vegetables, plus homemade dessert, as Alfred, Joan, and Dean played Ping-Pong on the porch to determine who would do the dishes.

Dean got so good at avoiding cleanup that he eventually won a state junior table tennis championship. But on the table at home, Alfred manipulated some of the games, letting his son catch up and win, other times beating him soundly to teach Dean values like never quitting and how to overcome adversity, traits his teams would personify. After Dean got thrown out of a Pony League baseball game for arguing balls and strikes, Alfred drove home the point of how much he had hurt his team.

Cursing, tobacco, and alcohol were taboo in the Smith household, although Dean would engage in the latter two later in life until he kicked smoking cold turkey in 1988 and cut back on his social drinking. That he never used profanity in a profession rife with blue locker-room language was as much a credit to his mother's claim that swearing demonstrated a lack of vocabulary as to his childhood household rules. Smith became so sharp with his clean words that his players often joked that they wished he would curse.

Thriftiness was another family value, which eventually made Dean Smith a great complement to Frank McGuire's freewheeling ways at UNC. Alfred often challenged his children by offering money if they made certain grades in school, but he also expected them to spend only one third of the reward and either save or donate the rest to charity. Dean occasionally chose a fourth option, giving any extra money he had to some of his friends who needed it the most.

Dean Smith (22) never started for Kansas, but as a senior he did appear in all twenty-five games of the 1952–1953 season, including this road loss at Rice. *(Courtesy of Rich Clarkson)*

Meanwhile, in Chapel Hill, Frank McGuire *(right)* was in his first season at North Carolina, having brought his old college coach, Buck Freeman, out of retirement to be his trusted assistant. *(Courtesy of North Carolina Collection at UNC-CH)*

LEFT: Lennie Rosenbluth's majestic hook shot over Wake Forest's Wendell Carr led to the three-point play that secured UNC's fourth win over the Deacons in 1957 and [RIGHT] kept the Tar Heels' dream season alive. *(Courtesy of Raleigh News and Observer)*

Frankie McGuire *(center)* was Carolina's lucky charm that season, as Rosenbluth *(left)* and his teammates were frequent guests at the home of Frank and Pat McGuire during their run to the national championship. *(Courtesy of North Carolina Collection at UNC-CH)*

ABOVE: Kansas grad Dean Smith *(right)* replaced Buck Freeman as McGuire's assistant coach in May of 1958; [BELOW]: three years and three months later, he was introduced by McGuire *(right)* and UNC athletic director Chuck Erickson *(center)* as the Tar Heels' new head coach. *(Courtesy of North Carolina Collection at UNC-CH)*

Ken Rosemond *(right)*, a reserve on the 1957 team, joined the UNC staff in 1958 and eventually helped Smith *(left)* recruit Pennsylvania high school star Larry Miller with promises of a new arena in Chapel Hill. *(Courtesy of UNC Sports Information)*

(Left to right) Ken Rosemond, Larry Miller, and Dean Smith in front of the construction site for Carmichael Auditorium, which opened in 1965. *(Courtesy of UNC Sports Information)*

John Lotz *(right)* and Bill Guthridge *(left)* were Smith's full-time assistants. *(Courtesy of UNC Sports Information)*

Eddie Foglcr *(left)*, Guthridge *(right)*, and Smith recruited some of Carolina's greatest players in the 1970s, and the NCAA allowed schools to have a third assistant in 1978. *(Courtesy of UNC Sports Information; Bob Donnan)*

Smith *(left)* tabbed the unknown Roy Williams *(far right)* as his "restricted earnings coach" for $2,700 a year. *(Courtesy of UNC Sports Information; Bob Donnan)*

Smith *(left)* won his first national championship in 1982, beating Georgetown in a thriller that came exactly twenty-five years after McGuire's Miracle. *(Courtesy of Hugh Morton)*

Dean Smith cut down the nets in New Orleans for a second time in 1993. *(Courtesy of Hugh Morton)*

By 1988 former All-American Phil Ford *(right)* had returned to the UNC program as an assistant coach. *(Courtesy of Jim Hawkins)*

After thirty-six seasons, Dean Smith announced his retirement in October of 1997. He departed with 879 career victories, the most of any major college coach at that time, and a resolve that it was time to step down and turn the program over to long-time aide Bill Guthridge. *(Courtesy of Dan Sears)*

The family's idyllic life ended shockingly on December 7, 1941, when their regular Sunday afternoon radio programs were interrupted by news of the Japanese bombing of Pearl Harbor. It changed Smith forever, as some of the high school players he had admired were enlisting in the armed services. For the next four years, the Smiths said good-bye and "God Bless" to many of Alfred's former players, who marched off to war while the family worked at the Red Cross Club, rolling bandages and preparing CARE packages for the troops, and contributed at home, rationing gasoline and learning to use honey and syrup in place of sugar.

Among Dean Smith's most sorrowful memories of childhood were the losses of human life, which far outweighed results on the fields and courts and gave him an early perspective on the games he played and later coached. When Alfred's former players came home safely, they faithfully stopped by the house, and they all mourned those who did not make it back. When Dean was twelve his best friend, Shad Woodruff, grew ill and died quickly from a virulent form of polio after both boys had sipped from the same soda pop bottle at the schoolyard. Dean stayed outside his friend's hospital room for hours and then grieved by assembling a scrapbook of Shad's life for the Woodruff family.

Thus, Smith learned early that important relationships were not always easy, but the bonding that occurred through sports seemed so much stronger than the frivolous friendships other kids made. He was becoming a coach from a formative age, and he long maintained that those kinships were the key to his thinking.

Years of tagging along with his father to practice and games sold Smith on his chosen profession. He became a quarterback in football, a guard in basketball, and a switch-hitting catcher in baseball—barking out signals from all three positions and unwittingly preparing to coach.

He wound up playing for his father for only one season, on the Emporia freshman football team, and took ownership in the role by constantly diagramming formations and showing them to Alfred for approval. Quarterbacks called most of their own plays in those days, and Smith began thinking two or three snaps ahead, trying to set up third down by what he called on the first two plays of the series.

When Dean was ready to begin high school, Alfred retired from coaching and moved the family to Topeka, the state capital, to take a job with the local VA hospital. During Dean's ninth-grade year at Emporia, Joan had scolded her little brother for acting like a "cocky junior high school athlete." Smith said the dressing down was timely because his natural ability had topped out, his growth spurt stopped at 5'10", and he wound up on the tail end of the athletic bell curve.

"I was the best athlete I would ever become in the ninth grade," Smith said. "I didn't improve much after that. I once thought I'd grow to 6'4" but never grew any more at all."

He started as a sophomore in all three sports for Topeka High but at 150 pounds, he hardly distinguished himself enough to command a college scholarship. His first touchdown pass in football went to a 6'3" gifted split end named Adrian King, who was black and later became a state champion in the high hurdles. Another archaic rule in Kansas high school athletics kept the basketball teams segregated to avoid interracial dances following home games at night.

Smith was aware that he was playing in the same Topeka gym where his father's team had won the 1934 state title after being forced to leave its only black player, Paul Terry, back in Emporia. He complained to Topeka principal Buck Weaver but never acted on his instinct to mobilize the student body to try to change the policy. He regretted it whenever he saw the motto above the door of the library that read: "By nature all men are alike, but by education become different."

Like most Kansans growing up in the 1940s, Smith avidly followed the state university's basketball team, and he listened to a young radio announcer named Curt Gowdy call the Jayhawk games. Kansas was coached by the famed Dr. Forrest C. "Phog" Allen, who had succeeded the game's inventor, Dr. James Naismith. The beautiful college town of Lawrence sat only twenty-five miles from Topeka and was a dream destination for Smith after he had visited there as a young boy and his father gave him photographs of the campus and football stadium. The comparison with Chapel Hill was not lost on Smith years later.

Smith dreamed of being recruited by Kansas, but he was only good enough to attract serious attention from several smaller colleges, in addition to Baylor and Kansas State, where Smith knew assistant basketball coach Tex Winter. On a recruiting visit to Manhattan, Kansas, Smith was offered a partial scholarship and a chance to earn extra money by selling programs during K-State football games. He went home to think about it and talk to his parents.

Although Smith had met Dr. Allen through his father, he didn't dare call him. But he contacted assistant coach Dick Harp, who knew of the scrappy guard on the Topeka team that finished third in the state tournament. When Harp heard what K-State had offered Smith, he said Kansas could match it with an academic scholarship based on Smith's strong high school record (he was thirty-seventh in a graduating class of 647) and a similar chance to make extra money.

Smith peddled programs during KU home games and made $40, sometimes $50, a week. He also worked in the equipment room at the campus gym, a job Smith liked because he could study while working, hardly looking up from his book when he had to hand out towels.

And, oh yes, Harp told Smith he was welcome to try out for the freshman team. Smith became a starter and played well but without any realistic prospect of starring on the varsity level. Smith also had gone out for freshman football at KU and was the third-string quarterback and safety, which led him to contemplate quitting the sport he admittedly liked best.

Kansas did not have a freshman baseball team, but that spring something more important occurred with the outbreak of the Korean War. Unknowingly choosing the same service discipline as McGuire, Smith joined the Air Force ROTC so he could finish college before being drafted. Following graduation, he had to serve four years of active duty, where he would form the most important relationship of his professional life.

In August of 1950, about the time Smith was preparing to return to Lawrence for his sophomore year, a baby boy was born to Lallage and Babe Williams in Marion, North Carolina, near where they lived in the one-stoplight hamlet of Spruce Pine and so far removed from anything except Appalachia that his entire story seems somehow out of a Victorian novel.

From the beginning, even after his family moved close to the "big city" of Asheville, Roy Williams and his older sister were raised in a world apart from the tumultuous streets of New York City that fortified Frank McGuire and the nurturing neighborhoods of small-town Kansas that reared Dean Smith.

Indeed, the odds that Roy Williams would ever escape the life he was born into were more daunting than the Appalachian Mountains themselves. Williams' heritage was more of Cherokee Indians proudly trying to hold onto their land, of Daniel Boone blazing a trail through the Cumberland Gap, of the natives and French battling side by side to repress British colonialism, and, because there were so few slave owners in Appalachia, of a conflicted Confederacy that retained many loyalists to the Union Army.

The Civil War brutalized the region, often pitting family members and brothers against one another. When carpet-bagging businessmen recognized the wealth of resources in the mountains—coal, timber, and natural gas—many Appalachians sold their land and mineral rights for up to fifty cents an acre. Then the impoverished people were hired for pennies to work on the land they once owned. Their legacy became a lifestyle of backwoods housing and one-room schools, driving many men from their families and toward the cities to seek work and a better life. This was no normal childhood by any stretch for any boy.

Grain alcohol, which turned boredom to belligerence in the boondocks, tore apart Williams' family, which consisted of thirteen aunts and uncles on his father's side and ten on his mother's. During father Babe's binges, Lallage (or Mimmie to her family) sometimes spirited her two children away to one of her siblings or to a room at the Shamrock Court Motel, which was owned by another relative. The three of them spent one summer crammed into a small single-wide in a trailer park.

"Things were really tough, and it wasn't pleasant," Williams said. "Back then I didn't understand it, or like it, but I didn't let it dominate my life."

They always returned to their house on Warren Avenue, helplessly enabling the alcoholic father, before it ended for good, when Mimmie and her two children moved to a tiny, two-bedroom rental on Reed Street near Biltmore High School. Babe had taken up with what would be his second of five wives. Finally, his family had a place of its own that he couldn't destroy. The new home gave Mimmie and her children some peace of mind, but they had no money to live on.

Mimmie was not averse to hard work, having picked cotton as a child with her brothers and sisters and now putting in a full shift at a shoe factory, but she could not make ends meet on one job. She cleaned houses on the weekends and took in other people's ironing and darning, attacking the pile of clothes after cooking biscuits and gravy for Frances and Roy and putting them to bed.

"My mom had to battle every day to make things go, so on Friday she could pay this bill and that, and then have enough left for food," Williams told *Sports Illustrated* in 1997. "Some of my worst memories were coming home from school and finding her ironing. Ten cents for a shirt, ten cents for a pair of pants, and this after she had worked all day. You don't think that was hard to see? I knew that a lot of moms didn't have to do that, and I didn't want to watch her. So I'd just leave."

But he always returned to care for Mimmie. While Frances sometimes stayed with girlfriends, her little brother never spent a night away until he was in high school. "He felt he needed to be there," Frances, who died in 2007, once said. "He was like a protector to her."

At first, young Roy had no father and no father figures—no big brothers, like McGuire, or a police precinct looking out for him, and a universe away from Smith, who had the ultimate mentor in a father and coach.

In fact, his family was in such a daily struggle that he had no time for frivolities like following sports. Williams said he "knew nothing" of the University of North Carolina, had never heard of Frank McGuire and how his Tar Heels took on a seven-foot giant from Kansas in 1957.

Of his numerous cousins, only one of them played organized sports. Roy was the second when he joined a team in the seventh grade and eventually became the first high-school athlete in his family. He was also the first Williams to ever think about going to college, but he never had that as a realistic goal growing up because they were so poor.

Roy made friends easily and spent every day after school with them, "losing myself" in the games they played in the Biltmore schoolyard before they walked home for supper. That a young, charismatic senator from Massachusetts had been elected president of the United States about that time and excited much of the country meant little to a youngster in the mountains of North Carolina.

Unlike young Frank McGuire and young Dean Smith, faith did not play a big part in Roy Williams' childhood. Mimmie took her two kids to church on Sunday mornings when she could but, frankly, there was not a lot to have faith in. From those beginnings, Williams never embraced a formal religion.

"We were just trying to get by, one day at a time," he recalled.

His only frame of reference was a life of near-poverty and examples, both good and bad, from his parents. Children of alcoholics invariably go one way or the other, turning into heavy drinkers themselves or refusing to touch the stuff. Harboring low-level anger at the ne'er-do-well father who made it so hard on his mother and a fear that it could happen to him, too, Roy chose the latter and never had so much as a beer. He so loathed the alcohol that ravaged his family that, as a high-school student, he jumped into friends' cars at night and served as the designated driver long before the beer companies coined the phrase out of self-defense.

Williams also found a hero in Mimmie, whom he has called an angel to this very day. She taught him the value of nose-to-the-grindstone grit, and she was always doing something to earn an extra dollar; the high-energy, multi-tasking millionaire coach of today came as much from that channeling as anything he learned from his male mentors.

One day, while riding the bus home from high school, Frances saw her kid brother hanging out with his buddies at the corner store. When Mimmie found out and asked him what they were doing, he said they had stopped to get a Coke after playing ball.

"But you don't have money for a Coke," she said.

"I just drink water," Roy responded.

From that point on, Mimmie ironed one extra shirt and left a dime on the kitchen table before going to bed so Roy could buy a Coke with his friends the next day. That led to the true story of how Roy Williams had a refrigerator full of Coca-Colas in his garage when he finally could afford to buy them himself.

Despite an exceedingly hard life that ended in 1992 from a heart attack while undergoing chemotherapy treatment, Mimmie left her son with a guidepost that was to steer him. Of the choices he would confront, she always told him: "Do the right thing. You'll make it work."

Radio and the *Asheville Citizen-Times* gave Williams, the teenager, his first glimpse of the outside world. He now knew about the basketball team at UNC, five hours down the mountain in Chapel Hill, and the names Billy Cunningham, Bob Lewis, and Larry Miller, and their coach Dean Smith. But he never thought they would mean anything to him.

Roy stayed in school, did his homework and used sports as his lifeblood. He played Little League and Pony League baseball and discovered basketball and, ironically, Ping-Pong at the local YMCA, where he spent his Saturdays. He loved basketball best because, even alone, he could still work up a sweat on the court by running incessantly—shooting and fetching the ball. Losing himself.

He became so competent with the round ball that he finally found his mentor and the man who changed his life in Buddy Baldwin, the coach at T. C. Roberson High School, which had opened after the merger of Valley Springs and Biltmore in 1962. Baldwin met Williams when Roy was a freshman and Baldwin loved his work ethic, his sincerity, and the manners Mimmie taught him. "I liked Roy's attitude, his competitiveness, the way he always said 'Yessir!' and 'Nosir!' and how he played both ends of the floor and tried to do everything you told him," said Baldwin, who became a best friend for life. In turn, Williams said Baldwin was the "first person to give me confidence, to believe in me."

Williams grew into a solid, if small, basketball player at 5'9" and 135 pounds, always hustling and squeezing every ounce out of his ability to earn a starting position as a sophomore at Roberson, where he went on to average 16 points a game and be named team captain as a senior.

"He was pretty hard-headed, even back then," Baldwin said. "He knew what to do on the court, what was needed, and I didn't need to call a timeout to tell him."

Summers were spent mostly working wherever he could find a job, like loading baggage for Piedmont Airlines at the Asheville Airport. Although earning extra money was the priority, Roy also found time to play nights and weekends in the summer leagues Baldwin had started.

An avid golfer, Baldwin introduced Williams to the game that turned into his enduring second love. Baldwin's regular foursome often drove out to Sapphire Valley, a new course that required the golf carts to stay on paths, so they brought Roy and a buddy along to carry their bags.

Years later, when it dawned on Williams that the group could have easily hired caddies at the course, he realized, "Coach just wanted to put a few dollars in our pockets more than anything. But I was intrigued with the game."

Idolizing Baldwin, who had graduated from UNC and briefly played freshman basketball, Williams decided even earlier than both McGuire and Smith that he wanted to coach. He first discussed it with Baldwin during his sophomore year in high school.

"He started talking to me about college, something as fundamental as that," Williams said. "It became the first thing I thought about in the morning and the last thing I thought about at night—the most important thing in the world to me."

Baldwin displayed what he called "extreme North Carolina bias" because he had grown up a basketball fan and enrolled at UNC a year after McGuire's 1957 team finished undefeated and won the national championship. "The reason I went to Chapel Hill was to watch great basketball," said Baldwin, who had played on Valley Spring's 1-A state champs his senior year.

So naturally he later wanted Williams to follow the same path—study education and, maybe, hang around the athletic department long enough for something to rub off on him. Then, during his junior year in high school, Roberson nominated Roy for a Morehead Scholarship to UNC. Williams did not advance beyond the early screening, but it gave him confidence in his ability to succeed in college.

By then, Williams had met Wanda Jones in algebra class and, while they remained mostly friends, she was already helping complete the circle broken when his parents split up. Mimmie, Roy's sister Frances, and Wanda restored his belief in family values, and the intense, fiery Baldwin balanced the women with a competitive atmosphere in school sports.

After making all-conference and all-county, Williams turned down several basketball scholarship offers to small schools—the biggest being Western Carolina—and a full academic ride from Georgia Tech. That riled up at least one of his teachers, who admonished the girls in her class to pay no attention to Roy because he would rather be a coach than an engineer.

"He was going to Georgia Tech to study engineering in their co-op program, where you went to school a year, then worked a year," Baldwin said. "But one day he told me that's not what he wanted to do. He was determined to be a coach, so I encouraged him to go to Carolina and study education." He and Wanda were both accepted at UNC and made plans for their freshman year, when they would officially begin dating.

The summer after his high school graduation, Williams played what he thought was his last organized basketball game when he captained an all-star team in the North-South game at Greensboro. Several weeks later, UNC assistant coach Bill Guthridge liked the hustle he saw in the youngster from the mountains during tryouts for the freshman team. Roy was able to put on the North Carolina uniform as the last man for a squad that featured the highly recruited Bill Chamberlain, Steve Previs, and Dennis Wuycik.

Williams barely knew who these big guys were. He hadn't followed college basketball, and certainly not recruiting, closely from the mountains, and he never witnessed a Carolina game in person until he arrived in Chapel Hill.

"Growing up, watching North Carolina play basketball just wasn't part of our family's deal," Williams said. "The first ACC basketball game I ever saw in person was when we played the preliminary game in the Charlotte Coliseum as freshmen."

He rarely got off the bench during the 1968–1969 season, mopping up in eleven of the seventeen games and taking a total of seven shots (he made two). In the team picture, he looked more like the mascot than one of the players, the frail kid at the end of the back row, shorter than both student managers. Indeed, his playing career was over.

Williams was a certifiable gym rat, and he went to work for the campus intramural office, umpiring softball games so well that he was promoted to supervisor of all officials. He ran a Woollen Gym schedule that included more than fifty basketball and volleyball games a day for dormitory teams, fraternities, and graduate schools. He also picked up a few bucks keeping statistics for Smith during varsity games, a tiny figure sitting in the corner of the catwalk, high above the Carmichael Auditorium playing floor.

Williams worked twenty-four hours a week doing what Mimmie had taught him because he needed the money to stay in school. He became so adept at managing student referees, controlling the highly contentious intramural games, and earning respect as the pint-sized czar of Woollen Gym that Guthridge again took notice. Guthridge recommended to Smith that Williams be hired to ref games at the Carolina Basketball School, the summer camp for hundreds of young kids and a few hotshot college prospects.

During those intramural days of winter, walking between courts at Woollen and the old Tin Can, Williams occasionally stopped at Carmichael Auditorium and poked his head through a portal to check out varsity practice. When a manager who was supposed to keep everyone but players and coaches out of the building told Smith "It's Roy up there watching," the boss nodded and let him stay.

By the summer of 1973, Williams was in grad school and watching Smith's practices more regularly, sitting in the stands at Carmichael with a legal pad and treating it like a lecture from the grand master. He watched with amazement the Friday afternoon that Smith threw the band Fleetwood Mac out of the auditorium for making too much noise while setting up for a concert that night. Smith and Guthridge also hired him as a full-time counselor at the Carolina Basketball School, and Williams impressed them with not only his energy but the same power of recall for which the head coach was becoming famous.

"In two days, he knew every camper in his gym by name," Smith said. "After the first year, he was the head of a gym, which was the quickest I had ever put anybody in charge of his own gym." One evening, Guthridge assigned Roy to referee an important camp game that included a sought-after rising senior from Rocky Mount, North Carolina, named Phil Ford. The highest-ranked point guard recruit in the country, Ford had dazzled fans at the Raleigh Times and Hillside holiday tournaments and already was widely known in the state.

Smith sorely needed Ford to get the Tar Heels to the same level as the vaunted N.C. State teams that had two other native North Carolinians—David Thompson and Tom Burleson. Smith wanted Ford, who was being pursued by schools from Maryland (coached by Lefty Driesell) to South Carolina (now coached by Frank McGuire) to have a good experience at the UNC camp. Williams' job was to make this particular game fun.

He had been made an unofficial part of Carolina's basketball program. "They knew who I was," he recalled.

When Williams eventually joined the UNC staff as a part-time assistant five years later, he talked incessantly about "my high school coach, Buddy Baldwin." After Baldwin visited Chapel Hill, Smith realized it was the same Buddy Baldwin who had to leave the freshman team so he could stay in school, graduate, and some day become a mentor to other young coaches and give someone like Roy Williams the chance of a lifetime.

This completed the connection to the Tar Heels among three men—McGuire, Smith, and Williams—from the most uncommon of backgrounds but with common values of family, hard work, loyalty, and love of team. The twists of fate that bound them would perpetuate a program for fifty years as perhaps the greatest sustained success story in American sport.

2

Born to Coach

THE same three men had mentors. The fatherless one wanted to be like his brilliant-but-troubled college coach. The son-of-a-coach sat on the bench in college and studied the man who wouldn't put him in the game. The alcoholic's kid took the advice of his first father figure and found the man he admired for a lifetime.

As a boy growing up in New York City, Frank McGuire knew he was either going to become a cop, a priest, or a coach. He liked how the policemen stood watch over the neighborhood and admired the men of cloth at his parish. But he also *loved* sports.

Ted Carroll and Marty O'Malley gave him a blueprint, and his coach at St. John's, Buck Freeman, became his first basketball mentor. It also helped that Freeman was a devout Catholic, thus winning favor with Anna McGuire, who was assured that her son's tuition, books, and meals would be covered by a college scholarship.

Because St. John's, a Vincentian school founded in 1870, was still located in Brooklyn at the time, McGuire lived at home during college. He got up every morning, put on a jacket and tie, slicked back his wavy red hair, and joined the other students for Mass. Then he went to class, becoming so proficient in Latin that he wound up tutoring classmates during his senior year.

Freshmen were ineligible for the varsity in 1932, so McGuire and his fellow frosh waited patiently during the season and played pickup games before the big team practiced. McGuire often hung around and watched how Freeman taught changing defenses, setting screens, and maneuvers like the old give and go, prodding players with praise and criticizing them through sarcasm.

Freeman was a coaching genius who would be with McGuire for a lifetime, but because St. John's played only teams from New York, Freeman never received national or even regional recognition despite winning more than 80 percent of his games. His "Wonder Five" of the late 1920s was well known around the city, and Freeman was on the way to his own elite coaching career until he began drinking heavily.

"Buck was always a confirmed bachelor, but he was married to the sport of basketball," McGuire recalled years later. "It was hard for him to understand why anyone would put something ahead of that. It bothered him for the players to have distractions like girlfriends, although it was tough to get caught in New York City."

During the spring, McGuire worked out with the St. John's baseball team, and Freeman arranged for several Brooklyn Dodgers to stop by practice on off-days. Whether or not he was a true major league pitching prospect, McGuire had enough potential to catch the eye of Dazzy Vance, a big right-hander who was in his last season with the Dodgers and nearing the end of his Hall of Fame career.

McGuire stayed in Greenwich Village during the summer, working on the docks and playing schoolyard games organized by Ted Carroll. One afternoon, Carroll brought young, handsome Joe Louis to Greenwich House to meet the residents. Louis was a Golden Gloves champion, and McGuire never forgot seeing him for the first time. A year later, Louis turned professional and, as the famed Brown Bomber, beat boxing legends Primo Carnera, Jack Sharkey, and Max Baer at Yankee Stadium, on the way to a heavyweight championship shot against James J. Braddock, the Cinderella Man from nearby Bergen, New Jersey. Louis beat Braddock and went on to defend his title twenty-five times in eleven years (including his famous first-round knockout of German Max Schmeling in June of 1938, which McGuire and Carroll watched from ringside).

McGuire started as a sophomore in the 1933–1934 season, becoming Freeman's defensive stopper while averaging a little over three points for the 16-3 Redmen. The game was still painfully low-scoring at the time; John McGuiness led the team with a 6.9 average. The next season, St. John's played in the first collegiate doubleheader at Madison Square Garden, losing to Westminster on December 29, 1934. NYU beat Notre Dame in the other game. Playing in the Garden brought big-time prestige to college basketball, owing to the large crowds the games attracted and to the press coverage they commanded.

The Redmen played three more times at the Garden that season—losing to City College of New York (CCNY) and Long Island but defeating Manhattan—on their way to a 13-8 record, Freeman's worst as a head coach. Bringing college ball to the Garden was the brainchild of twenty-nine-year-old sportswriter Ned Irish, who rented the building for the first doubleheader and, after it drew 18,000 fans, quit his job at the *World-Telegram* to enter the promotions business. McGuire later befriended Irish, another reason his teams were always welcomed back to what became known as "the world's greatest arena."

McGuire averaged nearly 6 points a game as a junior, playing with leading scorer Joe Marchese (7.3) and best buddies Java Gotkin and the unselfish Reuben "Rip" Kaplinsky. For years after that, McGuire's teams would hear him bellow out, "Play smart like Kaplinsky!" even though most of his players thought he was making up the name. McGuire's colorful yarns most often mixed fact with fiction.

As a senior, McGuire led St. John's to an 18-4 record, including five more games at the Garden, which had started hosting major intersectional matchups. In a Garden doubleheader that January, McGuire and St. John's played in one game while Ben Carnevale starred for NYU in the other. (A few years later, McGuire and Carnevale met in North Carolina and became fast friends for life.) The following December, Long Island University was the forty-third consecutive victim of Stanford, which featured Hank Luisetti, popularly credited for introducing the one-hand shot to basketball.

Because Freeman was so well known in New York, Ned Irish also gave St. John's a chance to play heavily promoted games against teams from outside the city. One of them was a narrow loss to a rough-and-tumble opponent, after which McGuire threatened to take on the entire team in the runway to the locker room before coaches intervened. He had an Irish temper in those days and carried it with him into young manhood until learning, and eventually mastering, that he could get further in life by not showing his emotions.

Besides being the next-to-last season of a jump ball following every made basket, it was the end for Freeman, by then a full-fledged alcoholic in need of help. His sad departure overshadowed an amazing head-coaching record of 177-31 at St. John's. The school replaced Freeman with another up-and-coming coach, Joe Lapchick, who had a great record at Iona Prep outside the city.

Belying his flamboyant persona of later years, McGuire was actually an honor student whose academic record attracted an immediate offer from Xavier to teach English and help coach the football and baseball teams at his high school alma mater. He was not talented enough for major league baseball, and pro basketball was just getting started, so McGuire began his coaching career at Xavier. He wound up teaching Latin, an entrance requirement for St. John's and other colleges. In his spare time, he supplemented his $4,000 salary by refereeing and playing in the old American Basketball League.

In 1938, at age twenty-five, McGuire was named head basketball (and baseball) coach at Xavier; his eventual nine-year record was 126-39, winning better than 76 percent of his hoops games. He had also become a man about town in New York, joining other young people in the swing craze popularized by big band leaders Benny Goodman, the Dorsey brothers, and Glenn Miller. He and his pals frequented dance clubs, where they did the risqué Big Apple and Lindy Hop.

On one such night out, McGuire got serious with Patricia Johnson, whom he had known since high school and throughout college. An accomplished dancer, Johnson had been a childhood actress and member of the original "Our Gang" comedy troupe that included Spanky McFarland and Jackie Cooper. The ensemble was eventually renamed "The Little Rascals" for movie serials and television.

McGuire and Pat Johnson began dating and were married in April of 1940. Pat had become a prominent fashion model, and with FDR having rebuilt the nation's confidence, the newlyweds lived a carefree lifestyle as New Yorkers on the move.

After the Japanese bombed Pearl Harbor in 1941, McGuire

and his boyhood buddy Jim Fitzpatrick volunteered for the Navy air corps. "Fitz" had just graduated from Annapolis and had to serve somewhere, and they agreed on naval aviation. McGuire entered six weeks of ROTC training after the Xavier season ended and received his commission as an ensign with three possibilities of where to attend Navy V-5 flight school. He and the very pregnant Pat were sent to Chapel Hill, North Carolina, a serendipitous assignment that he originally did not like.

"That was my last choice," McGuire said later. "But I'm thankful that the Navy ignored my other choices because I met people there who would become lifelong friends."

One of them, former NYU star Carnevale, had also become a coach and came to be acquainted with many people in the UNC athletic department. He wound up coaching the Carolina jayvee squad in his spare time, and McGuire occasionally sat on his bench during games.

The college town of Chapel Hill turned into a virtual wartime Who's Who from the sports world, including young Paul "Bear" Bryant, who landed his first college football head-coaching job at Maryland right after the war; Boston Red Sox slugger and soon-to-be renowned Navy pilot Ted Williams, the last major leaguer to hit .400 (.406 in 1941); and a future Yale baseball player, George Bush, years before he entered politics. In 1944, Otto Graham, who was third in the 1943 Heisman Trophy balloting after originally going to Northwestern on a basketball scholarship, attended the same flight school.

After a month or so, McGuire was on a first-name basis with almost everyone he met in town, including the local high school basketball coach, who needed help with off-season motivation for some of his players. McGuire happily drove over to the old Chapel Hill High School on Merritt Mill Road a couple of nights a week, watched scrimmages, and talked to players about the game he loved.

One afternoon, McGuire drove the eight miles to Durham and Duke's Gothic campus, where a magnificent gym had been built in 1940 with the money the school's football team made from its 1939 Rose Bowl loss to Southern Cal. The biggest basketball arena south of the Palestra in Philadelphia, Duke Indoor Stadium's seating capacity of 8,000 included 6,000 theater-style chairs in a balcony above student bleachers that ringed the court.

McGuire also visited N.C. State in Raleigh and saw the aborted "eighth wonder of the world"—a steel skeleton of a basketball coliseum bigger than Duke's. The bombing of Pearl Harbor halted construction, and State remained unsure what to do with the Erector set of an eyesore on the edge of campus.

On another trip to Raleigh, McGuire met entrepreneur Joe Murnick, who went on to found professional wrestling in North Carolina. They remained friends, and ten years later Murnick made the initial call to McGuire about coming back as UNC's head basketball coach. In the loyalty-based hierarchy McGuire later built, Murnick's son, Elliott, was named a team manager as soon as he enrolled at UNC.

McGuire's first child, Patricia Jean, was born in Chapel Hill in late April of 1942, and he returned to New York to resume his teaching and coaching at Xavier High School.

Meanwhile, Carnevale saw active duty for two years and nearly died when his PT boat was torpedoed in the Pacific. He returned to flight school in Chapel Hill to serve out his commission, and UNC asked him to become its twelfth basketball coach. The Navy agreed to pay his salary to succeed Bill Lange, who had resigned suddenly.

During Carnevale's two seasons with the Tar Heels, McGuire stayed in touch and attended the 1946 NCAA semifinals at

Madison Square Garden, where Carolina edged Ohio State in overtime before losing the championship game 43-40 to big Bob Kurland and Oklahoma State. UNC had a gangly twenty-six-year-old forward named Horace "Bones" McKinney, who had begun his college career before the war at N.C. State. From there, Bones went into preaching and coaching because he couldn't make ends meet in either profession, and he wound up at Wake Forest, where he would engage in some legendary ACC sideline battles.

Football was still king at Carolina at the time, and Carnevale proved to have great insight about the future of his sport. After the war ended, a scatback named Charlie Justice arrived in Chapel Hill from Asheville, and the Tar Heels enjoyed a brilliant four-year run with Carl Snavely as head coach. Behind the triple threat nicknamed "Choo Choo," they won thirty-two games and two Southern Conference titles, reaching the Sugar Bowl twice and one Cotton Bowl.

The football team played beneath the tall pines at scenic Kenan Stadium on glorious autumn weekends. Perhaps the greatest of those occasions came on the opening day in 1948, when Justice and Carolina crushed Texas before an adoring, shirt-sleeve crowd of 45,500. After the 34-7 loss, Longhorns coach J. Blair Cherry said he only wanted to "get this game over with" and go back to playing "real ball" in the Southwest.

Meanwhile, the basketball team shared Woollen Gymnasium with the student body and intramural programs, and the coach's office was in the ticket booth. Clearly, basketball was just something between football seasons in the South.

Carnevale left for the head-coaching job at the Naval Academy, where he remained for twenty years as a commissioned officer and not an employee of the athletic department. This protected Carnevale from getting fired, a strategy McGuire later shared with other coaches who were considering jobs at service academies. One of them, Steve Belichick, took McGuire's advice when he left the UNC football staff to be an assistant coach at Navy, a job he kept for thirty-three years. Belichick's young son, Bill, was born in Chapel Hill, and went on to become the controversial Super Bowl champion coach of the New England Patriots.

In April of 1947, Joe Lapchick resigned as St. John's basketball coach and moved to the NBA's New York Knickerbockers. Surprisingly, the school hired the thirty-four-year-old McGuire, who was welcomed back despite relative inexperience. Lapchick had led the Redmen to eleven straight winning seasons and seven NIT berths, but many alumni were embarrassed that he had only a sixth-grade education and basically had been a basketball orphan ever since. The 6'5" Lapchick grew up on the schoolyards of the city, turned pro at nineteen, and played for the original Celtics before going into coaching

By contrast, McGuire gave St. John's everything it wanted—a fine academic background, pedigree, and reputed local knowledge of how to recruit the best players to keep the Johnnies on top. Although he loved coaching high school, McGuire could not turn down the offer of a $7,000 salary, which the school increased to $7,500 as soon as he accepted. Due to the elevated cost of living in New York, he was thought to be the highest-paid college coach in the country. But the young, dapper Irishman knew he needed help in his new job when he made the quantum leap from high school to college.

McGuire tried to hire Freeman at St. John's as his assistant and was rebuked because of Freeman's drinking problems. McGuire had remained loyal to the chronic alcoholic, helping him dry out after binges and keeping him connected to the one sport he loved more than the bottle.

Instead, McGuire tabbed former St. John's player Al DeStefano and used Freeman as a scout while he was on the wagon. Mc-Guire had never recruited before and had to learn how to identify the high school players with the most college potential. He also enlisted his old pal "Uncle Harry" Gotkin to steer the best prep stars in New York to St. John's.

The first target was Bob "Zeke" Zawoluk, a 6'6" stud of German descent, and McGuire began a tactic that would bolster his recruiting success throughout his career, wooing the family even more than the player. He went to see Zawoluk's mother, a tall blonde named Gussie who had been recently widowed when her husband died in a car accident. She had wanted her son to go to school away from New York City, but McGuire drank coffee with her on several morning visits and, on one occasion, waltzed with her in the living room of the family's comfortable brownstone. He convinced Gussie to let her son play for him.

The Redmen needed Zawoluk because Lapchick had not recruited well his last few years and left McGuire with little to replace the graduating Harry Boykoff, the first 1,000-point scorer at St. John's. One player who did return was scrappy guard Dick McGuire (no relation), who became the defensive stopper in much the same way Frank McGuire was for Freeman. Dick McGuire had a younger brother, Al, who followed him to St. John's. The McGuires, from the tough seamen's neighborhood of Rockaway, Long Island, went on to become Hall of Famers in basketball, Dick as a pro player and coach and Al as a college coach. Al won an NCAA title at Marquette, beating UNC for the championship in 1977, then turned into a colorful television commentator and continued to enjoy widespread fame.

When Zawoluk signed with St. John's after his senior season in high school, it took some pressure off McGuire, whose first team endured a tough year and had to win six of its last nine games to finish with a 12-11 record. He was uptight on the bench, yelling at players and officials. When he was on the way to Madison Square Garden one day, a Yellow Cab cut him off and at the next light McGuire wanted to confront the driver. Luckily, his friend Tom Paprocki of the Associated Press was in his car and restrained McGuire.

"You're a poor excuse for a coach!" Paprocki said. "If you can't control your temper any better than that, you have no right to be handling a team of kids. If my kid played for you, I'd yank him off the team."

McGuire remembered that confrontation. The next day he thanked Paprocki, who became an adviser on how to deal with the press along with first mentor Ted Carroll, the tall, slender black man usually seated behind the St. John's bench.

Image was already important to McGuire, who wore custom-tailored suits, diamond cufflinks, and shiny shoes and had manicured fingernails. He also had continued Freeman's policy that players had to be clean shaven with short haircuts or they couldn't even practice. He bought matching blazers and slacks for them so they looked like champions when they entered the gym.

In turn, the Redmen's play began to match the McGuire style, including a stunning upset of CCNY, which was coached by icon Nat Holman, at the Garden. "Nat Holman once said to me, 'Jesus Christ, do you pick guys for their looks?' " McGuire related. "I told him that when St. John's walked into the Garden, they were always a handsome group of guys. It was all in the way they dressed. I wouldn't stand for anything else."

With senior Dick McGuire named captain and Al McGuire moving up to the varsity, they promised to be better in 1949. Then, when Zawoluk and fellow recruits Jack McMahon and Ron MacGilvary reached the varsity the following season, St. John's was a

New York City power again, ready not only to win the NIT but earn its first bid to the NCAA tournament, which was expanding from eight teams to sixteen in 1951.

McGuire also coached the St. John's baseball team and took the Redmen to the NCAA championship game in 1949 before he ever did so in basketball. He was the only college coach in history to advance that far in those two sports. He thus made more life-long friends among his former players from the diamond.

One was second baseman Lou "the Lip" Carnesecca, who, ironically, did not play basketball but refereed scrimmages for McGuire's team and sat in the stands to observe practice. "Looie" later turned to the round ball and had two stints coaching the Redmen for a total of twenty-four seasons, eventually being named to the Basketball Hall of Fame.

Another was a wise-cracking infielder named Mario Cuomo, whom McGuire threw off the team for insubordination. "He was a great third baseman," McGuire recalled, "but we needed a catcher. When he refused, I told him to get behind the plate or I would take away his scholarship. He said I couldn't do that because he was on an academic scholarship. I made him turn in his uniform. He was an Italian kid who wouldn't listen to me. If I knew he was going to become governor of New York, I never would have chased him off the team." After reconnecting as New York power figures, Cuomo and McGuire laughed about their first encounter, and St. John's eventually awarded Cuomo his letter in baseball at the school's athletic banquet.

"Whatever Frank wanted in the state of New York for ten or twelve years, he could have it, within reason," Al McGuire once said. "All he had to do was call the governor. The favor would have nothing to do with him—it was always to help someone else."

During McGuire's second season as a college coach, another

daughter, Carol Ann, was born to Frank and Pat. They decided to try for a third child, hoping for a boy.

When Dean Smith enrolled at Kansas in 1949, Phog Allen had already coached the Jayhawks for thirty years and was coming off two consecutive non-winning seasons for the second time ever. Allen was in the twilight of his unconventional career in which he used his degree in osteopathy to try to prevent injuries to his players. He earned the nickname "Doc" largely because he carried his massage table with him and got his and other athletes to lie down so he could adjust their backs. Doc Allen became so renowned in this little-known art that professional stars sought his treatment, including a young outfielder from Oklahoma named Mickey Mantle.

It was an optimistic time in America, and especially in the Midwest, because favorite son and Missourian Harry Truman had stunned New York governor Thomas Dewey in the 1948 election. Thousands of veterans went to college on the GI Bill and produced Baby Boomers that swelled the nation's population. Students on campus were more interested in drinking beer and dancing, and some coeds even dared to bring the newest fashion craze, the bikini, back to school.

The year was so fulfilling for Smith that he formed his career-long stance on freshman eligibility. More than twenty years later, when freshmen became eligible to play varsity sports, Smith opposed the rule change. He always advocated for the old system as in the best interests of college athletes.

During Smith's playing days at Kansas, schools expected freshmen athletes to spend most of their time getting acclimated to college life and working on fundamentals. Practicing every day but playing limited games gave him the chance to sink his teeth into academics and also enjoy his newfound social freedom. He joined Phi Gamma Delta fraternity, where he ran the Coke machine to pick up some extra money and began saving to buy his first car. Life for the son of conservative Kansas schoolteachers was better than ever.

Gil Reich, his teammate and frat brother, said Smith demonstrated early recruiting talent when he convinced students rushed by Phi Gam to join the house. "He was a salesman, I guess you could say," Reich recalled. "He always showed the ability to get along with all kinds of people."

While Smith played for the freshman team, KU's varsity rebounded from losing twenty-seven games the two previous seasons to become co-champions of the old Big Seven Conference behind sophomore sensation Clyde Lovellette. The league title was Doc Allen's first in five years. Smith watched from the stands as the Jayhawks lost to Bradley in the 1950 NCAA district playoffs at Kansas City and finished with a modest 14-11 record.

That spring, Smith made the first major decision of his life by simply using his head over his heart. Secretly, he loved football most because of the creative strategies involved on both sides of the ball. But, as one of six quarterbacks on the freshman team and being too small for any other position, he knew his chances of playing for the KU varsity were minimal. On the other hand, he was good enough in basketball to contend for playing time, and by now he was at least pondering a career in coaching.

For years, Smith would counsel ambivalent players and friends to make the same kinds of logical choices. He had a big forward at North Carolina, Mark Mirken, who promised his dying father that he would become a doctor. But Mirken struggled mightily with pre-med science courses, and Smith urged him to take aptitude tests that confirmed he would be much happier pursuing a law degree. Smith convinced Mirken that his deceased father would want his son to be successful, even if it meant a profession other than medicine.

As a sophomore at Kansas, Smith made the varsity and rode the end of the bench as KU went 16-8 with four juniors and a senior in the starting lineup. But they failed to win the league and reach the NCAA tournament. He was living the dream of wearing the Kansas uniform every day even though he appeared in only five games. Smith considered it a mixed omen when Allen asked him to work with the football players who came out late for the team, sending them to the opposite end of the court to teach the offenses and defenses they had already taught the other players. "Coach [Dick] Harp told me it would save time and give me practical coaching experience," Smith recalled in his autobiography, A Coach's Life.

Smith worked exceptionally hard that summer, thinking he had a chance to replace graduating senior Jerry Waugh. He ran, played endless pickup games, and spent hours alone in the empty Topeka gym trying to get his funny-looking two-hand jump shot to fall consistently. His father showed up occasionally to feed him the ball so he could practice using his quickness to get off his shot or drive around his man. He also did drills that would help him become a better defender.

But when the Jayhawks opened the 1951–1952 season on a thirteen-game winning streak—with senior Lovellette averaging more than 28 points and shooting nearly half the team's free throws—Smith languished as the seventh or eighth man, appearing in only every few games. He spent most of his time alongside sophomore LaVannes Squires of Wichita, who was Allen's first black player. Having lived through his father's racial strife back in Emporia, Smith was proud to be Squires' teammate.

The open guard spot went to another Dean—Dean Kelley. He was a 5'11" junior from McCune, Kansas, and good friend to Smith when they were not competing ferociously in practice.

Conservative and slow to substitute because he thought his players were in shape and should not tire, Doc Allen put in a full-court pressing defense the week after losing at Kansas State and Oklahoma State. Kansas reeled off twelve more victories all the way to the Final Four in Seattle. The Jayhawks won two NCAA regional games in Kansas City, a similarity to Smith's first national championship as a coach exactly thirty years later, when his team won regional games in Charlotte and Raleigh to advance to New Orleans.

Smith averaged 1.6 points a game as a junior, but his shining moment came late in the semifinals against Santa Clara, when Allen called him off the bench to run the delay game and help salt away the 74-55 win. "Dean was sharp defensively and a good dribbler," said Reich, a football star who transferred from West Point and also was the Jayhawks' sixth man in 1952. "When we needed a delay, we brought Dean in. Against Santa Clara, we killed the clock and he pulled a real Phil Ford."

The Jayhawks captured the third national crown for KU and Allen, the first since they went back-to-back in 1922 and 1923. Smith played in nineteen games, including the final seconds of the NCAA championship victory over Frank McGuire's St. John's team. For the season, he took only 10 shots and was more interested in making assists and playing defense.

While trying to steer Smith toward medical school because there were "too many ups and downs in coaching," Allen knew his reserve guard was destined to follow his father's career. The guards ahead of him, Kelley, Reich, and senior Bill Hougland, were bigger and more talented, but Smith knew the game unlike anyone else on the team.

"It was really a case of two guards being better than Dean," Reich said. "We were all a little bigger and had an offensive dimension he didn't have."

Smith used his pine time to internalize Allen's coaching style for which elements he would embrace and what he would do differently if he ever got the chance to lead a team. Like Allen and Harp, and his own father, he became a coach who taught fundamentals first and did not favor players who had singular skills. He also adopted the well-known Allen philosophy that there was more to life than basketball. Allen often became an inspiration for his players beyond the court, and that resonated with Smith.

Conversely, Smith's later penchant for substituting freely, even giving five men the chance to come in as a unit, was likely forged during that frustrating time on the KU bench. Harp, the assistant coach who eventually ended his career on Smith's UNC staff, always marveled at his sponge-like nature to learn and retain information.

"He retained everything he learned and asked questions about everything because he was so interested in why we did things," Harp said. "Dean's talent of using his bench well was a gift that came to him. You have to have the courage to do it and also be smart enough to make it help you improve your chances of winning games."

In his senior year, Smith appeared in all twenty-five games as the Jayhawks attempted to match their feat of thirty years before by repeating as national champions. Lovellette graduated to pro basketball, but 6'9" B.H. Born became the next great KU big man, averaging 19 points. Dean Kelley's younger brother Allen moved up to the varsity and was the second-leading scorer with a 13-point average. Smith remained mostly a mop-up man. The team struggled early to gain an identity without Lovellette before finally winning the Big Seven title and qualifying for the NCAA tournament.

The Jayhawks had another tremendous advantage in the 1953 NCAA regional, playing two games in Manhattan, Kansas, where they edged Oklahoma City and Oklahoma State to advance to the Final Four in Kansas City. After the Jayhawks crushed Washington in the semifinals, Indiana nullified KU's crowd support in the title game with all the fans who had driven down to cheer on Branch McCracken's Hoosiers. The shootout was tied at the half, 41-41, then slowed down to a pair of two-man games between Born and Allen Kelley and Indiana's Don Schlundt and Charlie Kraak. Born finished with 26 points and Kelley with 20; Schlundt led all scorers with 30 and Kraak had 17. Despite three technical fouls, one of which got Dean Smith into the box score with a single free throw, the Hoosiers held on to win McCracken's second national championship, 69-68. That's how close Dean Smith came to having his name among those who had played for back-to-back NCAA title teams.

Smith's college career was over, but he did make the cover of one 1954 national preview magazine, which showed him and two teammates against Indiana. When it hit the newsstands, Smith was a volunteer graduate assistant at KU, helping Harp coach the freshmen, watching Doc Allen conduct varsity practices, and taking the first official steps into coaching. To support himself, he worked mornings for the Lawrence Paper Company before playing for the National Gypsum AAU team based in Parsons, Kansas, while awaiting his Air Force orders that spring as a second lieutenant.

By then Smith had also met two women who would have a lasting impact on his life. As a senior, he had dated Joan Guthridge from Parsons. She had a younger brother who, like Smith, idolized the Jayhawks and wanted to play for them after having grown up listening to their games on the radio. Also, like Smith, he was a 5'10" guard with more heart than skills. Bill Guthridge went to Lawrence occasionally while in junior high school, visiting his sister and hoping to hang around Hock Auditorium most of the weekend. One day, walking with Joan, he met Smith and began a big brother relationship that endured for the next five decades.

Guthridge wound up at Kansas State, receiving the same partial scholarship Tex Winter had offered Smith seven years earlier. He played on three K-State Big Eight conference champions, but as a senior in 1959 lost to a UNC team that included Smith as an assistant on Frank McGuire's coaching staff.

The night Smith graduated from KU, he met Ann Cleavinger, an occupational therapy student from Manhattan, Kansas. Smith and Cleavinger dated during his post-graduate year and were married just before he was shipped overseas to Germany. She spent six months on her last rotation at the Mayo Clinic in Minnesota before joining her husband at the base in Furstenfeldbruck outside of Munich, where Smith continued his basketball career by playing for and coaching the base team.

Luckily, Air Force General Blair Garland avidly followed college sports and had purposely assigned former college stars to Andrews Air Force Base outside of Washington, D.C. Relying on ex-Kentucky players Cliff Hagan and Frank Ramsey, and other college standouts, Andrews dominated military competition, convincing Garland that a strong basketball team in Europe would boost morale there as well. Smith was one of several former college players sent to Germany, and the team they fielded easily won the Air Force European title by going 11-0. They qualified for the Worldwide Air Force Championships back in Orlando, Florida, won, not surprisingly, by Andrews AFB.

Smith recalled: "We had seven air policemen, and one of the

guys was 6'7". I played myself all the time—everyone always gets better after they get out of college, you know! It was great fun and really whetted my appetite to coach."

During that season, Smith met another service coach, Bob Spear, in France. Spear was a pilot who flew a C-54 over Berlin in the airlift of 1948. He was also a world-class tennis player who loved to paint in his spare time. Spear had been an assistant to Ben Carnevale at the Naval Academy, which became an important association in Smith's coaching career.

Spear remembered how Kansas played pressure defense in 1953, and he picked the young Smith's brain on the strategy every time they saw each other. They attended a clinic together in Germany during the summer of 1955, where Red Auerbach, Bob Cousy, and Adolph Rupp lectured, and Smith even got to play one-on-one with "the Cooze." Spear kidded Smith that his defense could not do much with Cousy's driving hook shot. Although they were thousands of miles from home, these two coaches thirsted for all the basketball they could get.

Spear eventually asked Smith to consider joining him to start a team at the new Air Force Academy in Colorado. Smith, whose first daughter, Sharon, was born in Germany, saw it as an opportunity to move his family back to the States before the end of his active duty in April of 1956, when Doc Allen was set to retire and Smith had planned to join the Kansas staff of new head coach Dick Harp. Smith told Spear if he could work it out with the Air Force, he would go with him instead.

As a player-coach for half of the next European season—still giving himself many more minutes than Allen ever did—Smith led his team to an 11-1 record. He received his orders in December of 1955 to serve out the remainder of his tour at the Air Force Academy outside of Colorado Springs. His base team hated to see him go and the players presented him with a commemorative plaque and watch, touching Smith and reinforcing his decision to enter coaching full time.

Smith's first stop stateside was Lowry Air Force Base near Denver, where he and Spear cobbled together a basketball team while West Point grads trained the first class of Air Force cadets. This was a coaching Rubik's Cube because Air Force trainees could be no taller than 6'4" in order to fit inside the cockpits. Furthermore, academic entrance requirements were stringent. Suffice to say that no one enrolled at the Air Force Academy with dreams of playing professional basketball, and practice was a low priority for players.

Spear and Smith were more like colleagues trying to piece together a puzzle, and they managed to field their first varsity team in the 1956–1957 season. Running the old shuffle offense and a version of the Kansas man-to-man defense, Air Force posted an 11-10 record, remarkable in its anonymity among everyone but those in the fledgling academy athletic department. All coaches at Air Force worked together to recruit athletes for all of the sports, trying to dissuade them from attending West Point, Annapolis, or an Ivy League school. "They recruited me and said there would be great prestige to being in the second class that graduated from the Air Force Academy," said Lee Shaffer, who played for Press Maravich at Baldwin High School outside of Pittsburgh and prepped at the Manlius School in New York with many service-academy recruits before eventually going to North Carolina.

Early in that first season at Air Force, Smith's year-old daughter, Sharon, nearly died from a choking spell while his wife was full term with their second baby girl, Sandy. He raced through the streets to a hospital on an empty gas tank as Sharon began turning blue in Ann's arms. Luckily, they made it and an emergency tracheotomy saved Sharon. A week later, his wife and two daughters left the hospital together, aided by Smith and "Grandpa" Alfred, who flew in from Kansas to help the family.

After having spent four straight nights in the hospital chapel, Smith developed a new perspective on life. He began reading the Bible regularly, and studying theology became one of his passions. The traumatic incident in a young man's life contributed to the balance and composure Smith later demonstrated throughout his career—competing intensely but when the game was over understanding that basketball was never a matter of life and death.

In May of 1973, Roy Williams had two degrees from North Carolina in education but nowhere to go. He had turned down a spot in the doctoral program because he wanted to get out of the classroom and onto the court full time as a coach. He and high school sweetheart Wanda Jones were getting married that summer, but after that all bets were off.

Dean Smith made a bunch of phone calls on his behalf, but Williams was far down the pecking order of scholarship players always trying to crack the profession. Eddie Fogler, for example, had been a graduate assistant for two years and slid into the full-time opening after John Lotz left the UNC staff to take the head-coaching job at Florida.

Then came a call-back from Charles Lytle, the principal at Owen High School in Swannanoa, North Carolina, 10 miles outside of Asheville. When Lytle offered Williams the varsity coaching job at Owen, the principal experienced on a far smaller scale what the Kansas brass would encounter exactly fifteen years later.

"I was laughed at when I hired him," Lytle said. "Everybody told me, 'He's nothing but a statistician at North Carolina.' "

Owen hadn't posted a winning record in more than ten years, and the local alumni and citizens hoped the school would go for a bigger name to turn that tide. What they got was a miniature version of Dean Smith, on the court at least. He showed up at his first team tryout with a whistle around his neck and the practice plan written out by the minute. He had fulfilled his first dream: to coach high school basketball.

"I didn't know anything about shoe contracts or TV shows," Williams said. "I just really wanted to be like my high school coach, Buddy Baldwin, and that was it."

Like the owner who builds a successful restaurant chain by working the grill and washing dishes in his first store, Williams swept the gym floor, pulled out the bleachers, and wiped down the backboards, while Wanda often washed the team uniforms between games. He poured every ounce of himself into the job, believing it was what God had intended for him to do in the mountains of North Carolina.

From his first day as a head coach, Williams brought the practice plan that Wanda had typed out the night before to the gym. He began by gathering the team around him and presenting a thought of the day—just like Dean Smith did at Carolina.

Williams' first team beat what must have been a woebegone Drexel twice and finished 2-19. In his first two games against his mentor, Baldwin's Roberson team rocked Owen on the way to a 25-0 record and the state 1-A championship.

"We were pretty good that year, and they were down," Baldwin said, "but after his first season you could start to see the improvement in his teams and players."

Williams' preaching and teaching brought a change in attitude, culture, and finally the record at Owen, which was small enough that the basketball coach would not be fired after a couple of dud years. Some opponents laughed when the team that could not beat anybody arrived at road games dressed in coats and ties, but Williams had picked that up from Dean Smith (who had learned it from Frank McGuire) as a way of showing pride and building self-worth.

During that time, Williams also helped coach football and started the school's golf team. He taught physical education and was eventually named Owen's athletic director. By now, he and Wanda, an English teacher at neighboring Tuscola High School, had saved enough money to think about building a house.

All of this established Williams as a valued and trusted member of the community, where he began youth leagues and summer camps to form a feeder system into the junior high school and eventually to Owen. He privately tutored one young girl named Mary Ann Myers in ball handling, challenging her as much as any boy to reach her potential. She developed so well that her jersey eventually was retired at Miami of Ohio. Another youngster he pushed out of the nest was an awkward giant for his age named Brad Daugherty, who later starred at Owen and was eventually recruited by Carolina and Williams.

Owen basketball became an extended family presided over by Williams and his wife. Wanda packed up the sandwiches and snacks for road trips, hosted cookouts outside their tiny garage apartment, and made comfort food for the occasionally troubled player who came over for one-on-one time with the head coach. The Owen basketball culture sprang from the Carolina basketball family that Williams had observed in Chapel Hill, and it reflected how Buddy Baldwin had coached at T. C. Roberson.

"I felt like a part of his family," said Porky Spencer, a former player. "My father drove a truck and wasn't around much. Roy was like my father."

Williams was as tough on the court as he was compassionate off, another Baldwin bromide. He wanted his players to dive after loose balls and spill their guts trying to get into shape. As they did at Carolina, players had to run a mile in under seven minutes before they could officially join practice, and the coach was out there exhorting them to set and reach goals they once considered impossible.

He never got used to losing in his first two seasons, slamming clipboards and throwing his jacket, and he continued to take defeats like stomach punches, even after Owen posted his first winning record—14-6—in 1976. The Warhorses made it to the state playoffs for the first time in fifteen years, eliminated on a half-court heave at the buzzer.

That loss stayed with Williams for years, just like Kansas' defeat to Arizona in the 1997 NCAA regional when the Jayhawks were ranked No. 1 in the country, and the Tar Heels' loss to Georgetown in 2007 when they were six minutes from the Final Four. Yet Williams also felt pain for the coaches he beat, stemming all the way back to that first year.

"If you're not familiar with North Carolina, I-40 runs east and west through the state," he said recently. "Even now, when I'm driving on it, I like to go through Drexel. We beat Drexel both times my first year. And I wonder what happened to that coach."

Thirty years later after winning his first national championship in his fifth trip to the Final Four, Williams cried with his family and then sought out losing coach Bruce Weber of Illinois to console. He had seen Dean Smith do the same thing to Georgetown's John Thompson in 1982.

The Owen high school players who endured those first two years have remembered them fondly, especially the night Roy and Wanda had the team over for pre-game meal during a losing streak while the few local alumni who did care were still muttering about the statistician the school had hired. "There were fifteen, eighteen of us packed in there, crawling over each other to grab pieces of chicken," Porky Spencer told the *Raleigh News & Observer* in 2008. "He thought we needed to get closer, know what one another smelled like."

Williams has insisted those five years at Owen, like his playing days under Baldwin, shaped his attitude toward coaching individuals beyond their points and rebounds. He figured out how much building relationships meant to creating a winning team.

During the fifth season of a high school coaching career that would end with an overall 45-64 record, Williams began contemplating a bigger challenge. He wanted to coach basketball full time and not have to worry about teaching physical education classes and certifying students for mandatory activities they really did not like very much. "That's when I decided that maybe I should try to get into college coaching," he said, "because there that's all I would have to worry about . . . coaching kids to get better in basketball."

Following All-American Phil Ford's graduation from Carolina in 1978, the NCAA approved expanding Division I coaching staffs to include a restricted-earnings assistant—someone who would essentially work full time for part-time pay (an unfair labor practice that resulted in a successful multimillion-dollar lawsuit against the NCAA twenty-five years later). The UNC position began at a whopping $2,700 a year.

When discussing how to expand what was already hailed as the best coaching staff in college basketball, Smith, Bill Guthridge, and Fogler overwhelmingly agreed on the first person they would ask. "He had done well in high school," Smith reasoned, "and it was already in the back of my mind. This is the guy I want on my staff."

Williams had been a de facto part of the UNC program for more than ten years. He kept stats and observed practices as an undergraduate and helped Guthridge run the Carolina Basketball School during the summers between his seasons at Owen.

Aspiring to join the coterie of coaches that Smith developed, Williams was surely interested. But he and Wanda made a combined salary of $30,000, which was pretty good in the late 1970s. They had an infant son and were paying a mortgage on their first home.

After Smith extended the offer, Williams went to Baldwin first. "I knew how driven he was, how much he wanted to be a college coach, and always felt he would be successful at anything he tried," Baldwin said. "I told him, 'If this is what you want to do, just go tell Wanda to pack.'"

It wasn't quite that easy. "That's absolutely the dumbest thing I've ever heard of," she said. "We've got a new house, a new child. I'm getting ready to go back to work, we're going to be making decent money. I'm from here. You're from here. Our friends are all here. For $2,700 a year?"

The look on her husband's face suggested he didn't want their nice life in the mountains to be the last stop. "When do we leave?" Wanda said, giving in.

They sold the home in Swannanoa, strapped their one-year-old son, Scott, into their old blue Mustang, hitched a U-Haul trailer to the back and moved to a tiny apartment at Glen Lennox about a mile east of the UNC campus. "He had less money than me, and I was a student manager," recalled Chuck Duckett. "He had duct tape on the windows of his car, had one suit he wore all the time and a pair of two-tone shoes that were right out of Mayberry."

The NCAA naively thought these new positions would be

part-time jobs, so it was OK for Williams to work elsewhere to supplement his state salary. The results were sixty-, sometimes eighty-hour workweeks for the third assistant on the UNC staff. Because restricted-earnings coaches could not recruit or scout high school prospects, Williams had mostly clerical and organizational duties around practices and games. And he coached the Carolina junior varsity team of walk-ons, which kept his motivational skills sharp.

"Coach Smith gave me a lot of responsibility, a lot of freedom to do some things, and that was very satisfying," Williams said. "Each and every day he prepared all the assistants to become head coaches. He got us involved in every aspect of the program. It wasn't like you were just an academic guy or just a recruiter."

Every Sunday during the fall and winter, Williams left Chapel Hill at 5:00 A.M. to drive film canisters of the UNC football and basketball coaches' TV shows to stations in Greensboro, Charlotte, and Asheville. He had a home-cooked breakfast and a visit with Mimmie, his divorced working mother, and then he drove down the mountain toward another workweek.

For the five hundred miles of driving each week—on his day off—Williams was paid $105.00 minus gas expenses. He did that for five years, and the job lasted until they started transmitting coaches' shows via satellite.

In his other part-time job, he peddled Carolina basketball calendars after a third party proposed the idea of promoting the team with a poster that had head shots of the players and coaches, plus the schedule. Businesses could print their name and address in black and white (or Carolina blue for an extra twenty bucks) on the three-inch strip across the bottom.

The first year, Williams logged nine thousand miles and sold ten thousand five hundred calendars and made another $2,400. He eventually fired the middle man, who Williams said did not drive a mile or make a phone call and still made money on every calendar he sold. With the help of Wanda, who had a high school teaching job for $9,000 a year, the calendar business helped keep Williams' coaching career afloat.

By the time their daughter Kimberly was born in 1980, Roy and Wanda had pieced together an income that, along with their savings, allowed them to buy a house on the south side of Chapel Hill. After eventually, and in due course, acquiring wealth that enabled them to own beach homes in Charleston, South Carolina, and Wilmington, North Carolina, and signing a contract that paid him in excess of $2 million annually, Williams once calculated that during his first eight years in college coaching his family income averaged less than $40,000.

Even after his income swelled into the millions, Williams was reluctant to give up some of the habits of his success, almost as if he were afraid of losing everything he had earned in his improbable journey from a life of near poverty. At Kansas and Carolina, he recruited all of the primary targets himself, every year, meaning he has made most of the phone calls, written most of the letters and, even after a player signed a binding scholarship, still traveled hundreds of miles to watch him play during his last high school season.

That made Williams closer to McGuire in how they recruited— hands-on. Perhaps they liked to do it or did not trust anyone else to do it the right way. Or maybe they wanted to make doubly sure the kids they were getting came from the right backgrounds. McGuire relied on scouts like Harry Gotkin to identify players, but he never signed off on a kid until he met his family. With Williams, if crooked AAU coaches or so-called players' representatives were involved, he insisted on dealing directly with the parents or high school coach. Kansas and Carolina had the basketball clout to demand that.

In contrast, Smith eventually assigned his assistant coaches to handle the scouting, viewing of high school games, and early meetings with the top recruits, thus setting the stage for the head coach to go in and close the deal. Late in his career, when speculation swirled over his impending retirement, Smith encouraged players to pick Carolina because it was a top-notch university and had a great basketball program. Not because they were going to play for him. Of course, after all he had accomplished, that was easy for him to say.

The major common denominator for the city slicker, quiet Kansan, and the mountain man was their desire to help young people and show them the way. That is why as a Hall of Famer, the sixty-nine-year-old McGuire still treated an eighteen-year-old youngster he met for the first time with respect and dignity, inviting him into his penthouse at the St. Regis Hotel in New York, introducing him to his wife and offering him something to eat and drink. That is why as an embattled young coach at risk of losing his job, Dean Smith still had time to help a bewildered student in Woollen Gym find the drop-add desk. Also, that is why as a coach who had just won his first national championship, Roy Williams gave his personal vacation time to a fundraiser for his secretary's son, who had been diagnosed with childhood leukemia.

It was the way of their world with these three men. It was no coincidence that it also became the Carolina Way for more than fifty years.

3

The Irishman

FRANK McGuire always advised young coaches to cooperate with the newspaper guys and treat them all with respect, whether they were national personalities or local hacks. After learning to do it even better than his mentor, and to the dismay of many rival coaches, Dean Smith credited McGuire for sharing that wisdom. Smith's skill with sportswriters would often frustrate his coaching rivals, but it all began with the Irishman.

While coaching and teaching at Xavier High School, McGuire had the son of Associated Press cartoonist Tom Paprocki in one of his classes. Once after a Xavier game when McGuire grew angry with a local writer, Paprocki gave him the same kind of advice he would years later about the cab driver McGuire wanted to punch out.

"He told me that as long as I'm in the game, I would need the press and to get along with them," McGuire recalled. "He said, 'If you fight with them, you will run out of blood before they run out of ink!'

"Pap also told me, 'I'm your friend, but don't ever tell me anything you wouldn't want in the paper. That is my business, and it comes first.' "

McGuire gave writers nuggets of information that were harmless but which made them feel like he was confiding in them. In later years, Smith often began an aside to reporters with the qualifier, "Confidentially. . . ." The practice of telling them the truth—but not all of the truth—made McGuire and Smith masters of maneuvering the media into their camps, and it paid off handsomely with generally positive press coverage.

Although McGuire did not gamble, he knew those who did and who their bookies were. Once, when he ordered St. John's to hold the ball late in the game to protect its lead, beat writers who had bet on the Redmen to cover the point spread criticized him heavily for the ploy in the morning papers. From that point on, his teams kept playing and avoided the freeze. He was also careful to tell writers about any injuries that would hamper or sideline his star players. He wanted to be completely straight with reporters because many of them bet on his games.

At St. John's, McGuire also learned to invest time with the faculty to gain their support and assistance. He did it by reminding teachers of his own background as a good student, a St. John's graduate with honors, and convincing them he wanted his players to have overall success. One of his early recruits, promising freshman Jack McMahon, was flunking out, which would have made him ineligible the next season.

"Jack had a hard time adjusting, and I needed him in the worst sort of way," McGuire said. "I went to one of his instructors,

Father O'Riley, obviously a good Irish Catholic, and cried on his shoulder."

Father O'Riley was unmoved at first, because many freshmen eventually quit school and went to work. He even told McGuire that McMahon was not college material. Then the Father asked McGuire if McMahon was a good player. "He has a chance to be a great player," McGuire said, "the very heart of our team."

Because St. John's had become a New York City power under Joe Lapchick, Father O'Riley thought twice before casting out someone with the ability to keep the Redmen on top. He told Mc-Guire to have McMahon see him after class the next day, and from that point on McMahon stayed out of danger. He went on to star for St. John's and then enjoyed a long professional playing and coaching career.

Behind Dick and Al McGuire, the 1949 Johnnies improved to 15-9, beating Big Apple rivals Manhattan, NYU, Fordham, and Brooklyn College, but losing to CCNY in overtime at the Garden before another near-capacity crowd. They were back in the NIT, which in New York was considered as prestigious as the ten-year-old NCAA tournament, but fell to Bowling Green in a first-round game. McGuire vowed that would not happen again once his prize recruiting class moved up to the varsity.

Senior captain Dick McGuire led the team in scoring with a 12.8 average and was among the most ferocious defenders in the college game. Helped immeasurably by his coach's schmoozing of the press, Dick McGuire won the Haggerty Award as the top player in the metropolitan area and was picked by the New York Knickerbockers in the first round of the new NBA draft.

Coach McGuire flew out to Seattle for the 1949 NCAA championship game, the first played out of New York in seven years. McGuire sensed that the national tournament was ready to surpass the NIT in popularity. He set his goal for St. John's to make the field the next season, but knew that powerful CCNY would stand in the way. If not, then certainly St. John's would make it the following year, when players in his first recruiting class were juniors and the NCAA field would expand to sixteen teams.

Al McGuire set the tone for the 1949–1950 season in an exhibition scrimmage against Long Island University arranged by promoter Ned Irish, played one Saturday morning at a mostly empty Madison Square Garden. Frank McGuire and LIU coach Clair Bee were great friends and thought such a practice game would be good for their teams, which were not scheduled to meet that season. "We wanted to see our teams under game conditions, but I told my players that Coach Bee and I were close and I didn't want anything to happen that would affect our friendship," McGuire said in his biography years later.

Al McGuire was the opposite of his all-business brother Dick, who played the game without any lip. Al was always yapping at somebody, and though he did not actually *start* most of the fights, he never backed down from the ones he instigated. There were no referees in the scrimmage. Both coaches reminded their teams that it was an unofficial game, to play hard, but it didn't matter who had more points in the end.

Right after the opening jump ball, Al McGuire and LIU's Adolph Bigos went sprawling on the court, with McGuire landing on top and applying a chokehold around Bigos' neck. It turned out they were continuing a fight that had begun the night before in a New York City club.

The coaches ran onto the floor, and Frank McGuire ordered his player to let go because Bigos was turning blue in the face.

"Not until he says, 'I give up,'" Al said.

"The guy can't talk as long as you're choking him!" his coach barked.

Al finally stopped strangling Bigos, and the scrimmage went off without further incident. That morning, Frank McGuire saw something he missed during Al's sophomore season, playing in the shadow of his brother. If he could control Al's temper, he would have a leader at guard to go with the star recruits.

New York City was still the hub of college basketball and, in 1950, CCNY won both the NIT and NCAA tournament championships—the only time one school won both in the same season. Lost in the CCNY excitement was that St. John's set a school record with twenty-four victories, including an upset of Adolph Rupp's Kentucky Wildcats at the Garden. This time the Redmen advanced to the NIT semifinals before losing to Bradley.

That summer, three CCNY players were among thirty-three collegians exposed for point-shaving in a sting operation. It was a public relations disaster for college basketball. The scandal weakened the long-standing city teams and left the door open for St. John's and McGuire to continue building their reputation.

The 1951 Redmen responded by winning twenty-six times and earning their first-ever bid to the NCAA tournament, which sent eight teams to the East Regional in New York and eight out west to Kansas City, with the championship game scheduled for Minneapolis. St. John's lost to Kentucky but beat N.C. State in the East Regional consolation game, after which McGuire and Wolfpack Coach Everett Case talked briefly about living in North Carolina.

Case had moved to Raleigh from Indiana, where he coached dominating high school and service teams. He had gained a commitment from N.C. State to complete Reynolds Coliseum and even had the school lengthen the building. This created rows and rows of horrendous platform seats behind the baskets and another 3,000 seats in the balcony that did not even face the court.

McGuire still had fond memories of his time in Chapel Hill during Navy preflight school. His third child, young Frankie, was born with cerebral palsy, and he and Pat had already discussed moving to a warmer climate with a less hectic pace. McGuire was now considered one of the bright young coaches in college basketball, well known beyond his native New York City, where he had escaped the stigma of the CCNY scandal.

St. John's had established itself as an attraction that drew large crowds to Madison Square Garden, the school's de facto home court. In 1951, McGuire had scheduled only four games at tiny DeGray Gym on campus and played thirteen at the Garden, including close losses to Kansas and Kentucky. That the thirty-eight-year-old McGuire was locking horns with prominent coaches such as Case, Phog Allen, and Rupp on basketball's biggest stage made him all the more appealing to schools looking to upgrade basketball.

While McGuire thought about relocating his family, New York would always be his turf and prime recruiting base. Through the contacts he had with former players who became high-school coaches, from Jack Curran at Archbishop Molloy to talent scouts like Howard Garfinkel and Harry Gotkin, McGuire saw New York as a fertile breeding ground. McGuire had already begun considering how he could rescue these prized recruits from a city with increasing crime and the lingering stench of the point-shaving scandal that threatened the game he loved.

As the 1951–1952 season began, after McGuire's annual summer vacation with the family to the Catskill Mountains, he sensed it could be his last season at St. John's. Even so, he was excited. His first recruiting class of Zawoluk, McMahon, and MacGilvary was entering its senior season, and playing so many games at the Garden gave the Redmen a decided home court edge against a schedule of opponents that would harden them into a championship-caliber club.

The NCAA was gaining strength as the ruling body of college athletics and began discouraging teams that accepted invitations to its tournament from playing in the NIT first. However, it did not schedule a single game of its event in New York for the first time in history.

McGuire chose to see this as an advantage, an opportunity to take a tournament-ready team on the road to play "New York City basketball." It is where McGuire first coined his famous phrase, "Us Against the World."

"His approach was that basketball is won by making a team," Al McGuire said. "He made a family out of the team—you became almost like a city-state, and you're going to fight them. He would form a group that would run through a wall for him. You became a neighborhood. The enemy is in the other locker room, and let's don't ever forget that. They're keeping score."

Frank McGuire also saw the recruitment of his first black athlete, handsome sophomore guard Solly Walker, who was the most valuable high-school player in New York City, as a galvanizing force. He fervently preached that they all stick together, especially during their sixth game of the season against defending national champion Kentucky in Lexington, where Walker was sure to hear taunts and slurs.

Adolph Rupp, so powerful that he had already chased off the most successful football coach in Kentucky history, Paul "Bear" Bryant, to Texas A&M, had told McGuire that he "can't bring that boy here." But, like Alfred Smith almost twenty years earlier in Kansas, McGuire said he was coming to Kentucky with his entire team and they all would eat and stay together at the same hotel.

St. John's took the train from Grand Central Station. The team checked into a hotel in downtown Lexington without incident and Walker played against the Wildcats in Memorial Gym, where he was jostled by the Kentucky players and harassed by their fans. The result was the most lopsided loss of McGuire's coaching career, 81-40. By the time the teams met again two months later, things had changed to the point where McGuire gave a successful audition to schools that might be thinking of hiring him as their next coach.

Recovering from that blowout, the Redmen won fifteen of their next sixteen games and secured NIT and NCAA bids for the second straight year. Using the NIT, and a quarterfinals loss to LaSalle, as merely a warm-up, St. John's was ready for the biggest challenge in its basketball history.

The NCAA assigned the Johnnies to Raleigh for the East Regional to face Southern Conference champion N.C. State at Reynolds Coliseum, with the winner to meet top-ranked Kentucky for the right to advance to the national semifinals in Seattle. For the first time, the NCAA was sending the final four teams to one site.

McGuire expected the rough reception in heavily segregated Raleigh to be hardest on Walker. They wound up eating one meal together in the hotel kitchen before McGuire arranged for a local parish priest to take in Walker for the weekend.

The on-court assignment, however, was right in McGuire's wheelhouse, and he knew his improved, battle-tested team was capable of pulling off twin upsets. Wearing his silk suit and tie, handkerchief perfectly folded in his breast pocket, McGuire strutted into Reynolds Coliseum in the alligator shoes he had just bought on Fifth Avenue.

The state of North Carolina took notice when the Redmen held off Case's Wolfpack by 11 points, as the red-clad crowd of 12,400 howled at Walker throughout the game. Watching from the stands were UNC athletic director Chuck Erickson and comptroller Billy Carmichael Jr., who were trying to decide whether to fire basketball coach Tom Scott after his second straight losing season. Their interest piqued, Erickson and Carmichael went back the next night for the East Regional championship game.

In the rematch against Kentucky, McGuire used the first game to his advantage because the Redmen had already struggled mightily against Kentucky All-Americans Cliff Hagan and Frank Ramsey and 7' center Bill Spivey. He also assured his team the Raleigh fans wouldn't be as bad as they were in Lexington because they did not care who won. And then he riled up his players by revealing that Rupp had already chartered a plane to the semifinals in Seattle and that hundreds of Kentucky fans had made hotel reservations out there. (Forty-three years later, Dean Smith used a similar ploy against Kentucky coach Rick Pitino in the 1995 NCAA regional final in Birmingham, telling his underdog team that the Kentucky victory party had already been scheduled at a downtown restaurant.)

"We rose to the occasion and played our best game against Kentucky," McGuire said afterward. "Great players seem to hit their peak in crucial games, and that was the case with 'Zeke' Zawoluk, who did everything you could ask by scoring thirty-two points and holding his own against their big men inside."

St. John's won 64-57 in a game that wasn't that close, and it convinced Carmichael and Erickson that UNC needed to go after McGuire as its basketball coach. They immediately put the wheels in motion.

Of McGuire's 550 college career victories, one at each of his three schools would be remembered as his best: the 1952 win over

Kentucky that catapulted the Redmen into their first final four weekend; North Carolina's triple overtime win against Kansas and Wilt Chamberlain five years later for the national championship; and the 1971 ACC championship win for South Carolina over UNC and his former assistant, Dean Smith.

After the adventure of flying across the country in a propeller plane that had his players just happy to be back on the ground in Seattle, the Redmen defeated Illinois in the semifinals and then faced Kansas and 6'9" All-American Clyde Lovellette, who led the nation in scoring with a 28.6 average and was unquestionably the best player at the first "Final Four." The game turned out to be a foreshadowing of five years later, when McGuire and North Carolina faced Kansas and the next Jayhawk giant, Chamberlain.

Just as it would be in Kansas City in 1957, McGuire's team was the equal of Kansas but had to figure out how to handle KU's big man in the middle. St. John's had already eliminated the top two ranked teams in Kentucky and Illinois but had not faced anyone with Lovellette's size and physical gifts. Kansas coach Phog Allen had an offense in which everything ran through the future Hall of Famer, who was so big that it was almost impossible to keep the ball out of his hands.

McGuire tried to counter by rotating Zawoluk and McMahon, but they gave away too many inches and could not contain Lovellette. Behind his 33 points and 17 rebounds, the Jayhawks built a big lead in the championship game, led by 14 at halftime, and allowed reserve guard Dean Smith to come off the bench and quarterback the delay game that ran out the clock. Lovellette has remained the only player ever to lead the country in scoring and win a national championship, and he went on to play for four NBA teams and in three All-Star games.

Following the 80-63 Kansas victory, McGuire sought out

Lovellette and the victorious Jayhawks and warmly congratulated them all. Smith's hand was among those McGuire shook. Disappointed, McGuire knew he had lost to a better opponent but had also propelled St. John's basketball to a new level, establishing it as more than just a strong New York City team and winning the first of his three national coach of the year awards, which came at three different schools.

He wasn't sure where he was going, but after five years and posting a 106-36 record at his alma mater, he knew it was time to leave home.

When Frank McGuire left St. John's after the 1952 season to coach elsewhere, he trumped Everett Case with an ace in the hole named Lennie Rosenbluth. At 6'5" and maybe 175 pounds, Rosenbluth was swarthy and almost spider-like, so skinny that as a sophomore and junior he was cut from his high school team, which was loaded with meaty war veterans. He became a vagabond player with any organized team that would have him.

After improving so much that he starred in the *Daily Mirror* AAU tournament, Rosenbluth was called back by his high-school coach and started for the rest of his junior year, leading James Monroe High into the city playoffs at Madison Square Garden. That's where he met Harry Gotkin, who invited him to the Catskill Mountains that summer to work at Laurel Country Club. Rosenbluth got to play regularly for Laurel when three older teammates were severely injured in a car accident, one of whom eventually died.

Red Auerbach of the Boston Celtics, among the college and pro coaches vacationing in upstate New York and scouting the summer games, watched Rosenbluth average 20 points with his uncanny shot, and Auerbach invited him to his team's training camp on Cape Cod. The shy seventeen-year-old roomed with Celtics star Bob Cousy and held his own on the court against big men Easy Ed McCauley and Bones McKinney. He also landed a contract offer from Auerbach.

"For a kid to play with the Boston Celtics?" Rosenbluth said. "Yes, I was ready to go." But the NBA banned Boston from signing a high-school player, sending Rosenbluth back home for what was to be his senior year.

By then the New York City high school coaches were on strike, relegating Rosenbluth's prep career to a half-dozen games and leaving him with little formal training in the game of basketball. Amazingly, he had still not gotten any skilled, orthodox coaching. Or any coaching at all, for that matter.

Instead, he played for Gimbels (against Macy's) in the New York industrial league and joined what was the all-black Carlton YMCA club led by future college and pro star Sihugo Green. The club, which once won sixty-five straight games, was coached by Hy Gotkin (Harry's brother), whose son Davey had gone off to N.C. State. They all arranged a tryout for Rosenbluth with Everett Case and the Wolfpack in April of 1952.

After a long train ride to Raleigh, and a tour of the campus with Davey Gotkin, and meeting Case for breakfast, Rosenbluth showed up in old Thompson Gym and found pickup games on two courts. He didn't know where everyone came from—some were N.C. State players and some from other colleges. Some were high-school kids, which was Case's way of hiding what were really illegal tryouts.

"I told Case I was out of shape from not playing," said Rosenbluth, who also smoked at the time. "He said, 'Don't worry about it, just get in there and play.'"

Rosenbluth continued, "I ran the court three or four times and couldn't breathe; I was dying. We were playing against State's varsity, and they're running up and down the court and it was hot as the dickens in there. I just couldn't do it."

Case then spoke with Rosenbluth's father, Jack, a former minor league baseball player who had ridden the train down with his son. "Scholarships are hard to come by, and I don't want to waste one," Case said. "I can't use Lennie."

Jack Rosenbluth could not understand it because Case had invited him to Raleigh for the Dixie Classic and 1952 NCAA tournament after having worked out his son against the State players in New York during a practice for the NIT the previous March. Jack called Harry Gotkin, one of McGuire's chief scouts, who told them to come back to New York. Upon their return, Gotkin took Rosenbluth to the St. John's athletic banquet, which was also a testimonial dinner for the departing McGuire, who had met Rosenbluth several times at Madison Square Garden.

McGuire knew Case favored faster players from Indiana over the more rugged kids from the Northeast. He figured Rosenbluth was raw and had yet to develop many bad habits and was well suited for his instinctive, freelance system. Revealing that he would be coaching at either North Carolina or Alabama the next season, McGuire offered Rosenbluth a scholarship as long as he could qualify to get in school.

"No matter where you go, I'm going with you," Rosenbluth responded, shaking McGuire's hand. Years later, he said of the moment, "I was just grateful to be getting a scholarship and going somewhere."

Rosenbluth wound up as one of McGuire's boys instead of playing and starring for N.C. State. Carolina fans more than fifty years old or so have cringed over the thought of Rosie wearing Wolfpack red.

The Tar Heels had fallen on hard times since Ben Carnevale's departure after the 1946 season and the loss to Oklahoma State in the NCAA championship game. Under Carnevale's successor, Tom Scott, they sank steadily in the old Southern Conference, from second to third to fifth place.

UNC fired Scott after his sixth season and two 12-15 records. They had failed to finish in the top eight and qualify for the Southern Conference tournament in either year. Worse than that, Scott had become Everett Case's whipping boy, losing all fifteen of his games against State, which was in the midst of a dominating 161-39 run and six straight Southern Conference championships.

These debacles versus State were far from close encounters. The Wolfpack won by margins ranging from 26 to 40 points. The names of Katkaveck, Dickey, Ranzino, and Terrill were as magical at State as Choo Choo had been in Chapel Hill. Raleigh, after all, was loaded with UNC alumni, and watching their team coming into Reynolds Coliseum (or suffering through games on the radio) had become cruel and unusual punishment.

Carolina-Duke *football* still might have been the most important rivalry at the time, but clearly, the Tar Heels were looking for someone to end the insufferable basketball embarrassment by the perennially powerful Wolfpack. Chuck Erickson and Billy Carmichael had targeted McGuire after his dramatic NCAA upset victories over State and top-ranked Kentucky, and they received a ringing recommendation from Carnevale, the head coach at Navy.

McGuire's decision to leave his native New York at age thirty-nine was a story in itself. The point-shaving scandals had already sent many high-school players scurrying south, but more of a factor was the health of his young son, Frankie.

"I asked myself, 'Why leave New York?' I had lived there all of my life, I had a good job coaching the school where I had graduated, and this is where all my friends were," McGuire said in his biography years later.

"However, when I thought of it in terms of my family, particularly Frankie, there were some negatives. We lived on the top floor of an apartment building in the Village, while St. John's was over on Long Island. It was very complicated to take Frankie anywhere. He couldn't eat out in New York City."

McGuire also visited Tuscaloosa, Alabama, where Floyd Burdette had just resigned after six years as coach, the last two finishing second in the Southeastern Conference behind Kentucky. But North Carolina was not in the deep South, and luckily McGuire already had a few friends and familiarity there. To someone reared on the asphalt of New York, the sand sidewalks and easiness of Chapel Hill touched McGuire in a way the town has many before and since.

After getting a call from Raleigh entrepreneur Joe Murnick, McGuire met in New York with the charismatic Carmichael, a UNC graduate and one-time Tar Heel basketball player who made millions on Wall Street and then returned home after the stock market crash of 1929. Carmichael had served in various roles for the Consolidated University, which included N.C. State, but he loved his alma mater most and wanted to give Case some competition. In charge of the purse strings, Carmichael was convinced he had finally found the right basketball coach for Carolina and offered McGuire the job.

In the same year that America elected a war hero, General Dwight David Eisenhower, as president, and television became the medium of choice with the *I Love Lucy* show, UNC hired its own dynamic change agent. "My decision was based on what was best for my family," McGuire said. "I didn't think of anything else. We could live in a house for the first time and have a swimming pool where Frankie could exercise. And we could go around town without it being such a hassle. It was just much better family surroundings than in a big city."

The notion that a handicapped child created "Carolina Basketball"—one of the longest runs of sustained excellence in the history of college or pro athletics—seems preposterous in the telling. But ardent dot-connectors have since seen how Frankie McGuire set off a chain reaction that led to a college dynasty. There was even a Frankie McGuire Day in South Carolina, where he lived most of his handicapped life until his death in 2009. It was a nice thing to do, noting his impact on the history of basketball.

Frank McGuire claimed that before accepting the job, he never gave any serious thought to the difficulty of luring players from New York to a university with no basketball tradition in a heavily Baptist state. Didn't most of his contacts run through the Catholic diocese, where every Father, priest, and altar boy knew who he was? How was McGuire going to get young people to leave that environment and move to the South, where Catholics and Jews were relatively scarce and Protestants ruled most churches, schools, communities, and families? The answer would determine how long McGuire stayed in North Carolina and certainly how close he would come to putting together a power like he had at St. John's.

"The people who recruited against me said to the Catholic families, 'Don't go to Carolina, they don't even have a Newman Club,'" McGuire recounted. "Eventually, I brought a Dominican father up from Raleigh to prove we had priests down there. It was tough breaking the ice, but once the boys saw for themselves and talked about it when they went back to New York we got it going."

Through the years, McGuire's Catholic players rued the start of practice on Monday. Then they each had to be clean shaven with a haircut and tell the coach which Mass they had attended or have a damn good excuse if they missed one the day before.

"They all believed Coach McGuire was at one of the services sitting in the back and Coach Freeman was at the other," former McGuire player Hugh Donohue said. "So if they lied about being in church, there was hell to pay."

McGuire, ironically, had earlier been part of the largest single influx of Catholics to Chapel Hill, where hundreds of aspiring aviators were sent for Navy pre-flight school in the 1940s. Mass was then regularly celebrated at the Hill Hall auditorium on campus.

Billy Carmichael, who had been one of very few Catholic students during his undergraduate days, led support for a Catholic church in town and began a building fund. Of course, McGuire was in front of the movement, in which W. D. Carmichael Sr. donated land on Gimghoul Road for a Gothic Revival church. It eventually became St. Thomas More, later moving to a larger tract outside of town to accommodate an adjoining school.

One early draw for recruits considering Carolina turned out to be that freshmen still were eligible in the Southern Conference. McGuire managed to have his scouts line up a couple of New York-area high school players to come with him. Unfortunately, Rosenbluth was not one of them. He lacked the credits in math and foreign language for admission to UNC. So McGuire suggested he spend a year at Staunton Military Academy in Virginia, where Rosenbluth played a post-graduate season in 1953. By then, McGuire was on the way to winning seventeen games in his first season at UNC and establishing himself as somewhat of a miracle worker in the eyes of Tar Heel fans.

Another import, a 6'4" Czech named Jerry Vayda from Bayonne, New Jersey, hit a driving layup in the closing seconds of McGuire's first game against Case, sealing an astonishing 70-69 upset over the eighth-ranked Wolfpack at a hushed Reynolds Coliseum. Although it would be two more years and six losses before McGuire beat State again, the first victory was enough to convince Carolina fans they had found their man to make them truly big-time in basketball.

On May 8, 1953, North Carolina and N.C. State were among seven schools that seceded from the Southern Conference to form the ACC. They joined Big Four rivals Duke and Wake Forest, plus Maryland, Clemson, and South Carolina in the new, smaller league created primarily to reap the rewards from football bowl games. (Virginia soon dropped its independent status to become the eighth member.) However, the ACC instituted two rules that had a big impact on its basketball teams—freshmen were declared ineligible for varsity competition, and the conference tournament champion, not the team finishing first in the regular season, would earn the lone bid to the NCAA championship playoffs.

Everett Case, so powerful that he had to approve N.C. State's participation in the new league, graciously offered use of his 12,400-seat Reynolds Coliseum for the ACC tournament. They didn't call him the Silver Fox for nothing.

Rosenbluth arrived in the fall of 1953, a nineteen-year-old freshman who was glad to have a college scholarship but found out that his sport was not a very big deal on campus. "Carolina basketball then was not Carolina basketball of today," Rosenbluth has said so often since his arrival in Chapel Hill. "Not even close to it. The first time we went down to Woollen Gym for freshman practice, it was locked and we couldn't get in."

Soon the students couldn't get into freshman games at Woollen, which outdrew a varsity that struggled to an 11-10 record in McGuire's second season. Students loved how "Rosie" shot from all angles and began backpedaling down the court on defense be-

fore the ball invariably went in. Rosenbluth's scoring explosions—
including 51 points against Chowan Junior College—gave the fans
great hope for the future.

Despite the Tar Heels' so-so record, State barely beat them in
their first two official ACC meetings during the 1954 season.
Case, dressed in his famous gray suit and sashaying the sideline
like a ferret, worked the officials unmercifully. In time, newspaper
coverage created a war of words that both coaches later called
a publicity stunt. "Nobody ever dreamed it," McGuire said, "but
Everett and I were really close friends until the nights we played."

McGuire's rivalry with Case, however it came to be, always
seemed to elevate Carolina's play. The 1955 Tar Heels shocked
State again at Reynolds Coliseum, 84-80. Rosenbluth averaged
25.5 points that season as a sophomore and the Tar Heels won eight
of their fourteen ACC contests, but their final record was 10-11.

During an embarrassingly one-sided loss to Virginia in Greensboro, a few fans were booing when McGuire turned to his old
coach and new assistant, Buck Freeman, whom he had brought
with him from New York, and asked what they should do.

"Get better players!" Freeman snapped.

"I already got 'em," McGuire shot back, "on the freshman team."

The most important recruiting class in the history of Carolina
basketball came down on what the *New York World-Telegram &
Sun* dubbed McGuire's Underground Railroad (Willard Mullins'
widely remembered cartoon showed starry-eyed, suitcase-toting
kids emerging from a subway station onto Franklin Street). Four
Catholic youngsters had been wooed by this irrepressible Irishman,
who promised their families he would take care of them in the scary
South.

Bob Cunningham, a 6'4" guard from Harlem, won McGuire's loyalty after he slipped in his family's apartment, severely cutting his hand on a broken window and missing most of his senior year at All Hallows high school. Two surgeries, plus one doctor's declined recommendation to amputate his thumb, scared away several coaches who had offered him a scholarship.

Cunningham came home one day from school, his hand heavily bandaged, to find McGuire sitting in his living room holding papers to sign. Freshmen were not eligible in 1954, so McGuire knew Cunningham would have plenty of time for the injury to heal.

That gesture of faith convinced Cunningham's friend and rival from St. Ann's in Manhattan, Tommy Kearns, to also sign with the Tar Heels as Cunningham's backcourt running mate. The curly haired Kearns, a 5'11" pistol who commuted to high school from New Jersey, showed such wizardry with the ball that McGuire had a hard time getting him to pass enough.

Pete Brennan and Joe Quigg, a pair of rugged forwards from Brooklyn, could shoot, and Brennan, a handsome 6'6" with wavy hair, could score in traffic. Quigg was 6'9" with room to fill out. He wore a crew-cut in high school that McGuire let him grow into a perfectly squared-off flattop.

Joining Rosenbluth, the Jew in the middle, these four Catholics thought they could conquer college basketball when they enrolled at Carolina in the fall of 1954. They also found a strange new world.

"None of us had ever been south of Baltimore," Kearns said. "North Carolina was almost a foreign country. It was beautiful, but back then there were signs on bathrooms, 'Colored' and 'White.' There were lines of demarcation, and that was a real shocker to a lot of us who really didn't know what segregation was all about."

Meanwhile, McGuire smartly filled out his roster with Baptists like Roy Searcy from Draper, North Carolina, and Methodists like Ken Rosemond from Hillsborough, who could help integrate the Yankees into their new surroundings. Most of the non-starters were not expected to play much, but it had less to do with their backgrounds than their basketball talent. McGuire just believed that the newcomers from New York spoke his language and, as first-generation children of immigrants, had the pride and toughness to withstand the culture shock of the South and rancor of the local rivalries.

The growing hatred amongst the Big Four schools was deeper than the twenty-five miles that circumscribed the quartet of campuses. Each of the three other rivals had a little extra aversion for UNC, the so-called state university with the majority of money and political clout among legislators and business leaders in the capital city.

Billy Carmichael was a political gadfly, pressing flesh and working the phones to see that the Consolidated University, mostly the flagship campus in Chapel Hill, got what it needed when the General Assembly went into session. For example, Carmichael, President Bill Friday, and Kay Kyser, another alum and famous big band leader, had successfully lobbied to start an educational television station that became UNC-TV. Besides being an influential politician, Carmichael was a brilliant quipster whose strategy could be summed up best in the funny-but-factual phrase he liked to throw around: "Make sure you don't liquor-up the wrong crowd!"

Duke was a small school funded by big bucks from its tobacco magnate namesake, James P. Duke. The Blue Devils owned the dominant football team for most of the 1940s and 1950s and, attending an elite private institution with a huge out-of-state enrollment, thought themselves superior to what they considered the backward (even redneck) residents of UNC and N.C. State. Their basketball rivalry also predated the ACC, when Dick Groat played for Duke and set season and school scoring records against the hated Tar Heels. Although it would one day take the national stage, the Duke-Carolina rivalry was bubbling long before men named Smith and Krzyzewski ever showed up at their respective schools.

Carolina and State had long shared the one-sided sibling rivalry of big brother liberal arts university versus what was a farming college until the 1960s. "Culture versus Agriculture" was the phrase coined by *Daily Tar Heel* writer Curry Kirkpatrick.

The Wolfpack's failure to field a competitive football team caused it to hire Case and concentrate on basketball, which in turn brought McGuire to the Tar Heels. Make no mistake about it, the State-UNC rivalry was forged by heat and it became permanent.

Even after Wake Forest moved from northeast of Raleigh to Winston-Salem on a grant from the Reynolds Foundation, the animosity among these schools did not diminish. One incestuous thread was that bizarre Bones McKinney began his college playing career at N.C. State, ended it at UNC, and then joined Murray Greason's coaching staff at Wake. When the inevitable succession occurred after the 1957 season, McKinney and the other Big Four teams staged some of the most heated and memorable games of all.

Each school still played in its own unique building, and that only turned up the heat, literally. Besides the home-cooking associated with long, rectangular Reynolds Coliseum, Duke had its intimate Indoor Stadium, UNC pulled the bleachers close to the court at Woollen, and Wake left grungy Gore Gym for dingy Memorial Coliseum in Winston-Salem, where McKinney always thought the head janitor watched practices and tipped off McGuire.

They staged donnybrooks at the old haunts—crowds cursing, throwing debris, and occasionally coming onto the floor to join in the fisticuffs between players. At the first UNC–Wake Forest game one year, McGuire allowed members of the Carolina football team to sit behind the visitors' bench and harass the Deacs. When the Tar Heels arrived at Wake for the rematch, they found Wake Forest football players—wearing full pads—waiting for them behind their bench.

So when Carolina opened the 1955–1956 season with a starting lineup of senior Jerry Vayda, junior Rosenbluth, and sophomores Quigg, Brennan, and Kearns, and won seven straight to grab UNC's first-ever top 10 national ranking, the ACC pecking order was the Big Four and the little four. The Tobacco Road teams formed a dominant top division before UNC and State tied for first place with 11-3 records; Duke and Wake Forest finished one game behind at 10-4.

The Tar Heels' only losses before the ACC tournament were at State twice (once by 22 points in the Dixie Classic and the other narrowly), at Duke and at Wake, and they went back to Raleigh for the conference tournament determined to beat the Wolfpack, win the ACC championship, and reach their first NCAA tournament in McGuire's tenure. Rosenbluth, All-ACC for the second straight year and now a second-team All-American, averaged 26.7 points and 11.5 rebounds a game.

Likely looking ahead, Carolina barely beat a 10-16 Virginia team in the first round before facing Wake, with which it split their home-and-home series. The Deacons had won by five at Wake Forest, the Tar Heels by four in Chapel Hill. Everyone expected another close game with the winner moving on to face N.C. State, which had beaten Duke in the first semifinal.

It wasn't much of a game. Wake's Jack Williams, Jim Gilley, and Jackie Murdock combined for 57 points, a total McGuire mentioned often during the following season in 1957.

Rosenbluth scored 26 points but missed 18 of his 28 shots, which was the best effort among the Heels. Vayda went 1-11 in his college finale, Quigg 2-7, Kearns 4-10, Brennan 0-7, and Tony Radovich 1-9, and the team shot a season-low of 25 percent from the floor. The Deacons won in a rout, 77-56, ending Carolina's season at 18-5 and on a sour note that McGuire would not forget.

"Never did I see him as hurt as he was after that game," reserve Ken Rosemond once recalled. "He lit into some people and probably set the groundwork for what happened the next year." Players who were there say the Carolina locker room after the Wake Forest game was a torture chamber.

Before that next season, McGuire needed to get a few things straight among his players, most of whom had been stars in high school and their respective team's leading scorers. He wanted Rosenbluth to take most of the shots—and for good reason.

"When I came to Carolina, I was the No. 1 shooter in New York City," Brennan said, "and then I averaged twenty-five points for the freshman team. When I moved up to the varsity, I believed I was the No. 1 shooter in the country.

"After I began playing with Lennie regularly, I wasn't even the No. 1 shooter on our team! He was the best shooter I ever played with or saw."

McGuire's mission was getting the entire team to see it Brennan's way. He began an early practice by rolling two balls out for a scrimmage, and when the team kicked one back McGuire rolled it out again.

"No, no, one's for the rest of the team and the other's for Tommy," McGuire said of the cocky Kearns. "If you want to hog the ball, take one for yourself."

It was part of McGuire's continuing attempt to turn a talented group of individuals into a true team, playing to its strength. He knew that to win championships they had to control their own egos and get the ball to their star, Rosenbluth.

"He let me play my game, and I was grateful for it," Rosie said. "Otherwise, I would have been lost."

"Feeding the animal," McGuire called it. He was determined to make it happen.

The loss to Wake Forest in the 1956 ACC tournament grated on McGuire all summer. He plotted ways to make his players think more as a team and less as individual stars and scorers.

They always watched McGuire carefully before starting to scrimmage to see if he rolled out that dreaded second ball for selfishness. It became a barometer of their progress.

As long as they worked on getting the ball inside to Rosenbluth, all was well. Rosie was an extraordinary talent of his time—lithe and liquid, with a hook shot he used against taller opponents in the pivot and a face-up jumper that he rarely missed. He was even known to take turnaround jumpers along the baseline, shots that would have given Dean Smith a coronary.

"When they conceded to use Lennie in the post, we finally became a good team," McGuire said. "In the beginning it was hard to convince Brennan, Kearns, Cunningham, and Quigg about Lennie. Kearns was so good with the ball he could go through the defense by himself and the others could all score, so that was a big concession for the kids. Lennie was a shooter, and they knew who I wanted to take the big shots."

Not only did "getting it inside" remain a staple of Carolina basketball through the Smith era, McGuire was faced with the same challenge when he later coached Wilt Chamberlain in the NBA. Even though fellow Philadelphia Warriors Paul Arizin, Tom Gola, and Guy Rodgers had been college All-Americans, McGuire insisted they defer to "The Stilt." They agreed but wanted team management to know about the deal so their contracts wouldn't be affected if their scoring averages went down.

When the 1956–1957 season opened at Carolina, the remaining Tar Heels had gotten the point about Rosenbluth. Furthermore, the starters found out they were going to rely heavily on each other.

Sophomore guard Harvey Salz, from Brooklyn, who was expected to back up Kearns, flunked out after his freshman year. Tony Radovich, who was on the team from McGuire's first year, had only one semester of eligibility left and was done after Christmas. McGuire and Freeman couldn't get starting center Billy Hathaway, a 6'11" banger from Long Beach, New York, to go to class and figured he'd be gone by the new year, too.

Fortunately, the other starters were intact and healthy, both physically and mentally. It was a good thing, since McGuire had only ten players he could use at all. There was almost no margin for error of any kind.

McGuire never took a player out for a mistake, but he showed his displeasure by straightening his tie and tightening the knot to his neck. When a player saw that, he knew he better do something to make up for it before facing McGuire at the next timeout.

"After getting killed by Wake Forest in the tournament, we were really embarrassed and came back in great shape, ready to play," Brennan said. "It was the only year that McGuire held most of our practices at night. Maybe he wanted to make sure we stayed out of trouble or were too tired to do anything but go to sleep."

Of course, McGuire and the other ACC coaches chafed at the conference's decision to play its tournament on the Wolfpack's home court every year, not to mention that the Big Four schools had to play the Dixie Classic in Raleigh. However, McGuire harbored a belief that a tough slate on the road, including a potential seven games at Reynolds, would better prepare the Tar Heels to be

ACC champions, which in 1957 was the only way to become national champs.

He scheduled only eight games at Woollen Gym, including the warm-up opener against Furman. Rosenbluth scored a school-record 47 points in the 94-66 romp. Then there were the seven ACC games.

The charmed life of the 1956–1957 Tar Heels began in the sunken Pit at South Carolina, which had the ACC's new top scorer and rebounder, Grady Wallace. On the way to Columbia, the designated "smoking car" with Rosenbluth and Quigg took a wrong turn and barely arrived by tip-off time. McGuire was miffed, but somehow they survived in overtime. Postgame, few observers would have guessed at what North Carolina would do over the next four months.

They opened their ACC home season by defeating a good Maryland team. Then they traveled north in terrible, wintry weather for a narrow 64-59 victory over NYU, which triple-teamed Rosenbluth and held him to 9 points at Madison Square Garden. The trip also included dates with Dartmouth and Holy Cross at the old Boston Garden, where McGuire first met a Massachusetts senator named John F. Kennedy.

McGuire was always looking for NCAA rules that gave him a bit of an edge. He uncovered a quirky provision that allowed him to pay personal travel expenses for his players if games surrounding Christmas were away from Chapel Hill. Thus, his schedules always included trips over the holidays, and after going home, his players reunited in Raleigh for the Dixie Classic before New Year's. By the time Carolina completed its northern swing in late 1956, the Heels were 8-0 and ranked No. 2 in the country, and Rosenbluth had already surpassed Al Lifson's 1,322 points as UNC's career leader.

They were scoring a lot of points by "feeding the animal" and swallowing their pride when the ball rarely came back out, as Rosenbluth built his 28-point average, a school record for one season that will likely never be broken. Their second-leading scorer was Brennan, who was money from the corner and hit for 14-plus per game. Everyone seemed to be hearing the McGuire mantra: Make the extra pass, hit the open man, find Rosie as much as possible, and treat the ball like it was gold.

"Controlling the ball is not freezing it," McGuire said. "Basketball is a game of mistakes, and by controlling the ball you tend to eliminate some of those mistakes."

Defense consisted of a loose man-to-man that quickly evolved into a funny zone with sixth-man Cunningham, the team's best defender, stationed between Rosenbluth and the basket. In effect, Cunningham's defensive brilliance was hiding Rosenbluth's relative indifference to guarding anyone.

Practices were mostly scrimmages, and the players often joked that they had one play, an out-of-bounds play. McGuire did end each day with situational drills for his team. He would blow his whistle and bellow through his megaphone, "We're down two with a minute to play; show me what you do." The same thing for being up by a point late in the game, which usually meant get the ball to the team's best free throw shooter, Kearns.

Carolina won its first Dixie Classic title under McGuire by beating Utah, Duke, and Wake Forest for the championship. This was the first of four close games that season against the Demon Deacons.

McGuire and his family flew back to New York for New Year's, while the team returned to Chapel Hill and a deserted campus. Most of the players picked up dates from Women's College in Greensboro (as UNCG was known then), jimmied the locks at the Sigma Chi house, and had a party they joked about for the next fifty years.

Spero Dorton, who was in his thirties and owned the Goody Shop on Franklin Street, where the team congregated after games, opened his restaurant to the hung-over Tar Heels on New Year's Day. At a private meal they pledged to not break training rules for the rest of the season, and they didn't, as far as anyone knew.

One rule not in effect was smoking, which McGuire allowed as long as the players had permission from their parents and he did not see them doing it. On one 1955 road trip, during bed check, McGuire knocked on senior Al Lifson's hotel room door to find five players puffing away. "Wrong room," McGuire said, as he shut the door.

Freeman called the team back together for practice the following week and pitched a fit to make a point before McGuire returned from New York. He threw the players out of Woollen and warned they had better be ready to go the next afternoon when McGuire was back. They laughed at Freeman behind his back but came to understand the good cop–bad cop routine.

"Buck would get madder than hell, then just throw everybody out of the gym," team manager Joel Fleishman recalled. "It always reduced the pressure and got everyone down from the clouds."

By New Year's Day, 1957, the Tar Heels had little depth left. With Hathaway, Radovich, and Salz gone, the rebounding load fell to Quigg and Rosenbluth, and Kearns was virtually a forty-minute man.

The manpower shortage also gave Bobby Cunningham a chance to move into the starting lineup, thus completing his improbable comeback from the hand injury that almost ended his college career before it began. Forever indebted to McGuire, Cunningham turned into the team's defensive stopper and sacrificial lamb on offense. He was among the most popular players, and he led by example (and probably minutes played, behind Rosenbluth and Kearns). This prompted McGuire's long-time penchant to play his five starters most of the game.

Although thin, the talent was unmistakable. The first game with State wasn't close, and it signaled the turning point in the rivalry. The cocky Tar Heels ran away from the Wolfpack by 26 points in Raleigh, easily McGuire's largest margin of victory over Case. The win gave them the No. 1 ranking after Kansas and Chamberlain, its 7'2" sophomore center, lost to Iowa State.

It also gave McGuire two out of the last three in ACC games at Reynolds Coliseum. UNC claimed a dominance that lasted until the arrival of David Thompson at N.C. State in 1972. An unparalleled tradition of Carolina success in road games endured into the twenty-first century, with the Tar Heels boasting the best road record in the country.

"McGuire loved to take the home fans out of it," Rosenbluth said. "His favorite expression was, 'Don't kick a sleeping dog.' Let's beat the hell out of them."

The closest call of the 1957 regular season came at Maryland, where an ACC-record crowd of 14,000 was in an uproar as the Terrapins held onto a four-point lead with a minute to play and their best free throw shooter at the line. McGuire felt torn between losing a game that would take the pressure off and shattering what he considered his team's fragile confidence. With the ebbs and flows of a college basketball season, McGuire did not take seriously the idea of going undefeated.

He called a timeout and said, "It looks like we can't catch them. But I want you to go down like true champions. If we lose, we lose just like we win. Be good losers as well as good winners, and people will think just as much of you."

The players weren't quite finished. Maryland missed the free throw. Baskets by Kearns and Cunningham around another Maryland miss sent the game to overtime. Although it took two extra periods, the Tar Heels survived for their 17th straight victory. After that, a sense of destiny sneaked onto the UNC bench and stayed there.

The modern tradition of the Carolina comeback—No matter how big the deficit or long the odds—was likely born that night, as well. McGuire was telling sportswriters who gathered around him in the locker room, "These guys don't have enough sense to get rattled—nothing bothers them." Then Rosenbluth walked by on the way to the shower and said, "Coach, we only have 15 more to go!"

"I could have strangled him," McGuire said. "He had the games counted!"

"Once we tied the game and it went to overtime, we knew we'd win," Rosenbluth explained later. "That was the kind of season it was. After that game some of us started sitting around and thinking, we're not gonna lose."

They almost did lose at home to Duke, which scored four quick points to tie the game with 21 seconds left. But Blue Devils guard Bobby Joe Harris looked at the hand-operated scoreboard at the corner of the court, and it still read UNC 73, Duke 71. Unsure of the score, he intentionally fouled Kearns, who made both free throws as the Duke bench erupted.

The manual scorekeeper from Carolina had been slow putting up Duke's tying two points, causing the confusion for Harris. Duke coach Hal Bradley argued vehemently, but officials said the electronic scoreboard overhead had been correct. Harris scored a meaningless basket as time expired, and the unbeaten season continued.

The Tar Heels swept State again and won two more close games against Wake Forest to run their record to 23-0 before the regular-season finale at Duke, where the Blue Devils were ready after the scoreboard controversy in Chapel Hill. McGuire belittled criticism of the first game by telling his fellas they would have broken the tie in the last 16 seconds and won anyway.

Despite a raucous crowd at Duke Indoor Stadium, they had little trouble in the rematch, winning 86-72 to complete the first undefeated season in ACC history. McGuire celebrated with family and a few close friends at his home on Oakwood Drive in Chapel Hill. Six-year-old Frankie, McGuire's good luck charm, said goodnight to the small gathering before Frank and Pat put him to bed. They were extraordinarily kind and patient with Frankie, who stayed in a wheelchair and required almost round-the-clock care at an early age.

While McGuire called it the "happiest night of my life," he knew the regular-season championship meant little unless the Tar Heels could also win the 1957 ACC tournament, because only the champion advanced in those days. He opened practice the next week by bringing out colored basketballs, putting 'Sweet Georgia Brown" on the PA system, and letting his team do some Harlem Globetrotters routines. Exactly ten years later, Dean Smith broke the tension before his first ACC tournament title by allowing his team to play volleyball instead of practicing.

Having loosened up the players, McGuire then baited them about losing to Wake Forest the year before, and he posted newspaper articles in which State's Case and Duke's Bradley predicted they could not keep it going.

"They're a fine club, but I believe someone will knock them off before the end of the season," Case said. Bradley chimed in, "North Carolina is a fine team, and I'm glad to see them ranked No. 1. It looks good for our conference. But I don't think they have a great team. They don't have the experience, and they've had too many scares."

Meanwhile, superstitions popped up all over Chapel Hill and around the state, where high-school basketball players began crossing themselves before shooting free throws just like the four Catholic Carolina starters did. UNC students grew beards and would not shave as long as the Tar Heels kept winning. Others traced and counted the exact steps they took to class each day. One who had illegally left his car downtown piled up the parking tickets, telling traffic cops that moving it would jeopardize the winning streak.

Fans began rituals of what they wore, where they sat, what they did while listening to games, creating a tradition that years later inspired longtime UNC radio announcer Woody Durham to tell his audience to "go where you go and do what you do" during the second half of close games.

Today's remarkable Carolina connectivity has been enhanced by technology but can be traced back to the cultlike atmosphere of the McGuire era. Tar Heel loyalists gather in sports bars and family rooms across the country to watch their heroes on high-definition television, while some of the younger set chat, e-mail, or tweet each other near and far on handheld gizmos, the lucky ones sending e-messages from the game site.

From the old grads of 1957 to the newbies of the 1990s and beyond, the habit of following Carolina basketball has extended friendships, kept regular reunions going, and spit out three generations that crave knowledge about the Tar Heels anywhere they can find it, from fanatical phone calling to maniacal message boarding and everything in between. The most superstitious believe what they do and even what they *think* can have an effect on their favorite team.

McGuire, himself, bought into the rituals. He never got a haircut on game day, a superstition Dean Smith continued, and had his lucky suits, hankies, and cufflinks. He never turned down fans on Franklin Street and kids on campus when they handed him nutmegs, lucky coins, and rabbit's feet as their dream season continued.

Eighth-seeded Clemson, which had won only three conference games and was 7-16 overall in 1957, proved an easy tune-up for Carolina in the ACC opener. Rosenbluth set a tournament record that still stands with 45 points, and after the game Clemson coach Press Maravich gave Rosenbluth his own rabbit's foot, as newspaper photographers moved in to snap the unusual picture.

By then, McGuire was already focusing on what he expected to be a fourth meeting with Wake Forest, which was playing N.C. State upstairs in another first-round game. He thought the Deacons were better and figured they would avenge a loss to State from the week before in the last regular-season game on the same floor. The two teams had finished 7-7 and tied for fourth in the ACC, but Wake Forest had the extra incentive of another shot at UNC and finally ending State's reign as the only champion the young ACC had ever known. The Wolfpack had won the first three ACC tournaments and six of the last seven Southern Conference crowns.

Wake ousted State to get its fourth crack at Carolina the next night. The three previous games had been decided by a total of 16 points. Wake Forest assistant coach Bones McKinney had played for the Tar Heels after the war and spoken to McGuire about joining his staff before going to Wake. The Deacons knew how to play against Rosenbluth, pushing him away from the basket, while their three top scorers, Murdock, Gilley, and Williams, hounded the Heels throughout their careers.

Playing the ACC tournament in Raleigh was by now familiar for the Tar Heels, who played seven times at Reynolds Coliseum that season compared to their eight home games. They stayed in

Chapel Hill between rounds and slept in their own beds, the best of both worlds for a so-called road trip.

On Friday, March 8, 1957, they ate their pregame meal of steak and baked potato (except for Rosenbluth, who had two shrimp cocktails) at the Pines Restaurant near Finley Golf Course about 2:30 P.M., relaxed for an hour or so back in Cobb dorm, and then piled into three athletic department station wagons for the forty-minute drive down Route 54. Rosenbluth, Quigg, and reserve Ken Rosemond trailed in the light blue wagon driven by manager Fleishman, puffing away and blowing smoke out the windows.

"Killed the nerves," Rosenbluth liked to say.

After watching South Carolina begin to finish off Maryland in the first semifinal game, the Tar Heels went down the steep set of stairs to their assigned locker room and got into uniform. They liked to kid among themselves while waiting to warm up, but everyone was unusually quiet, and McGuire sat alone at the end of a bench as the team filed out. He always stayed back to make his dramatic entrance just before tip-off.

"I never had an easy time against Wake Forest," he said years later. "They really got up for us because it was a big thing for them to beat Carolina. They would play like they were possessed. As long as Bones was there, the attitude never changed. He'd rather beat Carolina than anyone because he played in Chapel Hill."

The Big Four rivalries were already entrenched and passed on from one generation to another. Fathers would tell their sons about the 1957 ACC tournament and being there in the Reynolds din when Carolina and Wake Forest played for the fourth time that season. It was more than simple proximity among the schools; frankly, it was much worse than it became in later years.

Upstairs in the packed gym sat TV pioneer Castleman D. Chesley, who grew up in Asheville, North Carolina, but left the state after playing freshman football at UNC. He transferred to Penn, graduated, and then attended the Wharton School for business. He began producing regional football telecasts for ABC and NBC and the previous fall had done his first three ACC games, spending enough time back in North Carolina to get caught up in UNC's basketball season. Attending his first ACC tournament, his presence became another important element to what would morph into "McGuire's Miracle."

The Tar Heels filed down the basement stairs and returned to the locker room after warming up. Freeman, the tactician coach, had written the individual matchups on the board. Carolina would be facing a veteran Wake Forest club with four seniors—the 6'6" Gilley, 6'4" Williams, 6' guards Murdock and Ernie Wiggins—and one junior, 6'4" Wendell Carr. The Demon Deacons were 19-8 overall and ranked No. 20 in the nation, but they had lost a total of five close games to UNC, Duke, and State.

"Those boys had played a lot of basketball together," McGuire said. "They were quick, had balance, and Gilley was good underneath."

McGuire did not need to give a pep talk. He simply reminded his team one more time of how Wake Forest ruined their entire season a year ago on the same floor.

"We've had a great year, don't let those sons-a-bitches spoil it for you," McGuire said. He knelt to lead everyone in a prayer that ended with the Catholics on the team crossing themselves, just as they did before shooting free throws.

The players clapped and hollered and ran upstairs into the roar and yet another date with destiny. This time, really for the first time, everything was at risk.

4

"Deans" of the ACC

LONG before there was ever a Road to the Final Four, Tobacco Road was paved with the guts and glory of four schools that loved their basketball but hated each other. One of the schools wandered far enough off Tobacco Road to make these backyard battles seem secondary to something bigger—and their coach too big for his own silk britches.

The first season of basketball at the new Air Force Academy had been over for two weeks, and Dean Smith was back in Topeka, Kansas, visiting his parents with his wife and two baby daughters. He had been assigned to start a golf team at the academy, but he had to wait until the snow melted and the ground thawed in Colorado.

On Wednesday night, March 6, 1957, Smith listened on the radio to Max Falkenstein's call as Kansas defeated Kansas State in

Manhattan by seven points to clinch the old Big Seven Conference championship and reach twenty victories for the first time in five years.

Dick Harp had taken over for Phog Allen that season, and the Jayhawks' resurgence was due largely to their 7'2" sophomore phenom Wilt Chamberlain. Competing against many other college coaches, including North Carolina's Frank McGuire, Allen and Harp had gone to Philadelphia two years before and convinced Chamberlain to leave the city where he had become a high school hero at Overbrook and play his college ball at Kansas. Chamberlain had just as quickly begun building his legend in Lawrence.

Since he had been in the Air Force for almost four years, Smith planned to stay through the weekend and catch KU's last home game against Colorado to see Chamberlain in person for the first time. He had worked with Harp and the seniors on the current KU team during his post-graduate year and followed their success closely. Smith believed that the second-ranked Jayhawks still had to be the best team in the country, despite two-point losses at Iowa State and Oklahoma State.

Something else was on Smith's mind. His boss, Bob Spear, had invited him to the annual college coaches' convention at the end of the month in Kansas City, where the NCAA tournament semifinals and championship game were also being played. Spear told Smith they would share a hotel suite with three other coaches, among them McGuire, whose UNC team was ranked No. 1 and still undefeated that season.

Spear wanted Smith to go because McGuire might be looking for an assistant coach to soon replace the aging and ailing Buck Freeman. It dawned on Smith that if Kansas and North Carolina kept winning, they could end up playing against each other in what was not yet officially called the Final Four. So Smith eagerly picked up the newspaper on Saturday morning to read the account from Raleigh, North Carolina, and find out if McGuire's team was still alive in the ACC tournament it had to win to move into the NCAA playoffs.

What happened the night before at Reynolds Coliseum went a long way toward establishing the Atlantic Coast Conference as the preeminent college basketball league, and North Carolina as its superpower for the next fifty years. Today's ACC fans younger than forty have a hard time understanding just how much pressure and pride engulfed the ACC tournaments of old. They not only crowned the conference champion (there was no formal acknowledgement of a regular-season title in those days), but determined the league's one NCAA bid.

Combine that stark reality with the fierce rivalries among Tobacco Road teams and fans, along with the absence of any comparative sports affiliations—no major pro teams in the state and NASCAR still the dirt-track hobby of a zealous but small following. Losing the ACC tournament, especially for a team with an outstanding record, was a bitter pill to swallow. It made for a long off-season.

Supporters of the ACC champ, even if their team failed to do much in the NCAA tournament, would taunt fans of the other Big Four schools unmercifully through the summer before football kicked off.

For North Carolina, failing to win the 1957 tournament meant even more—the end of a dream season. Also, perhaps the end of the Frank McGuire legend before it began.

Wake Forest assistant coach Bones McKinney, who was all but running the team in Murray Greason's last season, was wise to McGuire's canniness. In fact, McKinney had taken the team to its old Gore Gym just north of Raleigh for an afternoon strategy session.

There, he could privately practice that evening's "fruit salad" defense without fear of the "Tar Heel" janitor back in Winston-Salem ratting him out to McGuire.

Before UNC had visited Wake back on February 26, McKinney had planned to use a full-court press because he did not respect the ball-handling skills of the Tar Heels' backcourt starters Tommy Kearns and Bob Cunningham. But when Carolina took the court with a three-guard lineup that included reserve Ken Rosemond, McKinney figured the janitor at Memorial Coliseum in Winston-Salem had tipped off McGuire.

"Preposterous!" McGuire claimed when told of McKinney's charge, reminding everyone that center Joe Quigg did not start because he was back in the UNC infirmary nursing a virus and Lennie Rosenbluth was coughing so badly before the game that McGuire jokingly told him he was not allowed to die anywhere but Chapel Hill. UNC still won, 69-64.

Losing to the Tar Heels three times that season already prompted McKinney to come up with another trick defense to stop All-American Rosenbluth, or at least keep the ball out of his hands as much as possible. Rosenbluth could not be shut down completely. He already owned the school's all-time scoring record in three seasons and kept it until Phil Ford broke it during his fourth year in 1978. Many sensational players followed, but Rosenbluth was the first in the so-called modern era of Carolina basketball who truly deserved the tag of superstar. He could hook from ten feet and jump shoot from fifteen with uncanny accuracy. As his senior year wrapped up, Rosie was the ACC's leading scorer and its second-most accurate shooter. In a word, he was deadly.

For sure, he wasn't a one-man team, or even close to it. That's why memories of "Four Catholics and a Jew" have remained in place through the years.

Joe Quigg, the prototypical post player, had a great nose for the ball, and Pete Brennan was almost as automatic as Rosie with his jump shot. And the guards, despite McKinney's assertion, were tough-as-nails competitors. Kearns was the better offensive threat and Cunningham was a lock-down defender who always took on the opponent's best perimeter player. Opponents simply could not afford to surround Rosenbluth because his teammates would take turns killing them.

The five perfectly matched starters gave McGuire a luxury that few other coaches ever would enjoy to such a degree. When four of them deferred to Rosenbluth as their leader and scoring star, they were in business.

The Tar Heels had an equally strong chemistry and affection for each other off the court. That's among the reasons why McGuire, who already treated them like champions—providing classy uniforms with tear-away warm-up pants, snappy road-trip blazers, and leather, monogrammed travel bags—did not want it to end in Raleigh. The head coach himself cut an awe-inspiring Godfather figure, a standard for looks and dramatic impact he had set for the entire program from the day he stepped foot on campus in 1952.

At the first meeting with his new team, McGuire sent senior Vince Grimaldi and junior Bud Maddie back to their dorms and told them not to return until they were clean-shaven and had cut their hair. As a result, North Carolina never had a shaggy-headed or a straggly bearded basketball player. McGuire had big plans for the Tar Heels and wanted them to look the part because he knew, someday, this air of confidence would give them an edge.

On this night, more than four years later, the nattily dressed McGuire appeared coldly calm, his tailor-made suit hanging just right from his shoulders and a blue handkerchief folded to a perfect square in his breast pocket. Diamond cufflinks winked out from his French cuffs. McGuire's shoes were as shiny as his wavy red hair. Everything was in its place as he strode onto the court for the first time, each step followed by the cheering, jeering crowd.

This was part of the "Carolina cool" that some saw as arrogance, and, as McGuire had hoped, later manifested itself as the "Carolina luck" that antagonists hated about the Tar Heels—the last-minute comebacks, hitting the big shot, getting the crucial call.

The Heels started fast and hot against Wake Forest, using a 10-point run that included four each from Rosenbluth and Kearns to build a 22-11 lead. There was no TV or official stoppage of action that killed momentum, so the clock moved quickly in the first half of these games before the fouls piled up and free throws began. To slow Carolina down, McKinney jumped up and signaled timeout with 8:32 left in the first half.

"Look, you didn't lose the lead in two minutes and you're not going to get it back in two minutes," he shouted. "Let's cut it to five by halftime."

"Keep working the offense," McGuire said while kneeling in the other huddle. "They've got to give us something, just keep working it."

Shooting percentages in basketball fifty years ago were not nearly what they became when players improved their skills and practiced year-round. Dean Smith's benchmark of hitting 50 percent helped his Tar Heels field the most proficient offense in the game. Teams of the 1950s might shoot eighty times in a game and make barely thirty of them, akin to a beach ball being tapped constantly up around the glass. That's why the great shooters, like Rosenbluth, often took as many as one-third of their team's attempts—they were so much better than everyone else. Some players on the court could not make a shot consistently from outside ten feet.

Wake Forest cut Carolina's lead to four points at the half. As the teams left the court, the crowd was so jacked up that Reynolds Coliseum reverberated with noise and shook, as a layer of cigarette smoke hovered about twenty feet in the air.

"This was the guinea pig half," McGuire told his team in the locker room. "It doesn't mean anything. We just played it because it was twenty minutes that needed to be played. You have to win the game in the second half."

He reminded them one more time how Wake Forest had rudely bounced them from the 1956 ACC tournament.

"They're going to come after us," he continued. "Don't ever forget what they did to us last year, right here in this building. I've never forgotten that and you shouldn't either. Play like men out there. No baby fouls, no three-point plays. If you commit a foul, make it a good foul."

McGuire had a reputation as a players' coach and not much of a tactician, but he combined a great feel for the game with sound preparation and savvy adjustments. For example, he had the 6'4" Cunningham follow the ball from the top of the Carolina zone, bothering the Wake shooters in the second half as UNC clung to a narrow lead.

The Deacons began driving to the basket and scored six straight points in 90 seconds to inch ahead 59-58 on two free throws by Jim Gilley. Less than a minute remained.

The crazed crowd stood and watched Carolina come up court for what looked like its last possession. McGuire disdained a timeout because his players knew what to do—get the ball to Rosie—and he did not want to give McKinney extra time on the sideline to draw up another special defense.

The ball went from Kearns to Cunningham to Rosenbluth, who cut from the left baseline to the top of the key to catch the pass. He was strangely wide-open because one Wake Forest player had tripped and Gilley wound up in the wrong place. Wendell Carr saw what was happening and raced from beneath the basket to guard Rosenbluth.

Rosie swept across the lane in one motion and collided with Carr. Upon contact, an official's whistle blew and Rosenbluth threw up a 15-foot hook shot. The question has been posed to Rosenbluth a hundred times since: Did he really plan to take a shot like that?

"Are you kidding me? I never would have shot a hook in that situation, but I felt the contact and heard the whistle," Rosenbluth said.

The ball hit nothing but net, and officials John Nucatola and Jim Mills conferred to make the correct call. It was either a basket and blocking foul, giving Rosenbluth the chance to complete a three-point play that put UNC back into the lead, or a charging foul that nullified the shot and gave the ball—and probably the game—to Wake Forest.

"The hook shot was perfect," McGuire recalled years later. "It went in like it had eyes."

The hushed crowd waited as Nucatola and Mills talked at the scorer's table. McGuire was on one side, lobbying from the corner of his mouth, and McKinney was on the other side, flailing his arms and pleading his case.

Mills finally said, "Foul on 25 gold (Carr), count the basket. One shot coming for 10 white (Rosenbluth)." After Rosenbluth made the free throw, Carolina led 61-59 and 46 seconds still remained.

On Wake Forest's last possession, Ernie Wiggins' 20-footer bounded high off the rim. Carolina's Cunningham came away with the rebound and dribbled to mid-court as the clock expired. Somehow, the Tar Heels had survived again and beaten Wake Forest for a fourth time that season, this one the closest of them all.

Back in Kansas, Dean Smith read the result in a newspaper and figured North Carolina would beat South Carolina easily in the ACC tournament final, and then be only three games away from Kansas City and a possible date with his Jayhawks.

Smith was right about who would win the 1957 ACC tournament, but there was another score to settle for Rosenbluth, who was locked in a personal battle with South Carolina's Grady Wallace. Even though Carolina and Bob Cunningham held Wallace to a season-low 11 points in Rosenbluth's last home game two weeks earlier, Rosie could not catch Wallace as the ACC's scoring leader, but he wanted to ring up more points than his rival in the tournament. Going into the final, Rosenbluth had 68 and Wallace 72 in their first two games.

The outcome of the championship game was never in doubt as the Tar Heels raced to a 50-23 lead at halftime. Forever loyal to his boys, McGuire let Rosenbluth play 39 minutes so he could finish with 38 points to Wallace's 28. Rosie's three-game total of 106 points remained an ACC tournament record for thirty-eight years until Wake Forest's Randolph Childress put up 107 points in 1995. Rosenbluth also wrapped up the ACC Player of the Year award, winning by a 43-4 voting margin over Wallace.

The anticlimactic, 95-75 win meant Frank McGuire was going back to the NCAA tournament for the first time in five years, taking the school that had not been there in eleven—since the 1946 Tar Heels, with Bones McKinney at forward, had lost to Oklahoma A&M for the title. The real drama, though, had come the night before against Wake Forest.

That game forever changed the course of the ACC. With a different outcome, North Carolina would not have won the league's first national championship, and Dean Smith might never have taken the job as McGuire's assistant two years later. The ACC would not have televised its games years before competitors and, consequently, gotten the leg up on regional recruiting.

If there was ever a single shot that fundamentally changed the history of a conference, it was Rosenbluth's hurried hook against Wake Forest in 1957.

Bob Spear was older than Smith, who was twenty-four, and already well connected in the profession. He attended the NCAA coaches' convention at the national semifinals each year, but always went alone and met up with coaching colleagues. This time, he planned to share a two-bedroom suite at the Continental Hotel in Kansas City with three other head coaches he knew from the service—Ben Carnevale of the Naval Academy, University of Denver coach Hoyt Brawner, and Frank McGuire, whose Tar Heels were playing that weekend and owned a perfect 30-0 record. After winning the ACC tournament, the Tar Heels had beaten Yale in New York and Canisius and Syracuse in the NCAA East Regional at the Palestra in Philadelphia behind 91 more points from Rosenbluth.

By now, McGuire was a media star. He was dogged daily by writers who watched Carolina practice, then cornered the coach afterward for witty insights into the magical ride on which his team was taking all of them, and an entire state. The Tar Heels had played twenty-two games away from home, selling out steamy gyms in Columbia, South Carolina, and Cullowhee, North Carolina, and pro arenas called "gardens" in Boston and New York.

McGuire amused writers with quips and quotes and at each stop charmed a few more scribes into his camp. By the time the Tar Heel express rolled into Kansas City for the Final Four, the Irish dapper dandy had become a giant of the game, even to the other three head coaches who shared a suite with him at the hotel.

Smith was the fifth wheel and slept on a rollaway cot in the living room. His mentor, Spear, especially wanted Smith to broaden his coaching contacts and to see if he and McGuire hit it off. Buck Freeman, McGuire's college coach at St. John's who followed his protégé south, was slowing down and could not do as much scouting and recruiting anymore. Freeman's last great find for the Tar Heels was Lee Shaffer, a strapping 6'7" forward on the 1957 freshman team whom Freeman coached at Clair Bee's summer camp before Shaffer's senor year at Baldwin High School in Pittsburgh.

However, McGuire needed a strong class to come in behind Shaffer because reigning ACC and national player of the year Rosenbluth was finished after the 1957 season and the other four starters would be gone the following year. McGuire wanted to spend more time on the road and knew he would have to replace Freeman sooner rather than later with a coach who could run the program while he went off recruiting. Thus, Spear's recommendation.

The fact that Kansas had also reached the 1957 Final Four made the blind date somewhat uncomfortable. Smith was also there cheering for his school, and several players he knew so well, plus his mentor Harp, to win the national championship.

McGuire and Smith met briefly on Friday afternoon before the semifinals. Their paths had crossed once before after the 1952 national championship, when McGuire coached St. John's and Smith rode the bench for Kansas. In any case, it was hardly a match made in heaven—wise ass New Yorker versus proper Kansan.

"Whoever heard of anyone named Dean?" McGuire said. "Where I come from, you become a dean. You're not *named* Dean."

Smith always remembered that story, especially after McGuire tried to arrange a higher salary for Smith by telling the North Carolina brass that he was a dean. Again, years later, Smith did not react to a ditzy young UNC cheerleader who always said, "Hello, Dean" because she thought it was his title, not his name.

McGuire, the suave storyteller who at forty-four years old was living the high life, regaled the group with a tale about Smith's old coach, the recently retired Doc Allen. After St. John's had lost to Kansas in that 1952 title game, McGuire and Allen roomed together while coaching a college team that toured against the Harlem Globetrotters.

Doc Allen had asked McGuire how he was doing, and McGuire said he had a headache. The Kansas coach, who had a degree in osteopathy, swung into action.

"Take off your pants," Allen had said, unfolding his massage table.

"Whoa! For a headache?" McGuire shot back. "Don't you come close to me!" At that, the coaches left the suite laughing on the way to Municipal Auditorium for the semifinals of the 1957 NCAA tournament.

That night, the Jayhawks spanked two-time defending champion San Francisco and advanced to the title game against UNC, which had survived Michigan State in triple overtime to keep the legend alive. The following morning, McGuire asked Smith perhaps the most important question of his young life to that point.

"So, Dean," McGuire said over omelets in the suite, "who will you be pulling for tonight?"

Smith swallowed hard and smiled thinly.

"I'm going to stay with the alma mater," he told McGuire.

"That's what I thought you would say," McGuire responded.

After breakfast, Smith went for a walk and called his father in Topeka.

"I might have blown my chance at the North Carolina job," he said, "because I told Coach McGuire I'd be rooting for the Jayhawks tonight."

"No, I don't think so," Alfred Smith said. "My guess is that Coach McGuire respects that kind of honesty and loyalty."

In leading the Tar Heels to the national championship game in 1957, McGuire took what had been a football school by a long shot and made it crazy over basketball, threatening the football program that hired Sunny Jim Tatum to build a national power. The two coaches were large, egocentric figures who both worked in Woollen Gym. McGuire had the tiny old ticket booth, while Tatum and his staff had an entire hallway of offices. As Tatum planned a resurrection of the glory days of Choo Choo Justice, McGuire one-upped him by creating an unprecedented diversion on the UNC campus and around the state.

"I was a senior that year, studying very little," said Hugh McColl, who went on to run North Carolina National Bank, which morphed into Bank of America. "Basically, I was just going to basketball games."

Jim Beatty, who became a world record-holder in track and an Olympian, was a UNC student in 1957. He called the Tar Heels' undefeated run a "nervous existence" for everyone on and off campus.

Spero Dorton, whose Goody Shop on Franklin Street was the team's hangout before and after games, nearly lost his business by being out of town so much following the Tar Heels. The same thing almost happened to McGuire's buddy and Chapel Hill's only veterinarian, Dr. Lou Vine, who angered pet owners by closing his practice so he could travel to away games.

Jim Exum, a UNC student who became chief justice of the North Carolina Supreme Court, drove twenty-four hours from

Chapel Hill to Kansas City with three buddies to see the ultimate road game against what many believed to be the best player in the country. Fewer than a hundred other fortunate fans from North Carolina joined Dean Smith and more than 10,000 Kansas rooters to watch a game that would go down in the annals of collegiate sport and, uncannily, tie two universities and basketball teams for the next half century and beyond.

Kansas had giant center Wilt Chamberlain, whom Frank McGuire had already tried to sign as the first black player at the University of North Carolina. They wound up working together in the NBA and remained lifelong friends.

Harp, who labored in a large shadow after succeeding the legendary Allen, had originally arranged the partial scholarship for Smith to attend Kansas, coached him on the freshman team, and then tutored him as a graduate assistant. He capped a distinguished, five-decade career working for Smith at North Carolina.

After Smith's own star rose, he steered two of his protégés, Larry Brown and Roy Williams, into the head job at Kansas. On at least two occasions, Smith declined to return home to coach the Jayhawks himself.

In what many later called a psychological ploy, but which was actually a last-second whim, McGuire sent 5'11" point guard Tommy Kearns out to jump against Wilt the Stilt to begin the 1957 championship game. The two would be linked for life by that quirky moment. Chamberlain later invested some of the millions of dollars he made through basketball with Kearns the Wall Street stockbroker.

"It was mentioned offhandedly in the locker room before the game, and I said, 'That's all right with me, no big deal,'" Kearns said. "That was the way we felt. It didn't make any difference who was jumping center against Wilt, because we were going to beat them anyway."

Even though he had been told that McGuire wanted him as an assistant coach, Smith remained fiercely loyal to Harp and Kansas. During the first half of the game, Smith sat between Spear and Carnevale, McGuire's good friends who rooted hard for Carolina. Smith saw it from the KU perspective and disagreed with Spear and Carnevale on almost every call. With his school falling behind, he became so agitated that he left his seat at halftime and watched the rest of the game from the Kansas section.

Someone down on the UNC sideline was changing seats, too. In the almost-casual days of the Final Four, when anyone could move around the arena with relative ease, North Carolina Governor Luther Hodges had come out of the stands and plopped down next to McGuire. Caught between the caustic spitfire of McGuire and Freeman, Hodges got up and moved to the end of the bench. However, when the salty language continued even down there, the governor returned to the stands.

Carolina carried a 29-22 lead into the second half, largely because it successfully kept the ball away from Chamberlain with a zone defense that had Quigg fronting the Stilt and Rosenbluth and Brennan between Chamberlain and the basketball. McGuire's strategy was working.

"Kansas can't beat you," he reminded his team in the locker room. "Chamberlain can beat you but Kansas can't beat you."

The Tar Heels nodded their heads. They respected Chamberlain but were not awed by him because of their own accomplishments and because Rosenbluth had played against Chamberlain in the summer leagues of upstate New York. Rosie continued telling his teammates that a thunderous dunk was worth the same number of points as the baskets they would score. So, they reasoned, keep the ball away from Wilt and just play their game.

However, with Rosenbluth falling into foul trouble, Chamberlain got free in the second half and the Jayhawks chipped away to eventually lead after Rosenbluth fouled out with 1:45 left to play. Substitute Bob Young, pressed into duty, made a jump shot that eventually sent the game into overtime.

Without a shot clock and the action slowing to a snail's pace, each team scored two points in the first overtime, and both went scoreless in the second extra period, which was interrupted by a scuffle and near fight between the teams. To the partisan Kansas crowd in dingy, smoke-filled Municipal Auditorium, it was agony. Smith remembers sweating, puffing a cigarette, and biting his fingernails—unlike the calm he would show as a head coach.

Kansas inched ahead and still led by a point with six seconds left in the third overtime, when Quigg drove the right side and Chamberlain swatted away his shot. However, an official whistled Gene Elstun for shoving Quigg from behind. Hissing and some debris then rained down on the court. Harp considered a timeout to ice Quigg, but McGuire beat him to it. He wanted to set up what would happen if Quigg dropped both free throws, made only one, or missed both.

"After Joe makes these foul shots, keep the ball away from Chamberlain and no fouls!" McGuire yelled to his team.

Freeman grabbed Young as they broke and said, "If Joe misses both, foul Chamberlain right away."

Quigg flipped the shots toward the basket from in front of his forehead. Bound for dental school, he later said those shots determined whether he would have a successful practice in North Carolina or back in New York. Both went in smoothly. "Bing, bing,"

McGuire was to say whenever describing how matter-of-factly Quigg did it.

"I'm glad it was Joe taking those shots," said Rosenbluth, who watched while standing at the bench with his blue warm-up jacket draped over one shoulder. "Every kid pictures himself shooting free throws for the national title and hitting them. Joe lived that."

Kansas inbounded the ball to Ron Loneski, whose pass to Chamberlain at the high post was underthrown. Hero Quigg slapped it away to Kearns, who imitated something he had seen West Virginia All-American Hot Rod Hundley do, flinging the ball in the air as the final seconds ran off the clock.

The images of Kearns beginning the game jumping against Chamberlain and ending it with his underhand heave skyward are engraved into Tar Heel basketball history.

Several players lifted McGuire on their shoulders and celebrated on the court, briefly and with little show. It was nothing compared to what has since happened at the Final Four's conclusion with streamers descending from the roof, bombastic music blaring, and "One Shining Moment" showing over video screens. In 1957, that was the stuff of Flash Gordon comics.

When team manager Joel Fleishman later tucked the small NCAA trophy into a gym bag with the smelly socks and jocks, he had no idea of the history that had just been made with UNC's 32-0 classic season. It was the second straight NCAA champion that had gone unbeaten. (San Francisco, with Bill Russell, was 29-0 the year before. UCLA teams would go 30-0 four times, but only Indiana in 1976 matched Carolina's thirty-two victories against no losses.)

Smith sat depressed, chin in palm, watching the Tar Heels cut down the nets. He went into the Kansas locker room to console Harp, and then he walked back to the hotel. The Kansas and Carolina players also walked in the rain, still in uniform, because there wasn't enough room in the tiny locker rooms for the players to even shower and dress in private.

McGuire soon entered the hotel suite with Spear, Carnevale, and Brawner. The Carolina players trickled in shortly after, all showered and dressed in their blazers and ties and ready to hit the town as national champs.

McGuire asked each of his coaching friends to say something to his team, and Smith replied that he was so upset with the outcome of the game that he did not feel like talking. McGuire insisted, almost as if he were putting Smith through another aspect of the interview process.

"You guys had it at the end," Smith recounted saying in his autobiography. "Congratulations. But I certainly wasn't cheering for you."

McGuire seemed impressed with Smith's honesty and then asked him for advice on where to take everyone—players, coaches, a few sportswriters, and cronies—for a postgame meal. Smith said the only place he knew that would still be open was Eddy's, an expensive nightclub. He felt somehow pleased that at least Carolina would have to pay a big tab for dinner.

Eddy's accommodated the large party, and McGuire told them all to order whatever they wanted off the menu. UNC athletic director Chuck Erickson eventually made McGuire pay $48 in cash for Roquefort dressing on the expense account that McGuire turned in. Twenty-five years later, after McGuire had been there for Smith's defining moment at the 1982 Final Four, Carolina's young AD, John Swofford, jokingly sent the retired mentor a check for 48 bucks to pay him back.

At breakfast the next morning in Kansas City, McGuire got to what had been on Smith's mind most of the weekend. He began by talking about Freeman, whom he had hired at North Carolina and saved from encroaching alcoholism. Freeman was a bachelor who had devoted his life to basketball, and if he couldn't coach he would sink into depression and drink. He was tall and handsome with white hair, almost a ghostly figure when he walked into a room, and he was connected to all the scouts and hustlers in New York.

But he was also a brilliant assistant, better with X's and O's than McGuire, and so dedicated to the players' welfare that he checked their curfews in the middle of the night and followed them to the movies when they skipped class during the day.

Freeman's condition was worsening, whether or not he stayed one more season. McGuire said it was up to Buck but eventually he would need an assistant who could conduct practice while he was recruiting in New York. McGuire did not seem to mind that Smith was from Kansas with no contacts in the Northeast. He had already been in North Carolina for five years, had it in his contract that he could spend summers at his lake home in Greenwood Lake, New York, and was clearly itching to log more time on the recruiting trail. His young son, Frankie, was now eight and doing so well that McGuire could leave home for longer stints while his wife, Pat, managed the three children.

Feeling awkward to be considered by the school that had just taken down his beloved Jayhawks, Smith answered uncomfortably that he didn't expect to stay in the Air Force long term but that his official discharge was not until April of 1958. McGuire said that was okay; if Buck stayed on one more season, the offer would still be good the next year.

Smith remained torn between his love for Kansas, where he might have a chance to return and coach with Dick Harp, and the fact that working for McGuire with the defending national champions would be a great learning experience. They shook hands, agreed to stay in touch, and see what happened.

Smith, Spear, and Brawner flew back to Denver that afternoon while McGuire and Rosenbluth caught a flight for New York and a national television appearance on *The Ed Sullivan Show* that night. The rest of the Tar Heels boarded their Eastern Airlines charter bound for North Carolina and a reception that became as legendary as what they had accomplished on the court that weekend.

TV entrepreneur C. D. Chesley, hooked on Carolina's miracle run, had patched together a network of stations that carried the Final Four games back to North Carolina. Unbeknownst to McGuire and his team, who figured about a hundred industrious UNC alumni and students followed them to Kansas City, thousands of people back home had watched their epic, triple-overtime victories on TV sets in homes, frat houses, taverns, and even rooms at UNC's Memorial Hospital, where they had brought in rented sets from local hardware and supply stores.

When the UNC charter approached Raleigh-Durham Airport about 1:00 P.M. on Sunday, March 24, 1957, the pilot had to circle several times because so many people were close to the taxiways. Anxious about safety, he came very close to taking his aircraft to Greensboro. As it was, thousands of fans flooded past security onto the tarmac and dangerously surrounded the propjet when it came to a stop.

Quigg, the crew-cut junior center whose two free throws and defensive play had secured the title, first stepped through the plane door and felt overwhelmed. People screamed at him, waved pens and pieces of paper in his face, and several women sobbed as he walked down the staircase that had been rolled next to the plane.

"My feet didn't touch the ground from the time I left the plane until I got into the car," said Quigg, who has several framed pictures of his hero's welcome ride. "We had no idea that so many people in North Carolina had watched those games on TV. All of them who weren't fans became fans forever that night."

In Chapel Hill, most of the students were sleeping off the Franklin Street party that has become a ritual after big basketball victories. Late Saturday night, hundreds of them had marched on the home of Chancellor Robert House, who came out to help celebrate.

And why not? The 32-0 season, capped by a totally improbable six overtimes on successive nights, would endure as perhaps the greatest sports achievement in the history of a state, region, and maybe even the game itself. Certainly, a university never has been the same.

"When we got back that afternoon, fellow students asked me for my autograph," said Brennan, whose last-ditch jumper at the end of the semifinals against Michigan State sent the game into overtime and saved the season. "That's when I realized we must have done something special."

A few days after McGuire returned to Chapel Hill, he was given a Carolina blue Cadillac sedan by appreciative alumni, boosters, and students, who were not permitted to contribute more than one dollar. The car shimmered on the sidewalk in front of Woollen Gym as a small crowd gathered. McGuire happily accepted, having long ago decided that nice clothes and a fancy car were the two biggest status symbols in America.

He also got two more unexpected gifts. One was a phone call from his old friend and rival at N.C. State, Everett Case.

"You lucky potato plucker. I guess I need to take you out to the Angus Barn to celebrate," Case said of the Raleigh steakhouse near the airport.

The other was a surprise visit from Jim Tatum. The Carolina football coach, who heretofore had seen basketball as a wintertime diversion between the end of his season and spring practice, might have sensed the pendulum swinging, a tipping point reached.

"He told me he had a confession to make," McGuire was quoted in his biography. "He told me that he had been silently hoping we wouldn't win the tournament.

"As a matter of fact, he told me, 'After the game against Kansas was over, I kicked a hole in my television set. I was so mad I broke two chairs in my living room. But I've decided that I can't beat you, so I'm going to join you!'

"And we shook hands right there, and that was it. He even started coming to basketball games."

The irony of that moment was sharp because Carolina was clearly a football school at the time. In fact, the antipathy between McGuire and Tatum had become such common knowledge that both men had to issue conciliatory press releases after a story in the *Daily Tar Heel* covered the conflict. The student newspaper reported that basketball was getting a raw deal at the athletic training table, among other places.

Tatum would have only two more basketball seasons to publicly support McGuire's team before being bitten by a tick in the summer of 1959 and dying from Rocky Mountain spotted fever at the age of forty-six. He and McGuire may have indeed fixed their feud, but they would have at least one other disagreement— over the starting salary of McGuire's new assistant coach.

Buck Freeman hung on through 1958 at UNC, which began ominously when starting center Joe Quigg suffered a broken leg before the first game and never played again for Carolina. McGuire told the story of his undefeated team over and over to writers from Smalltown, USA, to *Sports Illustrated*. He predicted there wouldn't be another undefeated season in college basketball "for a thousand years" and admitted his boys were blessed with the luck of the Irish. He said he hoped they would lose a game early to "take the pressure off" in the upcoming season. He recounted a recurring nightmare that had the Tar Heels going scoreless in their first loss. As it was, the Tar Heels' winning streak of thirty-seven ended on the road at West Virginia in their sixth game. Led by sensational sophomore Jerry West, the Mountaineers won 75-64.

Dean Smith remained at Air Force, which improved in its second year of basketball behind leading scorer Bob Beckel, who was an honorable mention All-American but won more military acclaim as a member of the Thunderbirds precision flying team. (Beckel, years later, took Smith for a thrilling test ride in the F-100 Super Sabre in Nevada.)

With no seniors and five starters ranging from 6' to 6'4", the 1958 Falcons basketball team used grit and guile to compile a 17-6 record and, amazingly, set an academy record with 72 rebounds in a game against Westminster of Utah that still stands. The two young Air Force coaches continued tinkering with and tweaking strategies to offset their intrinsic disadvantages. After Smith helped Ann put their two young daughters to bed, he often went to Spear's home to watch film and talk basketball late into the night. They used a defense that came from a bad habit by one of Smith's KU teammates, Al Kelley, who often left his man to charge at the dribbler. It drove Doc Allen crazy, but Smith appreciated the element of surprise.

Air Force sprang the maneuver after made free throws and when behind. Years later the ploy was known as the run and jump on Smith's Carolina teams. It often forced the ball handler to pick up his dribble in panic and throw a bad pass. Smith also devised the scramble defense out of it by continually double-teaming the ball while rotating the defenders, which left the open man too far away to be of any help to the player who was trapped.

Spear and Smith hungered to learn all they could from the so-called old masters. They took a page from Hank Iba at Oklahoma State and Bruce Drake at Oklahoma, slowing the game and running the clock with the shuffle offense, which was like the old weave. They also employed a sagging, man-to-man defense predicated on protecting the basket more than stealing the ball. Some of Smith's greatest Tar Heel teams defended that way and were criticized for being lackadaisical even though they held opponents to a low field-goal percentage.

Another mentor was Clair Bee, who coached Long Island University during its glory years in the 1930s and early 1940s before the point-shaving scandals almost ruined college basketball in New York City. Bee's hobby was writing, and he authored the famous Chip Hilton series that Smith had read as a teenager. After leaving LIU, Bee wrote basketball-coaching books and one of them on the 1-3-1 defense was the basis for the point zone adapted by Smith and used by most of his protégés throughout their coaching careers.

At the 1958 Final Four in Louisville, Smith again shared a suite with Spear and McGuire. North Carolina, weakened considerably without Joe Quigg, had missed a chance to defend its national championship by losing to Maryland in the ACC tournament final, the only title won by a non–Big Four team in the first seventeen years of league play.

Although McGuire was disappointed to miss the NCAA tournament, especially for his senior star, Pete Brennan, who led the ACC in scoring and rebounding and won player of the year, it gave him more time to spend with Smith, whose Air Force commission was ending. Smith remained torn between accepting McGuire's offer and returning to Kansas to join Dick Harp's staff.

The same four head coaches who had roomed together in Kansas City—McGuire, Spear, Ben Carnevale, and Hoyt Brawner—took Smith for a night out, and it was more like a fraternity rush. Spear thought Smith should leave Air Force and spread his wings, Carnevale had already coached at North Carolina, and Brawner believed working with McGuire would bolster Smith's résumé beyond going back to a system he knew at KU.

McGuire, who also had talked to his former player Al McGuire about the job, decided he wanted Smith, and, with typical Irish bluster and charm, promised to make him the highest-paid assistant in the country. Smith agreed to visit Chapel Hill in April, and that turned out to pretty much seal the deal. His reaction was similar to what McGuire found when he saw the quaint university village for the first time.

"When I arrived I fell in love at first sight," Smith wrote in his autobiography. "The town was in its full springtime glory with dogwoods and cherry trees in blossom and petals floating in the breeze and dusting the footpaths."

McGuire wasn't sure what he saw in Smith because they were so different—stylish Yankee and almost meek Midwesterner. Eighteen years the elder, McGuire recited in New York brogue while Smith talked in a pitched nasal. One thing McGuire liked was Smith's religious background, Baptist, which would appeal to those Southerners who were still counting the Catholics on the team even though McGuire had purposely filled out his roster with Protestant players.

After conferring with his wife, Ann, who was back in Colorado and pregnant with their third child, Smith accepted and agreed to a $7,500 salary. McGuire helped him scout for houses so it would be easier for Ann to choose when she arrived in North Carolina. The two coaches ate virtually three meals a day together and played golf and handball, getting very close very quickly.

"He never thought he was beaten in either sport," McGuire recalled years later. "In golf, he would hit a bad shot and scramble back for a par. He kept trying, and that was a quality reflected in his players. They were just like Dean, diving around and never quitting."

Having signed a new five-year contract for about $12,000 per year, McGuire grew angry when Erickson told him Smith couldn't make more than $7,000 because none of Jim Tatum's assistants did. Smith said the lesser salary was fine because it almost doubled what he made at Air Force, but McGuire would have none of it.

McGuire taught Smith an early lesson that, in all organizations, there are circles within circles and you fight to take care of the people closest to you first. It was a principle on which Smith built a network, a multibranched tree that grew into the fabled Carolina Basketball Family. Those in the inner circle went to the front of the line to be pushed for the best jobs and highest draft picks, and Smith was less likely to assist anyone without Carolina ties.

In 1958, his boss barged in to see new chancellor William Aycock and said that Erickson had denied his request on Smith's salary, although he never told Aycock the amount. Tatum had apparently been promised that his top assistant coaches would make more money than any of their counterparts at Carolina, and Erickson did not want to create more problems between his football and basketball coaches.

McGuire said Smith was a "dean" more or less flippantly and

a good Baptist. He said he needed Smith to replace Freeman and keep basketball at the highest level. Aycock phoned Erickson and told him to pay Smith what McGuire wanted, and if Tatum complained to have him call the chancellor.

"I explained to Erickson, on that very day, we had approved hiring two professors at a salary out of line with the faculty, because to get good people you had to pay them more than those on hand," Aycock said years later. "You just try to catch up with the others, and I told him we ought to do the same thing with respect to bringing Smith on board."

Smith, twenty-seven at the time, took on Tommy Kearns in a game of one-on-one at Woollen Gym while McGuire went back to his office. Smith beat Kearns, who was soon to graduate and head for a brief career in pro basketball. Kearns claimed he let Smith win to be a good host, perhaps discovering the concept of "customer golf" that Kearns later used many times while building his portfolio of clients as a stockbroker for Bear Stearns.

Smith has called McGuire's influence on him immense, beginning with an introduction to the New York City that tourists never see. McGuire had connections dating to his childhood and late father, Joseph, the policeman. He knew people at Tammany Hall. He knew the chief of police. He even knew a few people on the wrong side of the law, once cracking at St. John's that he needed tickets on both sides of Madison Square Garden so he could keep the cops and robbers apart.

McGuire's biggest effect on Smith might have been personal, from the way he dressed to how he handled sportswriters to "paying it forward" with niceties for people who could help out later. McGuire even had his own porter at Raleigh-Durham Airport that he tipped generously for information about any recruits the

Duke and State coaches came to meet. Although not that sneaky, Smith had people skills of his own.

He possessed an uncanny memory for names and faces. Through his long career, hundreds of acquaintances were astounded when Smith remembered them, and their spouses and children, after a chance second meeting. It made him seem even more sincere, just like McGuire managed to communicate when he looked in their eyes and shook their hands.

From McGuire, Smith learned the value of wearing a coat and tie every day. The appearance added respect to their profession and put them in a work mode. If unexpected visitors dropped by the basketball office, and it began to happen much more often, the coaches were always prepared to greet them. Despite relaxed dress codes as the new norm, every UNC head coach since McGuire has worn a coat and tie during regular-season games.

"That's something I will always do, that I got from Coach Smith," Roy Williams said. "I know he got it from Coach Mc-Guire."

McGuire had the same family values as Smith. After his young assistant's wife and two daughters moved to Chapel Hill and their third child, son Scott, was born, McGuire kept Smith close to home through the summer of 1958. He gave Smith the responsibility that Freeman had in organizing practice plans and lots of other detail work to prepare for the upcoming season, such as travel arrangements and worrying about the players' eligibility, along with coaching the freshman squad of scholarship players and student walk-ons.

The Tar Heels lost five seniors and four starters from their 1958 team, including leading scorer and all-star Brennan and All-ACC guard Kearns. Junior forward Lee Shaffer and rising sophomores York Larese and Doug Moe were the new nucleus, and keeping everyone eligible was imperative, especially in the case of Moe.

Always relying on families, McGuire and father Gunar Moe had decided where young Doug was going to college in the family's Brooklyn flat. "That was fine with me, I didn't care," said Moe, a great athlete who grew to nearly 6'7" by the time he was out of school. "I was one of those goofy kids; all I cared about was playing ball."

When Smith's first season at UNC began, McGuire made him feel like an integral part of the program by turning the team over to Smith for a few days so he could go recruiting in New York. As with Freeman, the players tested Smith and knew he meant business when he tossed Moe and fellow sophomore Lou Brown out of practice for being sarcastic.

Smith favored a full-court, pressing defense that could blow out teams early, and he thought the talent McGuire had on hand was athletic enough to use it successfully. He exhausted the players with lateral drills, believing a team that could not play man-to-man defense would have a tough time at the end of games if it was behind and had to chase.

McGuire preferred his 2-3 zone because it protected his players from foul trouble and, frankly, had won him sixty-nine games in the last three years, including two ACC regular-season titles and a national championship. However, Smith installed a version of the 1-3-1 point zone from his Air Force days, and when McGuire returned from out of town he found out that the players liked it more than their traditional zone. He encouraged Smith to speak up any time he had something to say, even in games.

"It will be my decision," McGuire said, "but throw out a lot of suggestions. Don't be offended when I choose to do something else."

Smith saw the difference in their coaching styles after Carolina's first defeat of the season, a loss to Michigan State in the Dixie

Classic in December of 1958. Behind several players left from the team that lost to UNC in triple overtime at the 1957 Final Four, the No. 7 Spartans whipped the third-ranked Tar Heels. The 75-58 shellacking in their home state so angered McGuire that he was incommunicado before the third-place game against Cincinnati and All-American Oscar Robertson, who with Michigan State's Johnny Green were the first blacks ever to play in the ten-year-old holiday tournament.

The Bearcats, who went on to win the 1961 and 1962 NCAA titles, had been upset by N.C. State in the first round. This set up a third-place game between the No. 2 and No. 3 teams in the country.

McGuire still had not arrived ten minutes before tip-off, so Smith wrote the point zone matchups on the board, emphasizing how Doug Moe was to shadow Robertson. Suddenly, McGuire walked into the locker room and erased what Smith had written in chalk.

"Forget about this bullshit," McGuire said. "Just go out there and play like you're in the schoolyard . . . like you're in the schoolyard."

At that, the Tar Heels did, winning a classic confrontation that Everett Case called the greatest game ever played at Reynolds Coliseum. Emerging star Shaffer dunked and got fouled in the final seconds to send previously unbeaten Cincinnati home from Tobacco Road with two losses in three games.

Despite McGuire's bluntness, Smith was thrilled how the Tar Heels used the point zone to beat defending ACC champion Maryland and whipped Case's Wolfpack twice on the way to seventeen victories in their first eighteen games and the No. 1 ranking, frustrating opponents with their new defense. Included in the eleven-game winning streak after the loss to Michigan State were two over unranked and struggling Wake Forest, the second ending with an all-out brawl in Winston-Salem that began when Wake's Dave Budd horse-collared Shaffer in front of the home bench. The melee involved hundreds of Wake Forest fans and went on for ten minutes. The officials were forced to send the starters from both teams to the locker room and let the subs mop up until the final buzzer.

Carolina's twelve-man roster had a talented mix of players, including sophomores Larese and Moe. Shaffer, who went on to become an NBA all-star, was one of six juniors, including guard Harvey Salz, who had returned to school. The only seniors, and leftovers from the national champions, were Gehrmann Holland and Danny Lotz.

The blip on the regular season was a fateful two-game road trip to Maryland and Virginia, sandwiched around a one-sided scrimmage in Annapolis against the smaller Navy team of McGuire's old buddy Ben Carnevale. The Tar Heels lost their rematch with the Terrapins by 18 points and then dropped a one-pointer at Virginia that had McGuire fuming at officials and telling his team, "Let's get the hell out of here and go home."

They finished 12-2 and tied for first with N.C. State but got the first seed in the ACC tournament by virtue of their regular-season sweep of the Wolfpack. This was important because State had been placed on probation for violations in the recruitment of Louisiana hotshot Jackie Moreland. Merely advancing to the championship game against the Pack meant Carolina had earned the conference's one NCAA bid.

McGuire saw little need in even playing the ACC title game. He figured the ultimate goal of making the NCAA tournament had been reached.

"We've already beaten them twice, so why do we have to play

them again?" McGuire answered back to snickering sportswriters. He had no interest in letting Case steal some of his regular-season thunder.

So he insulted ACC fans and some of his own by not playing his starters very long and essentially conceding to State. After the 80-56 loss, he claimed to be resting his team for its first NCAA tournament game three nights later. But McGuire, obviously uncaring about whatever bad publicity it caused, was really making a statement that the regular season should mean more than three games in March played on Case's home floor.

It is hard to disagree with that logic, and history has supported it. Since the NCAA opened up its field to more than one team per conference, most coaches—including Smith and Roy Williams—tolerated the ACC tournament as a money-making necessity and a last-ditch effort for teams that hadn't already qualified for an at-large NCAA bid to play their way in.

Regarding the controversy swirling around the infamous 1959 ACC title game, McGuire said, "They had a big lead midway through the second half, and that's when I decided to rest my starters. This was Saturday night, and we had to play again on Tuesday in New York." The Tar Heels' first-round NCAA tournament opponent at Madison Square Garden was, ironically, the same Navy team they had seen the month before.

The ploy of resting his starters backfired on McGuire because Carolina went into the Navy game supremely overconfident from having embarrassed the Midshipmen in the February scrimmage. McGuire took his team to New York early and let the players go home and spend the night with their families. They thought the Navy game would be a song and frankly did not take it very seriously. Carnevale's club was itching for revenge and somehow hammered the Heels by 13 points in the East Regional opener.

The disaster signaled the beginning of the end for McGuire's omnipotence at UNC. The season expired with a 20-5 record, a thud and a sour taste that lasted for the next two years. Almost as if it were unavoidable, McGuire went from hero to villain around the league and the quiet, competent Smith held down the fort.

Without question, a storm was brewing on the horizon. The controversy inevitably stoked speculation about whether Mc-Guire would leave Chapel Hill.

5

Perfect Storms

IN the summer of 1959, America's sunshine turned cloudy. Along with the fattest paychecks ever (the average suburban family earned $6,500) and long-finned convertible cars also came worries about Communism and the Cold War. More than a few people built bomb shelters in their backyards. Social upheaval that would change the country forever roiled the middle class during the near-decade of prosperity under President Eisenhower.

Martin Luther King Jr. organized the Southern Christian Leadership Conference. North Carolina evangelist Billy Graham drew more than 500,000 people to months of revival meetings at Madison Square Garden. Furthermore, rebels led by Fidel Castro overthrew the government in Havana, closing off one of the free world's favorite tourist destinations of the 1950s.

Unrest in the South that began with the Rosa Parks–inspired

Alabama bus boycott eventually reached North Carolina. Four black students from North Carolina A & T College in Greensboro made national news by refusing to leave the lunch counter at Woolworth's after being denied service.

The University of California at Berkeley won the 1959 national championship in basketball with an all-white team—the last time that happened. In Chapel Hill, Dean Smith discovered a newly formed Baptist church that spoke to his liberal leanings. It had both university and community families as original members and, most important, a congregation committed to all races.

Smith knew that UNC had gradually begun integrating its student body in the early 1950s and, like his boss, wanted that to happen in basketball. Frank McGuire, who coached a black player named Solly Walker at St. John's, had tried to recruit the first black scholarship athlete. Thus far, he had yet to find one who could gain admission to Carolina.

Dr. Robert Seymour was named first minister at the Olin T. Binkley Memorial Baptist Church. This graduate of Yale Divinity School took a liking to the twenty-eight-year-old Smith despite having no interest whatsoever in basketball. That intrigued Smith because Chapel Hill had been hoops crazy for three years. His discussions about theology and sociology with Seymour and his wife, Pearl, strengthened his belief systems.

Smith never forced or flaunted his faith, and he respected all forms of religion. Through the years, he slipped into a back pew at the funeral of friends and mourned alone. When someone he knew struggled with a personal matter, Smith often sent comforting passages from books and articles or an apropos favorite sermon he heard at Binkley.

As the civil rights struggle became more prominent in the South, the Reverend Seymour wanted to integrate a popular restaurant in

Chapel Hill. He needed Smith to help him break the ice at The Pines, owned by Frances and Leroy Merritt. It was McGuire's favorite restaurant, and the Merritts had been feeding Tar Heel players four hours before every home game since McGuire came to town in 1952.

Seymour asked Smith, after his first season as an assistant coach at UNC, to accompany him and a young black theology student, James Forbes, who had joined the Binkley staff, to a meal at The Pines. The steakhouse at the corner of Highway 54 and Finley Golf Course Road had remained segregated. Seymour figured that Smith's presence would force the Merritts' hand.

"Bob knew that I knew the management, and that they valued the business of the basketball team," Smith wrote in his autobiography. Smith agreed and, as expected, Frances and Leroy greeted the trio when they arrived for dinner. After an awkward few minutes, they were all seated and served without incident.

When Smith became famous in later years, the story grew to make it seem like he personally integrated other businesses all over Chapel Hill. He had helped Seymour in this single instance because it was the right thing to do. After all, the Smith family back in Kansas had taught their son some things about racial equality. Later on, Smith would have a much larger hand in another story—integrating UNC basketball and the athletic department.

During the summer of 1959, another special bond formed when Smith tutored Doug Moe, who had made All-ACC as a sophomore but failed trigonometry in the spring semester. Smith took it personally because he had awakened Moe each morning and escorted him to math class, unaware that Moe walked in the front door of the math building and immediately went out the back door. When Moe flunked out, UNC gave him a chance to repeat the course in summer school.

Moe needed a C in trig to regain his eligibility for next season, and again Smith took responsibility for Moe's progress. Moe promptly made an 18 on the final exam and had to sit out the first semester. Smith claimed it was his fault for not preparing Moe for a crucial aspect of the test, just as for years he deflected criticism of on-court mistakes by his players.

"Players win games and coaches lose them," Smith loved to say.

It was a tenet that both McGuire and Smith lived by—support your people in public at almost any expense and settle all issues within the family. McGuire was very much a godfather-figure to his players, but Smith actually earned the complimentary moniker. He made phone calls and twisted arms to improve their pro draft status, help them land jobs, or secure whatever kind of assistance they might need.

Smith became so determined about achieving those results that he occasionally misread the point of a player's visit or call. Sometimes they just wanted to talk without needing the head coach to step in to fix a problem.

"He always wanted you to call him," Hugh Donohue, who played on Smith's first team, said. "He didn't like it when you didn't call him."

Whether protecting the image of UNC basketball or simply to get the facts right, Smith spared no effort. Midway through his coaching career at Carolina, he thought a university system report on graduation rates so misrepresented his team that he called his own press conference and walked in armed with a stack of documents.

Smith's loyalty as McGuire's assistant grew in his early years in Chapel Hill, beginning with his first recruiting trips to New York.

Harry Gotkin, McGuire's old friend and chief scout, still recruited players for Carolina even though the NCAA had cracked down on such practices. McGuire told him to stop, but Gotkin kept contacting prospects and funneling the information to Chapel Hill, where Smith was trying to learn how to identify recruits on his own.

Rumors of point shaving, the scandal that had tainted college basketball in New York ten years earlier, began resurfacing along the East Coast and all the way down to the Carolinas. McGuire remembered how the scandals affected most city schools, costing coaches their jobs and beginning the migration of the best players. He asked Smith to research and put together a scrapbook about the controversy, then he had each team member read it and sign a pledge never to take money if approached by gamblers.

Because the point-shaving scandal had shifted south, the NCAA was looking more closely at certain colleges. McGuire was terrible at keeping good financial records, and in the days before credit cards, he took cash advances for recruiting and scouting trips but rarely collected receipts when he entertained. This further strained relations with athletic director Chuck Erickson, who was already angry with McGuire because his team had been involved in several on-court fights and had become the ACC's newest bad boys.

The growing antagonism toward McGuire was new to Smith, who had earlier played and worked for the universally revered Doc Allen and the respected Bob Spear. He supported his new boss, but he remained in the background, mapping practice plans and running workouts when McGuire took off for New York.

On campus, the luster of the 1957 season had worn off with some people, and attention turned back to football. Jim Tatum's stunning death the previous summer galvanized the university around newly promoted head coach Jim Hickey. The team Tatum assembled had crushed Duke 50-0 on November 26, 1959, in what remains the seminal game of the football rivalry.

The Tar Heels' 1960 basketball season ended in shock. Entering the semifinals of the ACC tournament in Raleigh, Carolina had already beaten Duke three times, each by more than 20 points. Carolina took them lightly and lost, 71-69. Led by ACC Player of the Year Lee Shaffer, the team could have made a serious run at the national championship; instead, it went back to Chapel Hill with an 18-6 record.

A disconsolate McGuire spent much of the off-season away from North Carolina. He was also quick to take Smith to New York City after Kansas coach Dick Harp had asked Smith to return to his alma mater. Harp wanted Smith as an assistant and promised that the head-coaching job could be his within four or five years.

McGuire called it a recruiting trip, and the twosome did visit a few high schools. But McGuire was really recruiting Smith to stay at UNC by showing him more of the world than he ever had seen. They went to a baseball game at Yankee Stadium, saw a Broadway show, and ate like kings every night at the Italian restaurant owned by Danny Patrissy, McGuire's former classmate at Xavier High School.

At the end of the trip, Smith realized how much McGuire had enriched his life. McGuire had also made him an integral part of the Carolina program, imploring him to offer suggestions and be a contrarian when he disagreed. Smith was unsure he would get all that if he went back to Kansas, where he might always be seen as Doc Allen's bench-warmer and Harp's assistant.

So Smith decided to stay at Carolina, securing the important coaching lineage that would have been broken had he left. On top of that, UNC's basketball future would have been uncertain when

McGuire eventually departed. Now, of course, the stage was set for Smith to play the central role in its preservation.

The NCAA had made a preliminary inquiry into recruiting expenditures, which McGuire shrugged off because the chairman of the NCAA Infractions Committee, Horace McKnight, came from Columbia University. McGuire believed McKnight was carrying a grudge against him since his days in New York City.

In the fall of 1960, Chancellor William Aycock received an official letter from the NCAA demanding an accounting of how Carolina spent its recruiting budget. Paying scouts was against the rules, because some of them passed the money on to high school players in exchange for their commitments to attend certain colleges.

Aycock called in McGuire and told him they needed receipts to document his budget. "We have to refute these charges," Aycock said.

McGuire reiterated that the claims were bogus and he didn't have time to compile the paper trail Aycock needed, mainly because the big spender paid for most everything in cash and had no receipts. When the chancellor forced the issue, McGuire said he would assign his young assistant to come up with whatever Aycock needed.

It is an old and revered story at Carolina, how Smith split his time between the basketball office and South Building to construct a defense for the NCAA hearing. Smith had seen firsthand how McGuire extravagantly treated his team, sportswriters, and some alumni on the 1959 swing to Maryland and Virginia. Smith remembered the trip well because it ended the Tar Heels' eleven-game winning streak and cost them their No. 1 ranking, and McGuire seemed to react with a devil-may-care attitude.

After getting blown out at Maryland, the team had spent two days in Baltimore and scrimmaged Navy in Annapolis. They ate at expensive restaurants, went to clubs with slot machines, and McGuire picked up all of the tabs before they headed down to Charlottesville for the second game and a one-point loss to under-manned Virginia.

The trip reeked of over-indulgence but broke no rules. Smith collected affidavits from those on the bus and whatever other documentation he could find, eventually traveling to San Francisco with Aycock to plead UNC's case before the NCAA.

The charges were returned to the Infractions Committee for further review, and it looked like Carolina would be cleared. Then the NCAA summoned McGuire to Pittsburgh for a final hearing the first week in January of 1961. The Tar Heels had rebounded from early losses to Kentucky and Kansas State by beating Duke and Art Heyman, a star sophomore who had originally signed with UNC, in the championship game of the Dixie Classic.

They had moved up to No. 6 in the AP poll and were preparing to play Notre Dame in Charlotte. The timing of the NCAA hearing angered McGuire, who flew to Pittsburgh but refused to answer many of the questions posed to him by the committee.

Two weeks later, a few days after John F. Kennedy was inaugurated as the thirty-fifth president of the United States, the NCAA placed UNC basketball on probation for the rest of the 1961 season, which rendered McGuire's most experienced team since the 1957 national champs ineligible to play in the NCAA tournament. McGuire so abhorred the ACC tournament that he managed to have the Tar Heels pulled from that, too. He set a new team goal to win the regular-season race and be done with it.

Carolina went to Duke on February 4, 1961, with a chip on its shoulder, and late in the game antagonists Larry Brown and Heyman triggered the infamous brawl that lasted for ten minutes and involved Duke students and football players who came onto the court. It began when Brown threw the ball and swung at Heyman after a hard foul in the closing seconds. Donnie Walsh led the charge of teammates coming off the bench.

The Tar Heels' Doug Moe took on all comers, tearing his jersey as he swung wildly at anyone who challenged him. McGuire walked to the other end of the court while Durham police broke up the brawl; in his typical above-the-fray manner, he whispered to Moe as they walked off the court, "Wait till we get them back in Chapel Hill."

Despite losing that game to Duke, and having Brown and Walsh suspended by the ACC for the rest of the regular season, the Tar Heels won the uneventful rematch in overtime and finished first with a 12-2 record. But they sat home dejectedly from both postseason tournaments as Wake Forest won its first ACC championship and made its first NCAA appearance with Bones McKinney as head coach and Billy Packer at guard.

By now, McGuire had deeply divided the Carolina community, the alumni fan base, and even the administration, which was under pressure to clean up the program and build some insulation from the unsavory elements threatening college basketball. It was no secret that men with underground associations had walked the halls of Reynolds Coliseum, occasionally approaching vulnerable players.

When news of the gambling scandal broke in the spring of 1961, UNC president William Friday canceled the Dixie Classic, cut the schedules, and curtailed recruiting at UNC and N.C. State. McGuire was devastated by the arrest of one of his own players, bench-warmer Lou Brown, who had contacted athletes he knew at other schools for the purpose of shaving points to affect the outcomes of games from 1959 through 1961.

Brown and four N.C. State players were charged with bribery

and granted immunity in Wake County Superior Court for testifying and helping to convict gamblers who had approached them. "You look at these kids in the eye and say, 'Why? Why?'" McGuire lamented. "These aren't boys you pass on the street. These are your own, your family."

UNC suspended Lou Brown, who transferred to another school. He went on to become a college professor at the University of Wisconsin in the Department of Rehabilitation, Psychology and Special Education.

McGuire still had some strong, loyal supporters, who claimed he was steadily and unfairly being forced out. Chancellor Aycock invited several influential alumni and members of the newly formed Educational Foundation to his office to show them a university report that detailed the problems and proved that no one was being unfair to McGuire.

Smith's presence made the coming transition easier for UNC. Aycock put McGuire on notice with a letter after the 1961 season. The controversy-shrouded icon eventually resigned in August to coach Wilt Chamberlain and the Philadelphia Warriors.

McGuire suggested Smith as his successor, but Smith obviously did not get the job because of his recommendation. Already Aycock's choice as the new coach, Smith was McGuire's opposite in many ways.

Erickson, who had grown tired of many elements of McGuire's power base, wanted to select the new coach and agreed with alumni who favored a national search for another big name. However, Aycock very quickly promoted the thirty-year-old Smith and said he valued a clean program and graduating players above the number of wins his team posted.

"The decision has been made," he told a disappointed Erickson. Had Aycock not befriended Smith and discovered him to be a capable coach—albeit unknown and far less flamboyant than McGuire—he might have let the alumni have their way, and North Carolina basketball would look far different today.

Someone coming in from the outside would have broken the chain. Perhaps this would have distanced UNC from the unbeaten 1957 team and left McGuire's Miracle more associated with a disgraced coach; magic he had concocted and taken with him. Smith would not have been there to bridge the relationship between McGuire's former players and the university, building on this young tradition and somehow saving it during the difficult years to follow and giving birth to the Carolina Basketball Family. It avoided a shortened dynasty in basketball, like San Francisco with Bill Russell, Cincinnati in the early 1960s, and the great Ohio State teams that never returned to the dominance of the Jerry Lucas–John Havlicek era.

McGuire left Smith at a crossroads when he moved on to the NBA. The new head coach began repairing the image of Carolina basketball while never turning his back on McGuire, who undoubtedly left with mixed emotions.

"Dean was the brightest young coach I'd ever seen, but I didn't see how he could survive at Carolina," McGuire said. "They were de-emphasizing basketball, they had canceled the Dixie Classic, and there was almost no way he could recruit."

Smith struggled early, beginning with the probation-strapped 8-9 team his first season, his only losing record as a coach. He rejected McGuire's suggestion to put his own stamp on the program by changing the uniforms and swapping bench locations at Woollen Gym. Smith decided to make his mark in practice sessions, which were tighter and more intense, with breakdown drills scheduled to the minute, a system he passed on to his own protégés with detailed, typewritten practice plans. He was dedicated to principle from the beginning, and it quickly became clear that his way of doing things was to be easier said than done.

Billy Cunningham, the 6'6" son of a Brooklyn fire chief and schoolteacher who had signed with Carolina because his father ordered him to play for McGuire, had left Erasmus Hall High School after his senior season ended and spent the spring of 1961 in Chapel Hill. Cunningham completed his high-school requirements and hung out with what was to be McGuire's last Tar Heel team.

When McGuire resigned, Cunningham was in Brooklyn for the summer and assumed he would not be going back to play for the assistant coach he barely knew. Smith went to New York to try to convince the New York recruits—Cunningham, Judd Rothman, and Billy Lawrence—to still enroll at Carolina.

Rothman stayed in New York and Lawrence returned to Chapel Hill, only to go back before practice began. Cunningham stuck it out and played on the freshman team, but he did not study much during Smith's first season as head coach. In April, gambling that he might have seen the last of his best player, Smith sent Cunningham home because he was on the way to flunking out. Fortunately, Cunningham's parents were furious at their son for being so lazy and, upon Smith's suggestion, made him take correspondence courses to save his eligibility.

The Cunningham situation was an early example of Smith deciding on where to draw the line and how he was going to manage his own program. More of his own man than it might have appeared to outsiders, Smith followed some of McGuire's lead, but not all of it. Occasionally, he incorporated what his mentors didn't do.

While riding the bench at Kansas, Smith decided that if he ever coached a team the subs would get more playing time than Doc Allen and later, McGuire gave the non-starters. Smith never wanted one player to be the focal point, which was a common practice with Allen and McGuire.

Predictably, McGuire carried most of his college coaching style into the pros because that was all he knew. He figured players wanted to win and would respond accordingly. He convinced the other Philadelphia Warriors to give Chamberlain the ball, just as he implored his 1957 Tar Heels to "feed the animal" and let Lennie Rosenbluth lead them to an undefeated season and national championship.

Playing for McGuire, Chamberlain scored 100 points against the New York Knicks in 1962. Barely 4,000 people witnessed the game at the old Hershey Arena in Pennsylvania. This remains the greatest single-game scoring performance in NBA history.

Besides insisting that Chamberlain have the ball 50 percent of the time, McGuire dressed the team in matching blazers and slacks like he had at UNC. He also mandated they be clean-shaven and well-combed, no surprise for a coach once honored by the Barbers of America for being among their ten best-groomed men.

McGuire's one season coaching the Warriors ended with a last-second loss to the Boston Celtics in the 1962 Eastern Division finals. In June, owner Eddie Gottlieb sold the club to a group of San Francisco businessmen, who promptly moved the team to the West Coast. McGuire might have gone with the Warriors had they beaten Boston, which went on to defeat the Los Angeles Lakers in seven games for a fourth consecutive NBA championship. But he was an Easterner at heart and felt more comfortable there.

"Looking at the pros and cons, including where my family would live, I made the decision not to go west," McGuire said. "I had never done anything but coach and teach, so I had no idea what I would be doing. But I felt that I would end up somewhere, college or pro."

McGuire stayed out of coaching for two years and grieved with the rest of the country when John Kennedy, the forty-six-year-old Irish-Catholic president, was assassinated on November 22, 1963. McGuire spent that Thanksgiving with family and friends in New York and watched the telecast of Kennedy's funeral service at St. Matthews Cathedral in Washington and the burial at Arlington National Cemetery.

When McGuire's 1957 team had played in Boston before Christmas, Kennedy was still a U.S. senator from Massachusetts and attended one of the games. The coach and future president had met outside the locker room in the bowels of the old Boston Garden. Only four years apart (McGuire was forty-three, JFK thirty-nine), they connected and talked of their fathers and mutual friends they had in New York.

Dean Smith, by now a devoted Democrat, was also moved to tears by the slaying of the thirty-fifth president as he went ahead with preparations for his third season. With Cunningham as a sophomore the year before, Smith's second Carolina team had improved to 15-6, including a huge victory over Adolph Rupp's Kentucky Wildcats at Lexington. His players called it the perfectly coached game—from Smith's pre-game talk that calmed a nervous team to his strategy of a box-and-one defense against Kentucky All-American Cotton Nash to his spread offense executed beautifully by senior point guard Larry Brown.

"The best game of basketball anyone ever coached," said Charlie Shaffer, a Morehead Scholar and reserve guard on the team and later a well-known Atlanta attorney who helped the city land the 1996 Olympic Games. Shaffer and his teammates believed that 1963 game at Kentucky showed what kind of a coach

UNC had, even if some of Smith's innovative strategies were accidental discoveries.

One day in practice during that season, Smith saw something beyond just another lay-up when Larry Brown was double-teamed at the foul line and hit Cunningham along the baseline cutting to the basket. The maneuver inspired the Four Corners offense, which became Smith's signature for years.

The 1963 Tar Heels went on to finish third in the ACC and lost by a point to Wake Forest in the tournament semifinals. That year, they graduated five seniors, including Brown and fellow guard Yogi Poteet, leaving Smith with another daunting rebuilding job.

Perhaps Kennedy's assassination the following November affected Smith's preparation for the 1963–64 season, which he has long characterized as "the worst coaching job of my career." He constantly juggled his starting lineup and had Cunningham play center while occasionally bringing the ball up the court.

"I tried everything and I shouldn't have. We were back to relying on hope," Smith said of the 12-12 dud.

"You couldn't believe some of the things being said behind his back," Cunningham recalled. "But it wasn't his fault. We were trying hard, we just weren't good enough."

The saving grace of the 1964 season was Bobby Lewis averaging 36 points for the freshman team, exciting the large crowds that watched him play, some of the fans leaving after the preliminary game ended. Lewis had first visited UNC after catching Cunningham and Carolina on TV against Notre Dame, and Smith proved he had learned well from McGuire by getting Lewis' mother to grant him stewardship over her son even with the wolves baying at Smith's door.

His honeymoon was now over, hastened by the success of UNC's Big Four rivals—Duke, N.C. State, and Wake Forest—that had won the last six ACC championships. The Blue Devils, coached by the dynamic young Vic Bubas, had also advanced to the last two Final Fours.

As far as coaching reputations went, it was still the Big Three and little one. Bubas' mentor, the venerable Everett Case, was winding down a Hall of Fame career at N.C. State, and Wake's Bones McKinney had back-to-back ACC titles and one Final Four under the belt that held up his raggedy trousers. Smith was not in their league yet.

Smith spoke occasionally with McGuire, who was still in Philadelphia and torn between going back to pro basketball and overtures from the University of South Carolina, which grew out of old Tar Heel connections. Unlike North Carolina, which had at least some basketball tradition when McGuire arrived, South Carolina had failed to post a winning conference record in eleven years in the ACC and was a dismal 108-172 overall in that span.

The offer first came up when McGuire visited Asheville, North Carolina, and ate lunch with several old friends at the restaurant of a big UNC fan named Buck Buchanan. Jeff Hunt, a Columbia businessman and owner of a Caterpillar heavy machinery dealership, took McGuire to see a new tractor and told him that South Carolina was getting ready to fire basketball coach Chuck Noe, whose players were suspected of using amphetamines.

"Why don't you come and coach our team?" Hunt inquired. McGuire said if Noe left and they indeed had an opening, Hunt should call him. Whether or not McGuire's interest hastened the decision, South Carolina canned Noe after the twelfth game of the 1964 season and replaced him with interim coach Dwane Morrison, a former Gamecocks player who later became head coach at Georgia Tech.

Talks with McGuire began almost immediately. "Just pay me what [athletic director] Marvin Bass is getting, build me a twenty-thousand-seat coliseum and I'll fill it up," he said. The Gamecocks announced the hiring right after the close of another losing season.

In turn, a now-sober Buck Freeman came out of retirement as his chief assistant. Freeman helped build a basketball team while the boss recruited and rekindled old adversarial relationships in the ACC.

McGuire and Freeman remembered the sentiment on Tobacco Road about the seemingly pathetic effort that schools from outside North Carolina put into the sport. The Big Four went into every season believing they had six "sure wins" against South Carolina, Clemson, and Virginia because none of the three were working very hard at it. Clemson, for example, lost its first twenty-six ACC basketball games in the first three and a half years of the league's history.

"We're fighting for respect," McGuire said. "I was on the other side of the fence and know what those [Big Four] people think of us."

South Carolina got lucky by hiring McGuire when it did. The financially strapped San Francisco Warriors finally traded Chamberlain—and his large contract—to the new Philadelphia franchise that had relocated from Syracuse. McGuire might have taken that job, but he and his family had already settled into a big home in Columbia with a swimming pool that had a brick safety ledge to avoid an accident with Frankie's wheelchair.

Smith visited the McGuires for dinner the night before they met for the first time as head coaches on December 5, 1964. They stayed up late reminiscing about their days in Chapel Hill. After the game, an 11-point victory for the Tar Heels, McGuire insisted UNC won because he had convinced senior Billy Cunningham, by then the best player in the ACC, to stay in Chapel Hill.

It was a happy time, one with little pressure on McGuire to win games, until his wife, Pat, was diagnosed with the cancer she fought for almost three years. Smith would stay close to the McGuire family, sending notes and making calls of encouragement to Pat throughout the summer and fall.

On January 6, 1965, after Carolina returned from Wake Forest with a 6-6 record and its fourth straight loss, Smith faced a lynch mob. A group of students hanged him in effigy as the team bus pulled up in front of Woollen Gym.

It had been a common practice around the ACC to burn or hang likenesses of unpopular coaches, but Smith's was the only such incident that attracted media interest all the way through his Hall of Fame career. In any case, the tasteless student prank added to Smith's first doubts about his ability to succeed on the college level.

"Maybe I should go back and coach and teach in high school," he said to Lou and Florence Vine. They were McGuire's old friends but eventually became two of Smith's biggest supporters.

Smith held rare individual meetings with his players the next day, and their support buoyed his basic belief in what he was teaching. Two days later, the Tar Heels upset eighth-ranked Duke in Durham for Smith's first victory after seven straight losses to Bubas' Blue Devils, who had marquee players Jack Marin, Steve Vacendak, and Bob Verga. A small crowd of students greeted the bus carrying the UNC team, with *Daily Tar Heel* writer Peter Gammons, in front of Woollen Gym in the late afternoon of January 9, not far from the site of the "hanging." They chanted for Smith to say a few words.

"I'd like to but I can't speak," he told the crowd sarcastically. "I have something around my throat."

That was the first and last time Smith publicly countered criticism from alumni and fans. From that point forward, he dealt with it privately and gradually unified a Carolina fan base that eventually grew into something called Tar Heel Nation, thanks to UNC's emergence coinciding with the college basketball boom on television.

The 1965 Tar Heels beat Duke again, finished 15-9, and were in a three-way tie for second place in the ACC, their best season since McGuire won five regular-season titles in his last six years at UNC. Smith and his team went to the ACC tournament in Raleigh thinking they could win the championship and earn his first NCAA bid. However, similar to what had happened to McGuire's young, talented team nine years earlier, Carolina got trounced by Wake Forest, 77-56. It was McKinney's last Wake team before he was forced to resign following the season because of alcohol and drug issues.

Smith was heartbroken for Cunningham, the league leader in scoring and rebounding. The ACC Player of the Year ended his career by missing 9 of his 14 shots against Wake Forest and clearly under-recognized outside the conference for never having performed on the national stage.

The coach who recruited him to Chapel Hill felt for Cunningham, as well. McGuire, returning to the ACC tournament he loathed—this time with his new school—met Cunningham after the game and gave him a pep talk about taking his extraordinary talent to the NBA.

Cunningham led the ACC in rebounding for three straight years, leaping to a then-school record of 1,062, an average of 15.4 rebounds per game (including 61 in double figures) for his career.

He was second to Duke's Art Heyman in scoring as a sophomore and then owned the ACC as a junior and senior, winding up an All-ACC pick for all three seasons of varsity basketball, twice unanimously.

In the early pollination of Carolina's family tree, it was McGuire who connected Cunningham to Philadelphia through Wilt Chamberlain. On McGuire's recommendation and the urging of Wilt, the 76ers made Cunningham their first-round pick of the 1965 NBA draft. The renowned Kangaroo Kid, McGuire's last recruit and essentially Smith's first, went on to his own Hall of Fame career as a player and, eventually, coach of the world champion Sixers before buying into ownership of two other pro teams.

By the end of the 1965 season, Smith's job was safe but hardly devoid of criticism. He boasted player of the year Cunningham and second-team all-conference sophomore Bobby Lewis, so any detractors looked at the coach. Cunningham played much bigger than his 6'6", but was still the tallest player on the team. And though another top recruit, 6'4" forward Larry Miller, moved up for the 1966 season, the Tar Heels remained small and undermanned after Cunningham graduated.

Meanwhile, UNC broke ground on an arena that had been discussed since McGuire badgered financial chief Billy Carmichael Jr. about Woollen's leaky roof during his glory years. After his team won the 1957 national championship, McGuire turned up the heat and even commissioned, on his own dime, some drawings of a building that would sit near the baseball field on Ridge Road.

One time, McGuire purposely gave Governor Luther Hodges tickets directly under the hole in Woollen's roof, hoping a forecast for rain by game time would come true. It did not, and when McGuire's run at Carolina ended six months after Billy Carmichael's death in 1961, talk of a new gym went to the back burner.

Smith had picked up the subject again with Bill Aycock before the chancellor stepped down after the 1964 season to return to teaching at the law school. By then, Aycock had shepherded a creative idea through the UNC Board of Trustees and legislature. The state was in a building freeze and not appropriating money for "new construction" at public colleges, but could approve expansion and renovation of existing structures. So Aycock and university engineers John Bennett and Joe Hakan proposed a three-sided auditorium attached to the east wall of Woollen Gym.

Smith showed prospects the model of the new arena, which sat in the main lobby of Woollen, and had his top recruits to date, Lewis and Miller, pose with hard hats in front of the construction site. This was the future of Carolina basketball, and Smith's message was that they would all be part of it together.

William D. Carmichael Jr. Auditorium, named for the man who had rebuffed McGuire's demands for a new arena, opened on December 4, 1965, with a strategically scheduled 14-point victory over weak sister William & Mary. After a 51-point throttling of Richmond four days later and a 9-point road loss at fourth-ranked Vanderbilt came the signature game in the history of what was soon called Blue Heaven.

With the crowd noise reverberating against the brick wall above the student bleachers that pulled out from an old exterior Woollen wall, Lewis played his career game. The acrobatic star scored early and often against Florida State on his way to a school-record 49 points, the UNC single-game scoring record that still stands.

Lewis hit 18 of 25 field goal attempts and 13 of 16 free throws before leaving the game with 2:01 remaining and 50 points clearly within reach. Smith might have left him in the game to gun for the then-ACC record of 55 points, but he took Lewis out after he surpassed the two highest UNC scoring records to date, Cunning-ham's 48 points against Tulane a year earlier and Lennie Rosen-bluth's 47 against Furman in 1956.

The Tar Heels did lose twice in their new home on the way to eventually winning 169 of 189 games played at Carmichael in the next nineteen seasons. Included in the 1966 season was a 34-point slaughter of South Carolina that marked the first sharp exchange between Smith and McGuire.

The Gamecocks, who had upset third-ranked Duke in December, were still young and fading toward another poor record when the Tar Heels overran them. Even then, the Heels kept pressing the Gamecocks long after the issue was decided. Smith knew Mc-Guire was mad. After the game, he went by his mentor's hotel to smooth over things. Smith knocked on the door but McGuire did not answer.

Still, their friendship endured through McGuire building his own powerhouse at South Carolina. Smith always honored Mc-Guire and his UNC heritage with open invitations for members of the 1957 team to come back for games. In the midst of what became a vicious rivalry between players and fans from the two Carolinas, McGuire and Smith never were caught criticizing each other in public and, conversely, somehow maintained a deep, mutual loyalty above the fray.

McGuire was constructing another "us against the world" wall around himself and his team that led to fights and ill feeling in the league, similar to what had occurred in Chapel Hill. Furthermore, South Carolina was an interloper, treading on the hallowed turf of Tobacco Road, whose teams had thoroughly dominated the ACC since its inception.

———

With UNC fewer than ten years removed from the Miracle of 1957, some Tar Heel fans were still seduced by McGuire's style and success. Smith had not won nearly enough to earn comparisons with the Irishman. However, the opening of Carmichael, a third-place finish in the conference that included two victories over McGuire's Gamecocks, and a controversial tournament game further established Smith's identity as a strategist capable of using the rules to his utmost advantage.

Smith's 1966 team suffered two double-digit losses to first-place Duke during the regular season, and Smith had a plan if they met for a third time in the ACC tournament. The Blue Devils were tough and talented, still led by All-Americans Jack Marin and Bob Verga, but they were also slow afoot and committed to a zone defense.

Smith decided to open the first semifinal game of the ACC tournament, the last to be played at Reynolds Coliseum, in the Four Corners he had used to upset Ohio State in Columbus the previous December. With Duke standing around and refusing to chase the spread, Carolina trailed 7-5 at halftime and both teams were booed leaving the court. But in the second half, with the pace quickening and the crowd still booing Smith's strategy, it became a nail-biter that severely threatened Vic Bubas' attempt to win another ACC championship and reach a third Final Four.

The flummoxed Blue Devils had fallen behind 17-12 when they began forcing the action and fouling the Tar Heels, who turned it over twice and missed enough foul shots to find themselves in a 20-20 tie with six seconds remaining. Duke sophomore center Mike Lewis stood at the foul line with two shots. One free throw would likely give the Devils their great escape.

After missing the first shot, Lewis took a deep breath, dipped down, and hit the second. Carolina threw the ball away again, and the epic ended at 21-20 as a fair number of fans now applauded Smith and his team as they left the court.

"We didn't want to keep it close," he said a few minutes later, "we wanted to win. Playing this way gave us the best chance."

It was Carolina's last loss to Duke for nearly two years, as Smith began reversing the one record that had him in the most hot water with critics—12-22 against his three Big Four rivals. N.C. State and Wake Forest were both in coaching transitions and sinking toward the second division of the ACC, leaving Bubas and Duke as the dominant program. Quietly, Smith and the Tar Heels had moved into a stronger position.

Smith's latest freshman class, which confirmed him as a recruiter of McGuire's ilk, turned out to be the cornerstone of the Carolina dynasty. Joining the varsity for the 1966–1967 season were 6'11" Morehead Scholar Rusty Clark and 6'9" forward Bill Bunting, both from North Carolina. Their presence allowed Larry Miller to rove as a small forward and Bobby Lewis to go back outside as a shooting guard.

Clark turned down basketball scholarships to Davidson and Duke to accept the Morehead at UNC. However, the fact that he had tracked the Tar Heels as a kid had something to do with it, too. "I used to follow the feats of York Larese and Doug Moe in those days, and I just hoped that I could tag along in their footsteps," said Clark, who was from the military town of Fayetteville.

Smith relied on a third sophomore, a 6'4" upstate New Yorker named Dick Grubar, to get the ball inside as the Tar Heels' first option, like most of the point guards to follow him at UNC. Smith finally had the horses to fill his first coaching canvas, fielding a lineup with both size and quickness that could spring the full-court defense he had wanted to use with McGuire's last few teams. With Clark under the basket as the intimidator and shot-blocker, the Tar

Heels extended the court to its full 94 feet and became the new scourge of the ACC.

They won their first nine games and climbed to No. 3 in the national polls before Princeton, with its best team since Bill Bradley led the Tigers to the 1965 Final Four, dealt them a 10-point defeat at hushed Carmichael. Seven straight wins and five weeks later, Carolina was back up to No. 2 in the polls.

The North-South Doubleheader weekend at the original Charlotte Coliseum on Independence Boulevard featured UNC and N.C. State against South Carolina and Clemson, swapping opponents on Friday and Saturday nights. They were conference games, which meant the teams alternated years in giving up a home date against one of the out-of-state rivals. In 1967, UNC wore its white uniforms against South Carolina, signifying the Gamecocks wouldn't be coming to Chapel Hill that season.

The Tar Heels beat McGuire's club by 25 in Charlotte but found a much tougher team waiting two weeks later at the Pit in Columbia. Northeast imports dubbed the Four Horsemen— juniors Gary Gregor, Skip Harlicka, Frank Standard, and Jack Thompson—stunned third-ranked UNC by 13 points, auguring the arrival of the first true ACC force outside of Tobacco Road since Bud Millikan's Maryland teams of the 1950s.

The South Carolina center was 6'9" senior Al Salvadori, a West Virginian whose son, Kevin, would play for Dean Smith twenty-five years later. McGuire's freshman class included a 6' guard named Bobby Cremins, who was from the Bronx but attended prep school in Virginia. Cremins not only became an important player for McGuire in his rivalry with North Carolina, but he was later the coach at Georgia Tech who tangled with Smith over star recruits from New York City and environs.

Upon returning to the ACC in 1964, McGuire had resumed his

campaign to move the conference tournament off the N.C. State campus. Smith and several other ACC coaches aligned with Mc-Guire, and the declining health of Everett Case left little opposition. Case grew gravely ill before the 1965 season began and after two games turned his team over to assistant (and former Clemson coach) Press Maravich, whose son, Pete, was making a mockery of high-school scoring records as a senior at Broughton High School in Raleigh.

Although the ACC would lose some revenue by moving out of 12,400-seat Reynolds, the athletic directors voted to hold the 1967 tournament at the one-story Greensboro Coliseum (9,000 capacity) and the 1968, 1969, and 1970 events at 11,500-seat Charlotte Coliseum while Greensboro added a second deck that would be ready for the 1971 season. With interest growing in the ACC tournament through television coverage, public ticket sales ended. Only students and athletic donors could attend the games, and booster clubs around the league became big business.

Carolina's super sophs took the burden off senior Bobby Lewis and junior Larry Miller to do everything, and the 1967 Tar Heels beat Duke twice to win the ACC regular season for the first time in Smith's tenure. Helping Smith's popularity immensely, they were a perfect 6-0 against the rest of Tobacco Road.

Smith earned another important victory when Charles Scott, the first black scholarship athlete at UNC, finished his freshman season in good standing. Smith, who had earlier tried to recruit North Carolinians and future pros Lou Hudson and Walt Bellamy, fulfilled his goal of integration with someone good enough to star on the court, smart enough to succeed in the classroom, and tough enough to endure the obvious racial prejudice that lingered in the South of the 1960s.

Scott was from Harlem but had prepped at Laurinburg Institute in North Carolina and originally committed to Davidson College, which was coached by Lefty Driesell. Several troubling incidents in small-town Davidson angered Scott, and Smith swooped in to show the 6'5" athletic phenomenon the more progressive sides of Chapel Hill's campus and community.

Smith's goal to break down segregation in his athletic department was born from his color-blind father. This commitment was nurtured by Doc Allen's signing of Wilt Chamberlain at Kansas and reinforced by McGuire, who had brought St. John's its first black players and tried to get Chamberlain, among others, to break the color barrier at UNC.

Duke's Bubas, whose school was slower to integrate, saw the writing on the wall. Noting a changing of the guard and recalling the protest that Smith survived two years earlier, Bubas quipped after the second defeat to UNC, "If they hang me, I hope they do it close to the library. It's more academic that way."

Duke defeated South Carolina in the semifinals of the 1967 ACC tournament, costing McGuire a chance to take his team back to New York. The ACC was allowing its tournament runner-up to play in the NIT for the first time, and either the NCAA or the NIT at Madison Square Garden would have been fine with McGuire.

The Tar Heels beat Duke for a third time to win the school's second and Smith's first ACC championship. They did it behind 32 points from tournament MVP Miller and 26 from Lewis. The Blue Devils took 18 more shots, but five players fouled out, and Carolina made 32 of 44 from the free throw line. With McGuire watching from the stands, the players carried Smith around the court before they cut down the nets.

After avenging the loss to Princeton and handling Coach Bob Cousy's Boston College team in the NCAA East Regional, Smith coached in his first Final Four at Louisville's famed Freedom Hall.

He stayed with his team, but McGuire, Bob Spear, Hoyt Brawner, and Ben Carnevale again shared a suite, this time toasting the decision that sent Smith to North Carolina in the first place. The unhappy footnote was that Carolina got trounced by Dayton and Houston, and finished fourth.

The 1968 season began just after Pat McGuire lost her battle to cancer in September. Smith was among the hundreds attending her funeral in New York. It was also a time of more upheaval in America, with much of the country growing concerned over President Lyndon Johnson's handling of the escalating war in Vietnam.

On the court, the Tar Heels again led wire to wire. UNC had clinched the ACC race by winning twelve consecutive conference games—twenty straight overall—when South Carolina visited Chapel Hill for the first time since the 104-70 blowout loss that had miffed McGuire. Many old friends and acquaintances in the home crowd knew he returned as a widower.

Carmichael was buzzing for Larry Miller's last home game. Smith took the microphone before the game and asked the crowd to treat McGuire and his team with respect.

Miller, an All-American on his way to a second straight ACC Player of the Year award, expected to go out a winner. But the steadily improving Gamecocks had notched another successful season and, based on their earlier four-point loss to the Tar Heels in Charlotte, arrived confident of pulling an upset. McGuire's penchant for a dramatic entrance gave the game a surreal start, especially considering Smith's request.

Even after his team came out for its final warm-ups, McGuire hung back in the locker room until just before tip-off. When the now fifty-five-year-old legend finally emerged in his requisite silk suit, nodding and waving to familiar faces in the stands and warmly embracing Smith at the scorer's table, the crowd's reaction electrified the auditorium. If McGuire was still a hero to some old guard in Carolina blue, younger or newer fans unaware of the back story only saw him as the enemy and a serious threat to Smith's hard-earned success.

The Four Horsemen were now seniors, and their pony was sophomore Cremins, a scrapper with unrefined skills. The Gamecocks shot well all night and led late when Smith told his team to foul Cremins and dare the 59 percent free throw shooter to protect the lead. Cremins went to the line 16 times and made 13, and South Carolina held on to win by one point.

After the game, McGuire was animated when he talked to sportswriters. He had taken off his gold cufflinks and held them between his fingers as he gestured, almost as if to say he was still the king. Sitting by his locker, Cremins was surrounded by men with notepads and pens for the first time in his career.

Cremins joined his coach as a hero to the state of South Carolina that night, and he has long since teased Smith about giving him the chance not only to ice the game but become the desire of coeds who swarmed him when he got back to Columbia.

McGuire's team tied N.C. State for third place behind UNC and Duke, but lost twice to the Wolfpack, which was now coached by former Everett Case player Norman Sloan. Press Maravich had moved on to LSU after his son Pete failed to score 800 on his SATs and could not attend State or play anywhere in the ACC.

The Gamecocks, thus, got the fourth seed in the 1968 ACC tournament in Charlotte, leaving them in North Carolina's bracket. They had to beat the Tar Heels to reach the championship game and at least be considered for the NIT, which with McGuire's sentimental ties to the Big Apple would have been a lock.

Despite falling behind early, South Carolina rallied with an

18-4 run in the second half that tied the game in the final seconds. Miller missed at the buzzer, but the Tar Heels won in overtime, 82-79. The key to survival was another philosophical coaching difference. Smith's freestyle substitutions allowed his bench to contribute nine points. The Four Horsemen and Cremins scored all of their team's points, underscoring McGuire's long-time tendency of staying with his starters and possibly wearing them down.

The winner caught a big break because N.C. State took a page from Smith's strategy two years earlier and held the ball on Duke in the second semifinal. Bubas again refused to come out of his zone ("We couldn't press a team of grandmothers," he said), and the most infamous ACC tournament game in history slowed to a crawl, with State winning the excruciatingly boring game, 12-10. In UNC radio announcer Bill Currie's famous description, the action on the court was "as exciting as artificial insemination."

In the championship game, Sloan could not do the same against the aggressive defense of the Tar Heels, who let the overmatched Wolfpack hang around in the first half. Smith walked into the locker room behind the end zone stands at the Charlotte Coliseum and simply said, "You know what you have to do." He walked out, and his team blew open the game to win by 37 points, locking down its second straight championship.

Duke again got the NIT bid, inflaming McGuire's hatred for the ACC tournament and leaving him to think that bolting the conference altogether would be an easier way into a postseason tournament. His former player at St. John's, Al McGuire, had proven that as coach at independent Marquette, which had its pick of bids from the NCAA or NIT. That Smith's team advanced to play another independent, St. Bonaventure with All-American Bob Lanier, before defeating Davidson to win the East Regional, supported Frank McGuire's theory that not having to win a treacherous conference tournament was the easier road to an NCAA bid.

McGuire went back to the Final Four, this time in Los Angeles, and watched his protégé coach the Tar Heels into the championship game against unbeatable UCLA with Lew Alcindor. After playing their own game of stall ball in the first half, the Tar Heels ran with the Bruins and were blown out, 78-55. Smith figured if they were going to lose anyway, why incur the bad publicity of continuing to stall on national television.

Even after being run over by the UCLA machine, the Tar Heels were able to find a silver lining. Assistant coach John Lotz even called it "a tremendous thrill to be in the field with UCLA."

The two-time ACC champions had finished No. 2 in the country, and most of the Tar Heels had experienced Los Angeles for the first time. Smith truly had arrived as a head coach, and he received the same gift as his mentor after the 1957 season—a Carolina blue Cadillac—presented to him by some of the same Rams Club officials on the front steps of Carmichael.

"I'm not the Cadillac type," Smith said. "I accept the gift because I'm certain you're really expressing appreciation for the fine play of the team."

Smith drove the car to the airport, where he used an old McGuire maneuver of parking at the Airport Motel across the street from the terminal in exchange for giving the manager a few basketball tickets. He flew to Pittsburgh to wrap up the recruiting haul that would keep Carolina on top—star guard Steve Previs and rugged forward Dennis Wuycik were joining an incoming freshman class that also included Long Island's Bill Chamberlain, the second black scholarship basketball player at UNC.

Richard Nixon was in the White House by the next basketball season, which was to take the rivalry of the two Carolinas to a new level of antagonism. McGuire had recruited some cocksure players from New York, who quickly bought into their coach's hatred for the ACC.

The Tar Heels were well seasoned and now had college basketball's most controversial player in junior Charlie Scott. He had received the third-most votes on the All-ACC team as a sophomore and had taken over for Larry Miller as the focal point of the 1969 team. Of course, Scott carried the extra burden of his skin color and the racist reaction it provoked.

Smith nearly went into the stands of the new Carolina Coliseum in Columbia after a redneck who called Scott a "big baboon." It followed a suspenseful, six-point victory for UNC, which avenged a loss twelve days earlier to McGuire's newly named Iron Five. The South Carolina starters had played all 40 minutes in the game at Charlotte and stunned the No. 2 team in the nation behind 38 points from their cocky sophomore star John Roche.

McGuire apologized for the crass act, fearing that his school was not ready for its first black player, Casey Manning, from the border town of Dillon, who was starring for the USC freshman team at the time. A pioneer like Scott, Manning said he could go an entire day and not see another black student on campus. He went on to law school and became a judge.

Just as Smith had made efforts to integrate before Scott, McGuire had tried to break South Carolina's color line earlier by recruiting such players as Gilbert McGregor, who became a star at Wake Forest. Scott, a member of the 1968 U.S. Olympic gold medal team in Mexico City, was sensational down the stretch of the 1969 season, motivated by an absurd All-ACC vote that had left him off of five first-team ballots. Scott was easily among the five best players in the ACC, and he demonstrated that by dropping 40 points on Duke to lead Carolina to a third consecutive ACC tournament championship.

A week later, Scott scored 32 and hit the winning shot against Davidson, knocking his once-to-be coach Driesell out of the NCAA tournament for the second straight year and sending the Tar Heels to yet another Final Four. However, playing without injured point guard Grubar, they lost badly to Purdue and All-American Rick Mount in the national semifinals back at Freedom Hall.

South Carolina, which went to the 1969 NIT and lost its second game to Army when the Cadets' senior captain Mike Krzyzewski held Roche to 6 points at Madison Square Garden, dominated the rivalry and everyone else in 1970 and became the focus of disdain at UNC and around the ACC.

"When I came to college, most of what I had heard about Frank McGuire wasn't good because [the Gamecocks] were the big rivals and the bad guys," said Roy Williams, who was a freshman walk-on in 1969 and then kept statistics for Smith the next three years. "After learning more about the history, that he hired Coach Smith, it hit me that Frank McGuire really started the basketball success at North Carolina."

The Gamecocks swept through the 1970 ACC season unde feated and had their own run to the Final Four set up perfectly. In the days when teams could play NCAA tournament games on their home courts, McGuire's spanking new coliseum was the East Regional site.

South Carolina's Roche, who stayed at the center of the Scott controversy by beating him out for ACC Player of the Year in 1969 and 1970, suffered a severely sprained ankle in the ACC tournament semifinals against Wake Forest. He told McGuire he could go and hobbled through the championship game against N.C. State, but the Wolfpack pulled off the shocker, 42-39, in double over-time. The most excruciating defeat of his coaching career further pushed McGuire away from the league.

Hooted off the Charlotte Coliseum court after N.C. State's crushing win, McGuire had all the hatred and antagonism of nearly twenty years in the ACC clenched in his craw. He knew he should not have played Roche—his team could have easily taken down State with its other four starters going all out—but he chose to somehow blame the loss on the sudden-death nature of the ACC tournament he abhorred.

"It's like Russian roulette, and we got the chamber with the bullet in it," he said. Rival fans celebrated the most devastating defeat in South Carolina history and also a very bad loss for the ACC. The Gamecocks would have cruised through two NCAA East Regional victories on their home floor and moved on to the Final Four on another familiar court in College Park, Maryland. This missed opportunity turned out to be McGuire's best chance to win a second national championship. Even a strong run would have solidified his legacy at South Carolina. The last ten years of McGuire's coaching career might have been vastly different had his team not lost that 1970 ACC title game to N.C. State.

Worse still, the Gamecocks could not even accept an NIT bid because of an archaic NCAA rule that kept the NCAA Regional host schools from participating in another postseason tourna-ment. Devastated by his second-ranked team's sudden demise, McGuire fled to Florida with some of his cronies.

Meanwhile, Cremins refused to join his teammates for spring break in New York and holed up in the North Carolina mountains for the rest of the semester. That delayed his graduation from USC, but Cremins developed such an affinity for western North Caro-lina that he gladly accepted his first head-coaching job at Appalachian State five years later at the age of twenty-seven. Following Cremins' senior year at South Carolina, the entire ACC stood on the brink of change if not a breakdown.

The on-field, on-court, and recruiting rivalries turned personal, and administrators squabbled over eligibility issues. The conference had maintained what Dean Smith and other coaches called a culturally biased minimum of 800 on the college boards for athletic scholarships, and both Clemson and South Carolina threatened to leave the league if the rule remained. South Carolina football coach Paul Dietzel claimed that only two of the ten in-state players he was pursuing had 800 on the SATs.

Duke University released results of an internal probe that denounced the escalating costs of big-time athletics and stoked support for the de-emphasis of intercollegiate sports or withdrawal from the ACC. So the league was hardly on the same page with Duke.

Smith and North Carolina faced other challenges. After averaging 27 points as a senior, Scott graduated and moved on to pro basketball. While his success spurred further integration of athletics at UNC, the liberal campus was flushed with antiwar sentiment. Protests rocked college campuses nationwide, before and after four students were killed and nine others injured by tear-gas-toting National Guardsmen at Kent State on May 4, 1970. Some Carolina athletes questioned their commitment to team discipline while their classmates smoked pot, grew long hair, and demonstrated on the main quads.

Trying to balance his personal beliefs with his professional mission to teach and coach, Smith supported self-expression by his players outside of practice and games. He asked them to remember they were also part of a basketball team and athletic department, in many ways the faces of the university. He wanted them to consider the possible ramifications of their actions.

Unlike at neighboring Duke, where most of the students came from outside North Carolina and basketball was in turmoil after the retirement of Bubas, the Tar Heels' sustained success made the games more of a rallying point at Carolina. Students worried about the war and being drafted, but they also saw Carmichael Auditorium as a place to escape, where they all gathered to cheer a common goal.

Because of Duke's decline and N.C. State's struggles since the Everett Case era, South Carolina became the hottest rivalry for the Heels. It had all of the irresistible elements, beginning with the legend of McGuire, the mentoring of Smith, and South Carolina's recruitment of some combative players who were seen as Yankees.

The Tar Heels, by contrast, had become a product of Smith's principled savvy and left all of McGuire's macho behind.

6

Defining Final Fours

IT'S hard to believe, but three ACC championships and three trips to the Final Four were not enough to convince some of the Carolina old guard that Dean Smith was heading for coaching greatness. A few of the old-line faithful still reveled in remembering Frank McGuire.

The hangover from Smith's shaky early years lingered. There were even some players around who believed *they* had turned it around and he was just along for the ride. Never mind that he recruited them!

As a senior in the 1970 season, Charlie Scott dominated so much that none of the younger players had emerged. He shot an average of 23 times a game, almost twice as much as anyone else on the team, while showcasing his talent for the upcoming NBA draft. Toward the end of the season, most of those shots missed.

"I'm in a shooting slump," Scott said. "The only way to get out of a shooting slump is to keep shooting." He hit barely 40 percent down the stretch as Carolina fell to an 18-9 record and first-round losses in both the ACC tournament and NIT.

Scott still was an All-American, and once he left Chapel Hill, Smith's success story was supposedly over. The next season, the Tar Heels were picked to fall back into the middle of the ACC race. Smith's goal was to prove the signing of one great class, plus Scott, was not an anomaly, that he could avoid the fate other schools had suffered after a run of a few good years. He also had to renew his lifelong belief in basketball as a team game; win or lose, the 1971 Tar Heels would play unselfishly, share the ball, take only high-percentage shots, and totally commit to playing defense.

As much as any other season, this became a tipping point in Dean Smith's career and one that moved his program from potentially strong to permanently superior. Ironically, it also kept McGuire's legacy alive while positioning Smith as the coach at Carolina for as long as he wanted to be.

One contrast with McGuire that Smith sought from the beginning was behavior control at all times. He wanted the players' energy expended on the defensive end and executing on offense, not in reaction toward the other team. Acting out, even undeserved technical fouls, always got a Tar Heel benched for at least a few minutes, often more.

The new season began with cautious optimism that juniors Bill Chamberlain, Steve Previs, and Dennis Wuycik, the top players in the 1968 high-school recruiting class, would replace Scott as the leaders and dedicate themselves to Smith's coaching philosophy. Wuycik was a rugged scorer and Chamberlain was equally as smooth, while the slick Previs sacrificed his shots and scoring average to concentrate on assists and defense. Previs played unselfishly, much like Bobby Cunningham had for McGuire, and how Jackie Manuel and Marcus Ginyard would for Roy Williams more than thirty years later.

After beating Virginia in the ACC opener, UNC's young squad stood 4-0 but still entered the new year unranked during the regular season for the first time since 1966. Now came the much-anticipated home-and-home series with Frank McGuire's team, which had resumed after Clemson and South Carolina pulled out of the North-South doubleheader.

When the Gamecocks arrived in Chapel Hill on Monday night, January 4, 1971, they were fresh off winning the Holiday Festival at Madison Square Garden. They were ranked first in one national poll, second in the other.

The years had taught Smith and McGuire much about each other. Smith wanted to run, press, and play his bench. McGuire preferred controlling tempo to avoid foul trouble, keeping his starters on the court, and still favored the 2-3 zone he had used for most of his coaching career. The Tar Heels might have been quicker the year before, but South Carolina had more size and skill and the Gamecocks had beaten UNC twice in the same season for the first time in ACC history.

But this was 1971, and Carolina had a corps of unproven players itching to show they belonged in the league. On the Tar Heels' first possession, sophomore point guard George Karl crossed midcourt, put the ball on his hip and stood there, smirking. South Carolina had lumbered back under the basket and into its customary defense.

There were no rules to initiate action at the time, something that changed in years to come. So it became a pissing match between old friends Smith and McGuire. The Tar Heels were not going to play South Carolina's game anymore, and they had the home crowd howling with approval.

McGuire sat between his assistants, veteran Buck Freeman and Donnie Walsh, a point guard he had recruited to UNC who wound up playing his last season for Smith. Anticipating the strategy, Walsh had convinced McGuire to let him work with the Gamecocks on man-to-man defense during practice. The three coaches looked at each other, nodded, and McGuire waved his team out of the zone with a sardonic smile. The Tar Heels spread the court and began playing.

Two hours later, they had run their interstate rival out of Carmichael. Using wide spacing, sharp cuts, and a bunch of backdoor baskets, North Carolina looked like the better team. Smith had counted on Scott too much toward the end of his career, and now he committed to a lineup of players with roughly equal talent.

Despite having already cut down the ACC championship nets three times, Smith finally exorcised McGuire's ghost on this winter night in Chapel Hill. The game was so intense, the overflow crowd so revved up, that Carmichael Auditorium overheated like it was summertime. Still, the proper Smith and McGuire never came out of their expensive suit jackets, and near the end McGuire had pushed his sleeves well above the French cuffs, looking out of sorts and frustrated as he waved his arms at official Jim Hernjak.

The 79-64 victory gave UNC a 2-0 record and first place in the ACC. It became a template for how other teams refused to play at the Gamecocks' plodding pace, forcing them out of their comfort zone with stalling tactics.

South Carolina had John Roche and, except for Cremins, the same cast that had gone undefeated in the ACC and 25-3 overall the year before. The Gamecocks suffered three more league losses and crossed the line the conference had drawn for physical play. One of the upsets was at Maryland, where new coach Lefty Driesell ordered his own stall. His team led 4-3 at the half and won a fight-marred 31-30 game during which John Ribock, one of McGuire's few players from the South, punched Driesell in the face.

"Lefty hit himself," McGuire cracked to the South Carolina medic the following week.

Thanks to the man-to-man principles he learned from Smith, Walsh taught the Gamecocks to play better defense, and opponents were forced to quit stalling. When the top-10 rematch with the Tar Heels in Columbia rolled around, it turned out to be the last regular-season meeting between mentor and protégé. It was also the most intense indoor game ever played in the state of South Carolina, more like combat than basketball.

On one exchange that nearly triggered a brawl, George Karl tried to draw a charge from Ribock, who kicked Karl after he had flopped to the floor. Several Tar Heels moved in to defend their teammate, and the officials separated the players before any punches were thrown. The Gamecocks won the bitter battle, 72-66.

Still, UNC captured its fourth regular-season title in five years, edging South Carolina by one game in the standings in what was immediately hailed as Smith's best coaching job to date. He easily won his third ACC Coach of the Year award.

The teams met three weeks later in the 1971 ACC tournament championship game in Greensboro—the rubber match and McGuire's last hurrah in a league he was ready to leave. In another tense, taut game marked by missed shots and mistakes, the Gamecocks won their only ACC title, 52-51, on a layup by Tom Owens off a botched jump ball between UNC's 6'10" Lee Dedmon and USC's 6'3" Kevin Joyce.

The crowd booed Roche and McGuire, who had become villains worse than any the coach had created at North Carolina, as they accepted their trophies and cut down the nets. Roche, who saw himself portrayed as the culprit in the Charlie Scott saga, cursed Smith as both teams left the court. From that point on, the ACC no longer required the runner-up to stay on the floor for trophy presentations after the championship game.

Hidden by all the hatred was the fact that McGuire had become the only coach ever to win ACC basketball titles at two schools.

The Gamecocks lost their first-ever NCAA tournament game, against Pennsylvania. Smith's broken-hearted team went to McGuire's New York City for the other postseason tournament, the NIT, at Madison Square Garden.

First, despite losing All-ACC forward Dennis Wuycik with a knee injury in the first half, his teammates destroyed Massachusetts in the last college game played by Julius Erving. They took down Providence with Ernie DiGregorio and Marvin "Bad News" Barnes, defeated Duke for the third time that season in the semifinals, and ran away from then-independent Georgia Tech for the championship. The once-forgotten Tar Heels had posted a stunning 26-6 record and were the first of nineteen consecutive Carolina teams to shoot better than 50 percent from the field. "Ever since our NIT championship," Smith said years later, "every team has done exactly what I've said, and they've believed it."

After UNC won the NIT, which still meant something because the NCAA tournament invited just twenty-five teams that year, star forward and New York native Bill Chamberlain discovered another good reason to be a Tar Heel that evening. Chamberlain and his fiancée, Carol Taylor, and two friends were held up at gunpoint by a man who followed them into an apartment building elevator. Told to give up their money and jewelry, Chamberlain asked if he could at least keep the Bulova watch he had just received for winning the NIT.

"You really play for the Tar Heels?" the robber asked Chamberlain as the other three cowered in the corner of the elevator.

"Yeah, I was the MVP of the tournament," Chamberlain said.

"Shit, man, I don't want to rob a Tar Heel," said the thief, who let Chamberlain keep the watch and gave back the money and other jewelry he had just been handed.

A month later, South Carolina announced its withdrawal from the ACC to become an athletic independent. Perhaps thinking themselves too good for a conference of haves and have-nots after going undefeated in the ACC in football and basketball in the 1969–1970 school year, the Gamecocks had reached their zenith in both sports.

The move was promoted mainly by athletic director and football coach Paul Dietzel, who wanted to lower his school's entrance requirements to build a national power, and disliked the idea of sharing bowl money with the rest of a sorry football league. McGuire agreed with Dietzel on the academics and figured his team would be free of the bitter ACC basketball rivalries and able to schedule more national opponents.

McGuire called in many favors from his friends and former players, like Marquette's Al McGuire, to schedule several high-profile opponents. But he still had to find replacements for fourteen conference games and a postseason tournament. Inevitably, the absence of the longtime rivalries sent attendance spiraling down at the Carolina Coliseum. Basically throwing away all McGuire accomplished to become known as a football school, South Carolina basketball fell into a slow, agonizing identity crisis which continues today.

In retrospect, the decision to bolt the ACC has been called the biggest athletic blunder any school has ever made, and after its mild overtures to rejoin the league were rebuffed a few years later, South Carolina entered the Southeastern Conference in the early 1990s. The Gamecocks' football team began selling out every home game but struggled against bigger SEC powers, and their mediocre basketball team remained mired in the middle of ACC country.

There was to be one more North Carolina–South Carolina, Smith-McGuire game before the programs headed off in different directions.

In 1972, the Tar Heels again finished first in the ACC, which was down to seven teams. They routed resurgent Maryland to win the ACC tournament, their fourth title in six years. UNC's first opponent in the East Regional at Morgantown, West Virginia, was none other than South Carolina, which had won twenty-four games as an independent and easily earned the NCAA bid that had eluded McGuire in all but three of his fifteen years in the ACC.

Smith had reloaded with good players and was still smarting from the ACC tournament heartbreak of the year before. The Chamberlain-Previs-Wuycik class was now Carolina royalty, and Smith had added his first junior-college transfer in center Robert McAdoo. The Tar Heels were ranked in the top five all season and had won twenty-three games with the highest scoring average and largest winning margin in school history.

They confidently went to West Virginia on a mission against the Gamecocks, who were not seasoned by what would have been a typically tough conference schedule. The anticipated rematch was over as soon as it began, and the Tar Heels won 92-69. They advanced to meet and beat Pennsylvania for another trip to the Final Four, cuing the Carolina pep band to begin playing "California, Here We Come" as the game ended.

But, in Los Angeles, they lost to a fleet, 10th-ranked Florida State team that had yet to join the ACC, missing a chance to face sophomore sensation Bill Walton and UCLA for the national championship. The ACC title and thunderous revenge over South Carolina were sweet nonetheless.

Smith's eleventh Tar Heel team defined him as an elite coach, joining Ohio State's Harold Olsen and Fred Taylor and Oklahoma State's Henry Iba as coaches who had led four teams from the same school into the Final Four. Kentucky's Adolph Rupp had gone six times, and UCLA's John Wooden made the ninth of his eventual twelve trips.

Carolina fans might have guessed what comes up almost always comes down, especially since the Tar Heels had lost David Thompson to N.C. State in a bitter recruiting battle. In a period that felt longer than it really was for Carolina fans, their school fell to the Thompson-led Wolfpack nine straight times in one stretch.

Still, Smith's success from 1967 through 1972 sustained the Tar Heels until a freshman named Phil Ford arrived in the fall of 1974 from Rocky Mount, North Carolina, to take them back to the top of the state and the ACC. Ford said his first basketball hero was Charlie Scott, whom his grade-school teachers cited as someone to emulate. Ford loved to watch Thompson play, but by then Scott had turned him into a hard-core Carolina fan.

The recruiting coup proved key to Smith's continuum because Ford was the next great player black youngsters in North Carolina idolized. Had Ford followed Thompson to N.C. State, James Worthy and Michael Jordan might have grown up pulling for the Wolfpack instead of the Tar Heels.

Ford became the first freshman to start the opening game for Smith, and late in the season he helped snap the skid against State, the 1974 national champion, which had lost one game in the previous two seasons. That Thompson had originally committed to UNC and State landed on probation over illegal recruiting inducements was paltry consolation. Carolina won forty-seven games in Thompson's first two seasons at State, but somehow seemed like an afterthought compared to the wondrous Wolfpack.

After beating the Pack late in the 1975 regular season, the Tar Heels faced State again eleven days later in the final of the ACC tournament, which had also been reduced to seven teams after South Carolina's departure. What McGuire hated about the tournament came back to help his protégé in this particular instance, since more than one team from a conference was now allowed into the NCAA tournament.

By virtue of finishing first in the regular-season race, surprising Maryland had locked up one of the two NCAA bids for the ACC (the other went to the tourney champion). When State upset the Terrapins in the ACC semifinals, it looked like Thompson would get a chance to defend his national title as a senior. He had left the Maryland game late with leg cramps, but he came back against Carolina the next night.

The Tar Heels had beaten both Wake Forest and Clemson in overtime to reach the championship game, and they led the hobbling Thompson's team by six points at halftime. State went ahead by three points late, but Ford and sophomore Walter Davis hit clutch baskets that regained the lead for Carolina. Smith called on the Four Corners, sending the Greensboro Coliseum into delirium. Ford's bounce-pass to a back-cutting Mitch Kupchak for the basket and accurate free throw shooting sealed the 70-66 win. In notching the automatic bid to the NCAA tournament, Smith's team made the most of its last opportunity to snap a two-year absence from the Big Dance.

After becoming the first freshman named the Everett Case

ABOVE: Frank McGuire *(right)* with his 5'11" guard Tommy Kearns, who jumped center against 7' Wilt "the Stilt" Chamberlain in the 1957 national championship game. [RIGHT]: McGuire later coached Chamberlain in the NBA and Kearns became the Stilt's stockbroker. *(Courtesy of Sports Illustrated)*

Dean Smith *(right)* and his 1993 national champions visited President Bill Clinton at the White House. *(Courtesy of the White House)*

The 2009 Tar Heels scrimmaged with Barack Obama before he was elected president and they earned their own visit to the Rose Garden by winning the first NCAA tournament of Obama's presidency. Here an admittedly "nervous" Roy Williams (left) and the president enjoy a laugh together. *(Courtesy of Jeffrey A. Camarati)*

ABOVE: Roy Williams cut down his first national championship net as UNC's head coach in 2005 after leading four Kansas teams into the Final Four. [INSET]: In 1999, he and his wife, Wanda, returned from Kansas to attend Senior Night at Carolina to watch their son Scott in his last home game as a Tar Heel. *(Courtesy of the Associated Press; Bob Donnan, inset)*

After Smith signed him in 1966 as the first black scholarship athlete at UNC, Charlie Scott (33) blazed a trail for more minority players at Carolina and prompted the greatest of them all, Michael Jordan, to call him the "Jackie Robinson of college basketball." *(Courtesy of Rich Clarkson)*

LEFT: *(standing on left)* Scott's brilliant career paved the way for future African-American stars such as Phil Ford (12) [CENTER], James Worthy (52) [RIGHT], and Michael Jordan *(seated)* [LEFT]. *(Courtesy of Hugh Morton)*

ABOVE: The Carolina-Kansas connection ran from *(right)* Frank McGuire's Miracle of 1957 through former Jayhawk Dean Smith *(center)* to Larry Brown [LEFT], who coached KU to the 1988 NCAA championship. *(Courtesy of Robert Crawford; Larry Brown courtesy of Bob Donnan)*

Smith *(center)* and Brown *(right)* looked on as Roy Williams, who spent fifteen seasons at Kansas, joined them in the Basketball Hall of Fame in 2007. *(Courtesy of Naismith Hall of Fame)*

Bill Guthridge, like Smith a native Kansan, led the Tar Heels to two Final Fours in his three seasons as head coach. *(Courtesy of Bob Donnan)*

OPPOSITE PAGE, TOP, CENTER: Michael Jordan *(left)* and Dean Smith at the reunion of the 1957 and 1982 teams. This was a highlight of the 2007 season at UNC that raised a new banner commemorating Frank McGuire and his undefeated team. Jordan thanked Smith with a kiss to the head [ABOVE], while the '82 Tar Heels told their 1957 counterparts, "We wouldn't be here without you guys." [OPPOSITE PAGE, BOTTOM]: That night, Jordan, a six-time NBA champion, gave a heartfelt speech, saying the 1982 Carolina team was "like no other team I ever played on." *(Courtesy of Robert Crawford)*

Tyler Hansbrough (50) was a tower of strength for four seasons, staying in school for his senior year to break numerous records and lead his team to a UNC-high 124 victories in four years. *(Courtesy of Robert Crawford)*

The Tar Heels capped spring 2009 with Carolina's sixth national championship, as junior point guard Ty Lawson (5) wrested ACC Player of the Year honors away from Hansbrough and overcame a painful toe injury to direct the team to the last five of six impressive NCAA tournament wins. *(Courtesy of Robert Crawford)*

tournament MVP, Ford cavorted across the court with his team-mates. He clipped the nets and made the cover of *Sports Illustrated* for engineering the "Upset in the ACC."

Although his team did not advance past the Sweet Sixteen, Smith had found North Carolina's next high-school star to succeed Thompson, the best player from the state to that point. Had Ford not gotten so hooked on the Heels in the Charlie Scott era and decided to wear red instead of light blue, the Wolfpack would have very likely remained the ACC's dominant team for at least four more years.

Ford replaced Thompson as the brightest star on Tobacco Road and lifted his team back to ACC royalty for the remainder of his career. Smith never has compared players publicly, but he has always had trouble holding down his praise of No. 12 because of everything Ford meant to the team beyond statistics.

Not only was Ford's enthusiasm for the game infectious but, as crazy as it seemed, fans identified with him because he was barely 6' tall and could not dunk. He seemed to will the ball into the basket with his unremarkable jump shot, and he masterfully ran the most infamous and controversial offense of its day. When he played, they called it the "Ford Corners."

Having learned to dribble on the dirt playgrounds of his home-town in Rocky Mount, Ford seemingly could keep the ball only inches off the floor as he darted and weaved around picks and flailing defenders. Against double-teams, he could always find the open man, go get the ball if necessary, and start over again. His control was so deft that even Smith called the ploy almost unfair in the days before the shot clock.

"When the rules are enforced and hand-checking is not allowed, Phil Ford is impossible to stop one on one," Smith said. "*Impossible* is the word used."

In no other sport could one team stop the game dead if it had the ability to simply hold onto the ball. Pro basketball had its 24-second clock, baseball had three strikes and you're out, and football required teams to advance the ball in order to keep it. In college basketball, before the shot clock was adopted in the 1986–1987 season, one team could play keep-away indefinitely. Ford, implementing Smith's deep freeze, was good enough to do it for long stretches that ran off large chunks of time and frustrated opponents into fouling the Tar Heels.

It was not foolproof, of course. One particular failure helped define Smith's career almost as much as all the victories and championships.

On the twentieth anniversary of North Carolina's 1957 national championship, Dean Smith threw a party for Frank McGuire's undefeated team. The Tar Heels were playing Duke at home on Saturday, January 15, 1977, and McGuire purposely did not schedule a game for South Carolina so he could be there with his former players, now mostly in their forties. It was also a celebration of sorts for McGuire's pending induction into the Naismith Hall of Fame the following spring.

Smith invited the media to a brunch at the Pines Restaurant so that newspaper reporters and TV sports anchors could properly recognize the stars of McGuire's Miracle. Though still loyal to their old coach, the 1957 Tar Heels had stayed connected to their alma mater and to Smith, who had befriended them all through the years. He asked two writers who were particularly close to Carolina basketball to stay for the private luncheon, and reminded them that everything said behind the closed door was "off the record."

Smith introduced McGuire, who said a few words and joked

how it seemed longer than two decades since the Kansas City triumph. He bemoaned the fact that his current Gamecocks squad was off to a 5-8 start, including a home loss to Alabama in front of barely 5,000 fans at the Carolina Coliseum.

South Carolina had not been invited to the NCAA tournament since 1974, and already McGuire acknowledged his school's mistake of leaving the ACC. Imagine the fiery Irishman still coaching in an ACC that had Smith, Driesell, Norm Sloan, Carl Tacy at Wake Forest, and two Bill Fosters (Clemson and Duke), all with nationally ranked teams.

"We didn't like the 800 SAT rule because it cost us some good players," McGuire said, and he began to laugh. "But right after we left, two Clemson soccer recruits threatened to sue the ACC, and they changed the rule. Just like that, for two Clemson soccer players!"

McGuire had since distanced himself from the departure decision, contending that it was done by Dietzel—who resigned in 1974 with a losing overall record—and the USC Board of Trustees. South Carolina's home attendance had declined from the lack of natural rivalries after going independent. Clemson was the only ACC team that kept playing the Gamecocks. Eventually, that was reduced to one game a season. He did not mention it that day, but everyone knew McGuire thought the ACC power brokers had it in for him and were glad he had left the league.

McGuire and his second wife, Jane Henderson, whom he had married in 1972, always stayed with old friends Lou and Florence Vine on Meadowbrook Lane, a familiarity that helped him think of Chapel Hill as his second home. A regal sixty-three years old, he could still captivate an audience with one colorful story after another about his childhood in New York and his coaching career. But this luncheon was more about his players than him.

They told old tales and inside jokes, including how Varsity Theater manager Andy Gutierrez let Lennie Rosenbluth sneak into the air-conditioned matinees when he knew Rosie should have been in class. Several mentioned junior team manager Bennie Lubin, who was Rosenbluth's roommate and best friend. The brilliant Lubin, who tutored Rosie and other players with their term papers and tests, went on to be a millionaire financial investor in New York.

Senior manager Joel Fleishman, by then a successful clothier in Greensboro, claimed that he was the one responsible for running Governor Luther Hodges off the Carolina bench during the championship game in Kansas City when the language got too blue. They kidded Joe Quigg about supplying teammates with cigarettes that season through his job as the Marlboro rep on campus.

That afternoon, Smith's fifth-ranked team took care of Duke, whose coach, Bill Foster, would replace McGuire at South Carolina three years later. The 1957 Tar Heels were recognized at halftime of Carolina's 77-68 victory.

McGuire returned to Columbia to finish out a 14-12 season that included his 500th career victory on February 9 against The Citadel. After the season, South Carolina gave him a testimonial dinner, which Dean Smith attended in the midst of his own team's seventh NCAA tournament appearance in eleven years. Famed New York Yankees broadcaster Mel Allen served as master of ceremonies and Pulitzer Prize–winning author James Michener, who had consulted with McGuire on his tome *Sports in America,* was a guest speaker.

In April, the Board of Trustees voted to name the Gamecocks' home court the Frank McGuire Arena, and in May the Basketball Hall of Fame inducted its namesake. In a sad commentary on what was happening back home, no one from South Carolina attended the ceremony in Springfield, Massachusetts. Smith was there, and McGuire's old friend Ben Carnevale introduced the honoree. After they had met in Chapel Hill at Navy flight school in 1942, Carnevale went on to coach the Tar Heels for two years and later recommended McGuire for the North Carolina job in 1952.

The beginning of the end came in June, when South Carolina hired James Holderman as its president. During his interview, Holderman acknowledged he could "fire a living legend" if he had to, even though McGuire had helped Holderman get the job through mutual friends in New York. With Dietzel long gone, and the athletic department in disarray, McGuire was the last link to the still-controversial decision to bolt the ACC.

A political situation grew worse in September, when Donnie Walsh left McGuire's staff to join former UNC backcourt mate Larry Brown as assistant coach and general manager of the ABA's Denver Nuggets, who were vying for inclusion in the forthcoming merger with the NBA. McGuire promoted black assistant Ben Jobe to replace Walsh, angering the family of second assistant coach Greg Blatt. The grandson of one-time South Carolina Speaker of the House Sol Blatt, the young Blatt left for a job at The Citadel.

At the same time, UNC's basketball legend kept growing. The Tar Heels, led by All-American Ford and precocious freshman Mike O'Koren, had finished first in the ACC and won their second ACC tournament championship in three years by outlasting Virginia at the Greensboro Coliseum. It was a game remindful of the McGuire era, with several members of each team cursing at each other as they left the court at halftime.

Despite suffering key injuries to starting center Tom LaGarde, All-ACC forward Walter Davis, and Ford late in the season, Carolina somehow managed to beat Purdue, Notre Dame, and Kentucky to reach the 1977 Final Four in Atlanta along with Cinderella

UNC-Charlotte, the UNLV Rebels of renegade coach Jerry Tarkanian, and the last Marquette team of Al McGuire.

The Tar Heels had not been back to college basketball's holy land in five years, and over that time the event had exploded in press coverage and fan frenzy. In the interim, astronauts had made their last trip to the moon, Richard Nixon left office in disgrace, American involvement in Vietnam ended, and the country turned 200 years old. The Age of Aquarius had given away to an oil crisis, double-digit inflation, and rampant unemployment. Yet college and professional sports kept growing.

Meanwhile, North Carolina became a constant in college basketball, through the end of John Wooden's era at UCLA and the emergence of Indiana under Bobby Knight. Smith's Tar Heels still sought the one prize that had eluded them in four previous trips to the Final Four: the NCAA championship won by McGuire's team twenty years earlier.

The national semifinals were now played on Saturday afternoon and the title game Monday night in prime time; tickets at the 16,000-seat Omni were almost impossible to get; they were scalped for ten times their face value of $15 (by comparison, tickets to the 2009 Final Four averaged $250 in face value). NBC was four years from the end of its contract to televise the NCAA tournament, which it eventually lost to CBS for five times more money.

When Carolina held off UNLV with the Four Corners in the second half, and Marquette used a last-second basket by Jerome Whitehead to edge UNC-Charlotte, NBC and the nation had their dream matchup. Thanks to constant television appearances, the Tar Heels were the latest edition of America's Team. Al McGuire had already announced his retirement from coaching, and that ended up making him the witty, wacky, sentimental favorite.

Smith's own evolving career as a coach became sports fodder

that night when he out-thought himself on the national stage. After his team rallied from a 12-point deficit at halftime to take a 2-point lead, he went back to the stalling strategy that aided its late-season run. By calling for the Four Corners and not taking a timeout, Smith left O'Koren, his best backdoor threat, who had scored 31 points against UNLV, sitting at the scorer's table. Unable to get into the game, O'Koren watched as Marquette regained the momentum.

The ill-fated maneuver turned the shy Midwesterner into a walking controversy, incessantly discussed by basketball fans and UNC alumni all over the country. For years to come, groups of Tar Heels could not gather without the topic invariably turning to Smith and why he did this or that. Social events, dinner parties, and weekends with the family resulted in the guys debating Carolina basketball while the wives fumed in another room. Without trying, Dean Smith was testing the old adage that the only bad publicity is no publicity.

One issue that always seemed to crop up was whether Smith too often put his players above his team. As an example, some argued that he did not call a timeout late against Marquette from fear of publicly embarrassing senior reserve Bruce Buckley by taking him out for freshman O'Koren. Buckley stayed in and made a nifty backdoor cut, but Marquette's Bo Ellis blocked his layup for the lead, thus enabling the Warriors to retake control of the game.

As for protecting Buckley, Smith was following McGuire's lead, just as Roy Williams would do later. Off the court, McGuire tried to keep them out of trouble by working on school officials and local police. In practice and games, however, McGuire's top five were always set in stone, and the subs knew they were getting into games only if foul trouble or injuries occurred.

"There were the white shirts [starters] in practice and the blue shirts," former player Larry Brown liked to joke, "and the only way that changed was a death in the family." Smith's strategic moves, which pretty much had gone unquestioned for years before the Marquette game, became fair game after the devastating loss.

Obviously, Smith was protecting a team that had overcome injuries to get there and still was banged up. Ford, for example, could not shoot from beyond 12 feet due to the hyperextended elbow he suffered in the Sweet Sixteen against Notre Dame. And Smith had used the Four Corners to slow the tempo and befuddle high-scoring UNLV in the national semifinals.

But Al McGuire was Smith's match in their head-to-head chess game, showing the savvy he learned on the streets of New York and from his mentor Frank McGuire.

The rules in 1977 made the team that was trailing force the action by penetrating the hash marks on offense or coming out to play defense against a stalling tactic. When Smith held up four fingers and the Omni crowd stirred with anticipation, it was Al McGuire who became the maestro of the moment.

The image of McGuire motioning his team to extend its defense just enough to satisfy the rules, and then fall back under the basket, is etched in the minds of basketball fans older than forty (and those who have since seen the game on ESPN Classic). Clearly, McGuire was not going to have his big front line chase the Tar Heels, so he played cat and mouse until the Warriors won a critical jump ball following an exchange of fouls by O'Koren and Marquette's Bernard Toone.

In the end, Al McGuire rode off into retirement on his motorcycle with the national championship. Smith was left to answer why his team quit playing fast when it had all of the momentum and then scored only four points during a twelve-minute span.

"If Ford hadn't hurt his elbow and could shoot from outside, we would have continued to play against their zone," Smith said. "Who knows, we might have won, but I've never been a believer in the what-if game about the past."

The irony of the 1977 title game was that the Tar Heels tried to make the deliberate Warriors play faster. When they finally succeeded and tied the game, that's when their head coach called for the stall. His players knew not to question the strategy, and indeed it usually worked out fine. They were stunned when it did not.

After the 67-59 loss, Smith went around the somber locker room and thanked each of them. He handed out soft drinks to the team that had overcome so much to finish 28-5 but fell painfully short of the goal it wanted for the coach more than each other.

This players-come-first rap dogged Smith with many fans— but not the families of players—for years, right through his insistence that James Worthy and Michael Jordan turn pro after their junior seasons, when their return would have ensured powerhouse Tar Heel teams. The coach did not get his way in the spring of 1977, when he suggested that Phil Ford do the same. Up until that point in Smith's career, Robert McAdoo was the only player to jump to the NBA before his senior year, but Smith thought Ford needed to go, too, at the top of his game.

Ford said no by asking, "Who's going to tell my mother?" Mabel Ford's only goal for her son was to see him graduate from college.

As a senior, Ford was ACC Player of the Year, ACC Athlete of the Year for the second straight time, won UNC's coveted Patterson Medal, and passed Rosenbluth as the school's all-time leading scorer, a record that stood until Tyler Hansbrough broke it in 2009. Smith did not make a big deal out of the scoring milestone, relying on one of his father's old axioms that a player's contribution should never be judged by points alone.

Ford went on to become NBA rookie of the year with the old Kansas City Kings and a league all-star before alcohol and drug abuse slowed and then shortened his pro career. Smith was ready to support Ford then, too, arranging stints in rehab and eventually rescuing him from a lower-level banking job to join his staff with no coaching experience. Ford repaid him by straightening out his personal life and becoming one of the best recruiters in the college game, helping Carolina sign such stars as George Lynch, Jerry Stackhouse, Rasheed Wallace, Vince Carter, and Antawn Jamison.

When Smith and successor Bill Guthridge retired, and the coaching staff turned over, Ford wound up working with UNC alum Larry Brown in three pro cities. He left owing Smith virtually everything he accomplished in basketball, including the very real chance of becoming an NBA head coach some day.

More than anything else, however, Ford will be remembered fondly for running the spread that may have made UNC fans fret but which tormented opponents.

Smith's fascination with clever innovation, especially involving creative use of the game's rules, was well known around the league. The 1977 game against Marquette exposed to the entire basketball world Smith's proclivity to at times slow the offense and go with the percentages.

It was a major difference between Smith and Frank McGuire, who literally rolled the ball out in practice and watched from the bleachers as his players scrimmaged until they were exhausted or swinging at each other. McGuire was more of a "feel" coach, flying by the seat of his silk pants, but his instincts were always pretty good.

Compared to McGuire, Smith played faster (and his disciple Roy Williams played even faster). People harping about the Four

Corners forgot (or never noticed) that Smith's teams were among the highest-scoring in the game, and that holding the ball at the end to protect a lead mimicked football teams that ran out the clock.

Then there was the long, arduous wait for Smith to "win the big one." After the 1977 Final Four, *Charlotte Observer* sports columnist Frank Barrows wrote an infamous opinion piece predicting Smith never would win a national championship. Barrows wrote that Smith's even-keel approach was better suited for just being very good every year, rather than suitable for winning the very big games. Smith tucked away the article, willing to wait for the right time to respond.

The charge stung many Tar Heel loyalists, who were frustrated by near misses like the Marquette loss and, two years later, a shocking defeat to Penn of the Ivy League. That happened during the still-unbelievable Black Sunday doubleheader in the 1979 NCAA East Regional, when Duke also fell to St. John's at Reynolds Coliseum in Raleigh.

Losing to Penn was particularly depressing for UNC's newest assistant, Roy Williams, who had left a secure high school job in the North Carolina mountains to join Smith's staff as a restricted-earnings coach, requiring him to drain whatever savings he had to support his young family. Williams barely could afford the old clunker his wife, Wanda, drove to her teaching job at Chapel Hill High School.

"I was so poor back then that I didn't even have a bicycle," Williams said of his rookie season on the UNC bench. "As we came back to Chapel Hill on Route 54, I asked the bus driver to drop me off at the Glen Lennox Apartments, where we lived. I was really depressed because it was my first experience with how swiftly a great season in college basketball could end. Just like that, it was over."

As was his habit growing up playing, and later coaching, Williams took losses harder than almost anyone around him. They nearly paralyzed him for a day or so, and he had to force himself to move on.

He also worshipped Smith and Carolina Basketball. The chance to coach at UNC was a dream come true that he could not turn down, despite the financial hardships it caused for his family.

Williams so believed the Tar Heels did things the best way possible that he could not imagine losing to eighth-seeded Penn on an ACC court with thousands of UNC fans in the building. He had not yet learned that twenty-year-olds sometimes were not as ready to play as the coaches were to coach, that they might have been college students hanging out on Franklin Street the night before, while he was fretting over Penn's matchup zone.

Carolina always began the season as very likely the best-prepared team in the country. The teachings of Smith and Bill Guthridge were consistent from year to year, and they recruited and signed up smart players who learned fast. Toward the end of the season, however, other teams tended to catch up with the Heels. Games hung as much on emotion as execution, leaving Carolina with added pressure when playing reasonably talented opponents like Penn.

That meant an added disadvantage for Carolina, because every athlete worth his salt wanted the chance to knock off the fabled Tar Heels of North Carolina. It has long been a Carolina problem other teams would like to have, but it's been a problem, nonetheless.

Smith did not have much use for Frank McGuire's "Us Against the World" theme that defined the Irishman at both North and South Carolina. He never worried about the big rivalry games or the few heavily favored foes he faced because he knew his players would get themselves ready. Admittedly not much of a game-time motivator, he always admired how McGuire raised the dander in his locker room with some cockamamie story from his childhood or anything that came to mind. With his team holding a big lead at halftime, McGuire occasionally faked anger toward his players while they hid their heads in towels to keep from laughing.

Like sister ships passing on opposite courses, Smith's ascent toward his defining Final Four coincided with McGuire's slow but steady decline at South Carolina. After McGuire and his attorneys fought President Holderman's move to force him out of coaching and into a bogus administrative job as athletic director over the state system, they all agreed to honor McGuire's contract through 1980.

In the fall of 1979, McGuire announced the coming season was his last. Rumors began that Duke's Bill Foster would succeed him even though Appalachian State coach Bobby Cremins, the former Gamecocks favorite, campaigned hard for the job. The 1980 Blue Devils, nationally ranked the past two seasons, won their first twelve games and moved to No. 1 in the polls. Then, Duke oddly swooned through the rest of January and February when Foster began stonewalling the media about his impending departure.

Duke went 7-8 over its last fifteen regular-season games, tumbling all the way to 17th in the rankings, while in Columbia McGuire told friends his successor had been named but he had no say in it. The biggest irony came on February 23, 1980, when UNC honored the retiring legend again at halftime of the Duke–Carolina game in Chapel Hill. Did Smith already know that Foster was going to South Carolina, and schedule the ceremony to unnerve the departing Duke coach? When asked years later, Smith said he did not recall doing any such thing.

The Blue Devils played that way, falling behind early and getting blown out in the last home game for Mike O'Koren, a player from inner-city New Jersey not unlike those McGuire recruited to build his teams at three colleges. "I just want to get the credit for one thing up here; I selected Dean Smith," McGuire told a cheering crowd at Carmichael Auditorium. "The A.D. said 'no,' but I went to the chancellor. Isn't it ironic? I began my coaching career in the ACC in Chapel Hill, and I was here on the day my career ended."

McGuire flew home for his last game as a head coach against nationally ranked Western Kentucky. Before tip-off, he was inducted into the USC Athletic Hall of Fame and at halftime was named the university's coach emeritus. Fittingly, his team rose to the moment and upset the NCAA tournament-bound Hilltoppers, 73-65 in double overtime.

The Gamecocks, who had gone 15-12 in 1979, finished with a 16-11 record, which was McGuire's fourteenth consecutive winning season but not good enough to get another contract at sixty-six years of age. He was mad at those who ousted him but he pledged to remain in Columbia and Myrtle Beach, where he owned homes and had family.

McGuire's forty-year coaching career, which began at Xavier High School and extended through 549 victories at St. John's, North Carolina, and South Carolina, plus that one memorable season with Wilt Chamberlain and the Philadelphia Warriors, had ended. In becoming the only winner of 100 games and national coach of the year awards at three schools, he left high school and college alma maters in his native New York City and turned two Southern states on to basketball. The exciting voyage began on the playground at Greenwich House in lower Manhattan when a boy became a man the hardscrabble way.

Although his retirement at South Carolina in 1980 was forced at the hands of men he barely knew, and never liked, McGuire's true legacy lived on with Dean Smith in Chapel Hill. He kept his old North Carolina friends and visited often. Two years later, he was in New Orleans for the greatest night in the professional life of the man he, in turn, made a Tar Heel.

Dean Smith fielded his consummate team—with experience, ability, and incentive—in 1982. The Tar Heels were the preseason No. 1 pick in the polls and by *Sports Illustrated*, whose college basketball preview cover showed the head coach and his four returning starters. They ripped off thirteen straight victories, including marquee matchups with two No. 2 teams (Kentucky and Virginia). Soon, it was clear their biggest foe was an overwhelming level of expectation.

Smith never had to ride herd on this group or worry about complacency. Junior James Worthy led by example, failing to accept any teammate not giving maximum effort at all times. Worthy made himself the driving force behind knocking the national championship monkey off his coach's back.

Worthy thought they had the ape dead in the water after a late-season run his sophomore year. The 1981 Tar Heels had risen steadily from No. 17 to No. 6 in the polls, won the ACC championship, and avenged two regular-season losses to Ralph Sampson and Virginia in the national semifinals by riding Al Wood's historic 39 points to a 78-65 win at the old Spectrum in Philadelphia. They were playing well enough to be favored over Isiah Thomas and ninth-ranked Indiana on Monday night in the last Final Four televised by NBC and the last to include a third-place game (Virginia defeated LSU, 78-74).

On Monday morning, March 30, 1981, John Hinckley's failed assassination attempt left President Ronald Reagan in a hospital and the title game in doubt for most of the day. Smith favored postponement, but by late afternoon Reagan's condition was safe enough that NBC and the NCAA decided to go on with the show.

Carolina led by nine points early before two phantom calls by official Booker Turner banished Worthy to the bench with four fouls. As Worthy fumed, Thomas and the Hoosiers took control.

Following the 63-50 defeat, Smith retained his perspective and consoled some sobbing players by telling them that losing a basketball game was just not that big a deal. He also used his favorite analogy that "millions of people in China" did not know, or care, about what happened.

Worthy and rising senior point guard Jimmy Black orchestrated a team pledge to get back to the Final Four the next year and win it all for Smith—which became their consuming goal throughout the 1982 season. The Tar Heels were 26-2 and still top-ranked when they faced a third game that season against Sampson and No. 3 Virginia for the ACC tournament championship at the Greensboro Coliseum. They survived a controversial slowdown to gain the best NCAA seeding, and by beating James Madison, Alabama, and Villanova without having to leave North Carolina, they fulfilled the first part of their pledge. After hanging on to defeat unranked Houston with Clyde Drexler in the semis at the Superdome in New Orleans, they were one step away.

The 1982 NCAA title game against Georgetown came down to freshman Michael Jordan's last shot, but it was Worthy's 28 points on 13-for-17 shooting that had his team in position to win in the last minute, even after the Hoyas took a 62-61 lead on Sleepy Floyd's basket. Carolina called a timeout with 32 seconds remaining.

"We're exactly where we want to be," Smith told his team.

Roy Williams, UNC's young assistant coach, glanced up at the scoreboard because Smith's words were so settling he thought the Tar Heels might actually be *ahead* by a point. Williams built his own coaching confidence around that moment in time.

Smith knew that Georgetown coach John Thompson, his old friend and assistant on the 1976 USA Olympic team, would play zone and never let Worthy or center Sam Perkins touch the ball. The Heels were going to have to win it with an outside shot, a drive to the basket, or an offensive put-back.

"Coach knew we would have to kick it out to someone," Jimmy Black, the senior point guard of the 1982 team, recalled. "He called our number-two offense, which we had run all year—actually all four years—against zones." Black threw the skip pass from just right of the key across the defense to Jordan on the left wing.

"It was an easy pass, one I had made all year," Black said. "Michael was open enough to get a shot off or put the ball down and penetrate."

When Jordan's 15-footer went up and in, Black said his only thought was "get back on defense quickly." Now, with the lead, the Tar Heels had to stop Georgetown's final rush of the game.

Black was in the lane, trying to stay between the ball and Patrick Ewing, the Hoyas' towering freshman center. The Georgetown bench was up, screaming and waving towels as the Tar Heels scrambled to pick up their men. Worthy actually made a poor decision, running right through the passing lane between Hoyas Fred Brown and Eric Smith.

Worthy picked off Brown's panicky, errant pass, which all but sealed the 63-62 triumph and left the Tar Heels feeling more relief than joy. Every Carolina fan, many watching around the world, thought first for Smith and his long-sought title.

In the postgame press conference, Smith was ready with the needle for Frank Barrows. "A very talented sportswriter from Charlotte predicted we'd never be here," he said of the article written five years before.

Smith hugged family and friends, and even several sportswriters, and spent a few warm moments outside of the UNC locker room with McGuire, who had been named to a public relations position at Madison Square Garden. UNC's second NCAA championship was perfect symmetry for the two men: Coming twenty-five years after McGuire's Miracle in Kansas City, it elevated Smith to the same distinction his mentor had in 1957.

It also created fervor with fans, who wanted something, anything, with Carolina written on it. Some schools had just begun licensing their official logos and marks and collecting royalties on sales, and the 1982 title convinced UNC it ought to be in that business, too. The school has reaped more than $50 million in licensing revenue since then.

However, like McGuire's national champs, Carolina's exalted status would be challenged on the court by other Big Four schools in the next ten years. Just as the 1958 Tar Heels began the season without Rosenbluth, the 1983 team did not have Worthy. Smith had urged him to turn pro as a junior, and he watched with pride as the Lakers made him the No. 1 pick in the 1982 NBA draft.

Both McGuire, who lost Joe Quigg to a broken leg before the first game, and Smith had three starters back in their bids to repeat. Jordan, Sam Perkins, and Matt Doherty still were around, and freshman Brad Daugherty joined the 1983 team; oddly, the

Tar Heels lost three of their first six games and then won eighteen straight to reclaim the No. 1 ranking.

History had repeated itself: Smith, like McGuire, was now bigger than life. Coming off the 1982 national championship, he had been inducted into the Basketball Hall of Fame and then led the ground-breaking on an eight-sided arena with 22,000 baby blue seats on the south side of campus that would eventually carry his name.

Also, just like McGuire's villains of yore, opposing fans loved it when Carolina suddenly dropped three in a row in February of 1983. One of the losses came before the raucous crowd at N.C. State, which had improved dramatically after guard Dereck Whittenburg returned from a broken foot. When the teams met three weeks later in the 1983 ACC tournament semifinals in Atlanta, fifth-ranked Carolina (26-6) played poorly and lost again, allowing State to begin a remarkable ride to its own national championship.

Jordan's last season, 1984, turned out among the most bittersweet of Smith's coaching career. What has long been regarded as the best starting lineup in school history—Jordan, Perkins, Doherty, Daugherty, and freshman Kenny Smith—opened by winning twenty-one consecutive games. Late in the seventeenth victory, an airborne Smith crashed into the seats and suffered a broken left wrist after being unnecessarily hit from behind by LSU's John Tudor.

The Tar Heels were never the same. They used swing guard Steve Hale while they waited for their fleet freshman, nicknamed The Jet, to heal. Smith made it back for the last week of the regular season wearing a half cast, but their earlier chemistry did not return with him. They still went undefeated in the ACC, needing double overtime to survive Duke in the last home game for Perkins, Doherty, and, as it turned out, Jordan.

A week later, they were 27-1 when they lost the lead to Duke in the ACC tournament semifinals and missed championship Sunday for the second straight year.

As with the loss to State in 1983, Smith thought his team would be ready to play. That was not the case in either game. Among other reasons, NCAA bids and top seeds had been locked up. Meanwhile, young and aggressive coaches like State's Jim Valvano and Duke's Mike Krzyzewski used Carolina's aura as motivation to help their teams post upsets that lifted both programs to greater heights.

The Tar Heels, who had maintained their No. 1 ranking for all but one week of the season, limped into the 1984 NCAA tournament without the same swagger and confidence. After struggling past Temple in their opener, they faced Indiana in the Sweet Sixteen in Atlanta.

This game firmly solidified Bobby Knight's genius in his prime and further stirred the debate about Smith. Behind freshman guard Steve Alford and an unsung cast playing dogged defense that frustrated Michael Jordan, the unranked Hoosiers shot 65 percent and, with Jordan plagued by foul trouble, sent the nation's No. 1 team home early.

As in their loss to Georgia the year before in the NCAA East Regional championship game, Smith stayed with a pressing, trapping defense against Indiana and lost to a disciplined opponent that moved the ball patiently and waited for the open shot in rhythm. Smith believed that the team with the best talent and deepest bench should keep forcing the action to increase the possessions, and the cream would eventually rise to the top. Critics claimed he should have occasionally called off the dogs and tried to kill the opponent shooters' momentum, hoping to win a close game down the stretch. That did not happen in what was to be Jordan's last game as a Tar Heel.

Smith left his press conference in tears, saying he still had the best team in the country and probably anticipating that Jordan would take his advice and turn pro. The defeat devastated Tar Heels everywhere and gave Roy Williams another lesson in what had become the unpleasant-but-true definition of a great college basketball season. Even a 28-3 record could be tainted by losing in the ACC tournament and the NCAA Sweet Sixteen.

More than any other game, the 72-68 loss to Indiana, in which Smith sat his best player for the last eight minutes of the first half with two fouls, helped hatch the popular trick question: Who is the only person to hold Michael Jordan under 20 points? Besides not being true—Jordan averaged exactly 20 points as a sophomore—it proved patently unfair because Michael became the game's greatest all-around player.

Jordan was the first to admit he never could have become a force on both ends of the court had he not combined his incredible natural gifts with Smith's fundamental teachings during his three years in Chapel Hill. Not only did Jordan become a six-time world champion with the Chicago Bulls (and a six-time MVP of the NBA Finals), he was a regular on the all-defensive team. He had 2,514 career steals and 893 blocked shots. He was almost always assigned to guard the other team's best perimeter scorer.

After Jordan flew off to the NBA, the remainder of the decade resonated with more success but similar painful setbacks. Steve Hale, now a key player, suffered injuries at the end of the 1985 and 1986 seasons, which contributed to losses in a regional final and Sweet Sixteen to eventual national champions Villanova and Louisville. Carolina won fifty-five games over two years but still had no ACC tournament championship or Final Four trip to show for it.

Certainly the 1987 season would be the one to end that trend. Kenny Smith led five returning seniors who were joined by bally-hooed freshman J. R. Reid.

In a racking reminder of Jordan's last season, the loaded 1987 team again ran the table in the ACC but lost the tournament final to unranked N.C. State, then fell one game short of the Final Four with an agonizing loss to Syracuse in the East Regional at the Meadowlands in New Jersey. The years since have proven that the Orangemen, with future pros Rony Seikaly, Sherman Douglas, and Derrick Coleman, had every right to win that game, but the reputation of Smith and Carolina Basketball made it seem like a major upset at the time.

A favorite for the national championship, the Tar Heels fin-ished 32-4 and went home to watch Indiana (with Alford, now a senior) win it all. The title came a season after author John Fein-stein gave an inside look at the Hoosiers in his book *A Season on the Brink*.

In late 1987, McGuire and Smith suffered through profes-sional and life-changing tragedies. A fire destroyed McGuire's home in Columbia. With it went all the personal memorabilia that marked his career—trophies, plaques, and, especially, photo-graphs. That October, Smith had to tell freshman center Scott Wil-liams his parents had died in a murder-suicide domestic dispute near their home outside of Los Angeles. While taking his player back to California for the funerals, Smith suffered severe nose bleeds and was ordered to quit smoking by his doctors. He quit cold turkey on the first day of practice.

Graduation left the Tar Heels with point guard problems and a less-talented team that overachieved and earned Smith his eighth coach of the year honor by finishing first in the 1988 ACC race. Three losses to Duke, though, including the ACC tournament title game, soured the season, especially after the Blue Devils advanced to their second Final Four in three years.

That UNC won more games in the 1980s than any other college program, but did not bring home another national championship, spawned further debate on the coach. With bids now open to virtually any team in the expanded NCAA tournament field of 64, shouldn't the talented Tar Heels make a serious run every season? Instead, they went the rest of the decade without reaching the Final Four.

Smith still won twenty-plus games but, at fifty-seven and compared to forty-one-year-old Krzyzewski, he was seen by some as the aging coach with a passé style of play. The Tar Heels needed to reinvent and redefine themselves as the 1980s were ending and the MTV era exploded with Duke emerging as America's new favorite team in the eyes of the X-generation.

The 1988 Final Four weekend was a glorious reunion in Kansas City for the men representing three eras of Tar Heels, even though UNC had lost to Arizona in the West Regional final. McGuire, Smith, and Larry Brown, a Carolina favorite son, were together as Brown's Kansas Jayhawks made an improbable run to the championship weekend at Kemper Arena.

McGuire was retired from coaching for eight years. However, he was there as part of the fiftieth anniversary of the NCAA tournament and his 1957 Carolina team's historic win over Kansas and Wilt Chamberlain at Municipal Auditorium.

Smith, who was honored in the 1980s decade celebration, always attended the NCAA coaches' convention when his team failed to make the Final Four, but he usually left after Saturday's semifinals. He changed his plans when Kansas upset Duke, and he stayed to watch his first coaching protégé lead his alma mater against top-ranked Oklahoma.

Larry Brown had coached UCLA in the NCAA championship game eight years earlier, and he was pursuing his own dream of winning the title. He always fantasized it would be at Carolina when his mentor retired.

That happened to another disciple of Dean Smith who coached at Kansas, but it wasn't Brown.

7

The Larry Brown Bond

IN the summer of 1938, Bobby Gersten was coming out of The Bronx. High school was behind him and he was ready to be a college basketball star. Gersten was barely taller than 5'9", but he was gifted with a ball in his hands. He had earned a full scholarship to George Washington, where he was set to enroll and play alongside a hotshot guard named Arnold "Red" Auerbach.

"At the last minute, my father said, 'You don't need that scholarship, why don't you go to North Carolina with your two friends,'" Gersten recalled. "Dad was down there all the time and could see me play."

Harry Gerstenzang had changed his last name to "Gersten" when he became a traveling salesman, hawking women's handbags in the 1930s. His territory was the Southeast, from the Carolinas to Florida, and he could afford to send his children to college. Bobby had two buddies who were going to North Carolina— Danny Geller and Roy Asche. The three Jewish kids could stick together in the mostly Protestant South.

So Bobby Gersten enrolled at UNC, where he planned to play basketball and try out for the baseball team. When he arrived, he settled into Ruffin dorm and soon wandered over to the basketball office at the old Tin Can.

"No one knew who I was," Gersten said. "My high school coach didn't even call down to Carolina, and I was the last man to make the 1939 freshman team roster."

George "Bo" Shepard had coached the Carolina varsity to a 23-2 record and the Southern Conference championship in 1935 before he retired to become "advisor to basketball" and look after the freshman team. UNC had already employed nine head coaches since it began fielding an intercollegiate team in 1911. That included Norm Shepard (Bo's older brother), whose one team in 1924 went 26-0 and eventually was voted national champion by the Helms Foundation.

When Gersten moved up to the varsity in 1939, the year UNC opened Woollen Gym on South Road between the football stadium and a cluster of dorms, Carolina had its eleventh head coach, Bill Lange. He produced a 23-3 winner and another Southern Conference crown in his first season. Gersten's job on the court was to feed the ball to All-American George Glamack, the famed "Blind Bomber," who could not see very well but essentially "memorized" his shots from various spots on the floor.

By then, the popular Gersten had become president of the Monogram Club, the organization for varsity athletes at UNC. He also developed some ways to assist in recruiting athletes and believed that few recruits could say no to Carolina coaches after getting a taste of Chapel Hill.

"I had the idea of writing letters to those recruits the football and basketball coaches invited to visit," Gersten said, "and telling them we'd be their hosts when they came to campus. We sold programs at the football games and put the money we made into the Monogram Club party fund, and we had the biggest bashes."

Gersten won the coveted Patterson Medal in 1942 as UNC's outstanding student-athlete, and he was responsible for making Carolina attractive to out-of-state recruits. After graduating in 1942, the summer Frank McGuire spent in Chapel Hill at Navy flight training, Gersten returned to attend graduate school, assist Lange, and await draft orders from the Air Force. In December of 1942, he left Chapel Hill for good.

Lange lasted through the 1944 season, when he was quietly asked to step down because of his penchant for shoplifting on road trips. Lange loved to bring home small gifts for his wife, and he was detained while walking out of several stores with items he had not paid for. When word got back to his bosses at UNC, Lange decided it was a good idea to move on.

The school hired Ben Carnevale, who was also at Navy flight school and who made some close friends at Carolina. In his second year, the Tar Heels were led by John "Hook" Dillon, Jim Jordan, and gangly forward Horace McKinney, nicknamed "Bones." They advanced to the 1946 NCAA championship game before losing to an Oklahoma A&M team coached by Hank Iba and led by All-American center Bob Kurland.

Carnevale's Navy connections eventually led him to take over the team at Annapolis, and he was replaced by Tom Scott, Carolina's thirteenth head coach. That unlucky number seemed emblematic of the school's inability to stabilize its basketball program. By the time the Tar Heels suffered back-to-back losing seasons in the early 1950s, several occurrences near and far from Chapel Hill were conspiring to change that luck.

After Gersten received his discharge from the Air Force, he landed a job as head basketball coach at Long Beach High on Long Island. His students soon learned how much he loved North Carolina, and Gersten began a sixty-year campaign as one of the university's biggest promoters and ambassadors. His standard line to an up-and-coming basketball player was always the same: "Work hard and listen to what I say, and you might be good enough someday to play at North Carolina!"

Gersten met McGuire, who by then had moved on to UNC after rebuilding St. John's into a college power, through the vast and well-connected Jewish community in New York City. Gersten befriended the Gotkin brothers—Hy, who coached YMCA teams in upper Manhattan, and Harry, who worked for the family's hat company in the garment district but spent most of his time scouting high-school basketball talent.

Long Beach, on the south shore of Long Island and protected by a large sandbar and accessed by bridge, was a popular summer destination for New York City residents. The town's population swelled after schools closed with families who rented apartments, bungalows, and homes along the beach and behind the boardwalk.

The Crystal family lived on Park Avenue, a large divided highway and the main street in Long Beach. The Crystal boys, three of them, spent hours out on the grass median tossing a football or baseball. The oldest, Richard, was an artist who became a high-school teacher; the middle brother, Joel, was the joker in the family, and he aspired to be a professional entertainer.

The youngest Crystal was Billy, and he was everyone's favorite.

He tagged along with his big brothers and hung out at his father's record store in the city. He saw everything, heard everything, and forgot nothing. Billy Crystal's comedy routines for decades to come always included bits about his relatives and hometown heroes.

One of the Crystal idols played basketball for Bob Gersten at Long Beach. He was a pint-sized point guard named Larry Brown. Even before Larry and his older brother, Herb, became well-known athletes in town, everyone knew their story because they lived with their widowed mother above Hittleman's Bakery on Park Avenue across from the Central School playground.

Ann Brown had come back to work at her father's bakery after her husband, Milton, died of heart failure. Larry was seven and Herb was eleven.

Although Herb Brown turned into a good left-handed shooter at Long Beach High, Gersten learned that Herb's little brother was almost a basketball savant. Larry always played with older, bigger kids on the playground, and he soon led and organized all of their pickup games. He seemed to have a sixth sense on the court, and the other kids clamored to be on his teams because they almost always won (and thus could keep playing). Notably, little Larry liked passing the ball to an open teammate for a layup more than scoring himself.

By now, Gersten was a tacit member of the "Jewish Mafia" in New York that helped McGuire identify players like Lennie Rosenbluth. Gersten, in fact, coached a traveling team with four Catholic kids from the metropolitan area—Pete Brennan, Bobby Cunningham, Tommy Kearns, and Joe Quigg. Harry Gotkin called Gersten regularly to check up on the foursome. With McGuire's network of priests and policemen helping out, all four were leaning toward leaving the city and going to college in North Carolina.

The "Four Catholics and a Jew" eventually led the Tar Heels to their undefeated 1957 season, which turned a football-crazy campus into a basketball school. The stream of players that rode McGuire's Underground Railroad south continued with the help of scouts Gotkin, Gersten, and Howard Garfinkel, who later began a summer all-star camp in the Pennsylvania mountains where coaches congregated to evaluate talent.

Meanwhile, Long Beach High was earning state playoff berths behind its 5'9", 130-pound point guard, although Larry Brown was not considered the best player on Long Island. That stature belonged to Art Heyman of nearby Oceanside High, who was a year younger than Brown but much bigger (6'4") and as loud and obnoxious as Brown was quiet and courteous.

Heyman and Brown competed ferociously during schoolyard games in the off-season and when Long Beach and Oceanside met twice in their league schedule. Early in Brown's senior year, Gersten invited Frank McGuire to watch Long Beach against Oceanside and asked him to stay for a reception at his home after the game.

For months, Gersten had been telling McGuire about Brown, whom he called "the best player under six feet in the country." When McGuire walked into the Long Beach gym before the game, his silk suit glistening, he was there primarily to see Heyman, but he wound up loving two players in the game.

In a rare performance of ball-hogging, Brown scored 45 points to Heyman's 29 and Long Beach pulled off the upset. Brown made 13 field goals and hit 19 of 20 free throws, and the Long Beach crowd chanted his name and rushed the court when the game ended. Heyman admired his older rival's popularity—Brown was also senior class president at Long Beach—and told him when they shook hands, "I'll follow you to North Carolina."

That night at Gersten's home, McGuire made scholarship offers to both players, even though Heyman still had another year at

Oceanside and Brown needed to attend prep school to beef up both his body and his grades. Soon, Heyman and Brown were planning on entering UNC together in the fall of 1959, two of another five star-studded recruits scouted by Harry Gotkin, as part of McGuire's latest freshman class.

Brown and Heyman, plus Kenny McIntyre, Rich Brennan, and Billy Galantai, all great players from New York, were supposedly signed and sealed, but back then the ACC did not recognize letters of intent dated before July 1. Only one of the five, Brown, eventually enrolled at UNC in September of 1959.

The biggest loss was Heyman, who chose to play for Duke and its new young coach Vic Bubas, a former assistant to Everett Case at N.C. State. Heyman's stepfather claimed Gotkin pressured Art to sign with Carolina. After engaging McGuire in a shouting match at the University Motel in Chapel Hill, Bill Heyman essentially reopened his stepson's recruitment.

Bill Heyman and his wife were swayed by Bubas' charm and promises to build his team around Art, who signed a binding scholarship with Duke and was a central figure in the fierce rivalry with Carolina for four years and beyond. Few Duke players have occupied the role of antagonist better than Art Heyman.

The experience made McGuire's young assistant coach, Dean Smith, see the perils of relying on just one recruiting pipeline. After Heyman's defection, Rich Brennan, Galantai, and McIntyre all failed to gain admission at UNC and had to attend Wilmington Prep for a year, while McGuire scrambled to sign up New Yorkers Marty Conlon, Jim Donohue, and Ken McComb. Then came a late commitment from Norfolk, tough guy Dieter Krause, to fill the freshman class.

Billy Galantai did eventually go to Chapel Hill. As a freshman, he had eligibility problems from having played in semi-pro leagues during the summer and did not enter a varsity game at North Carolina until the 1963 season, originally to have been his senior year. He had a small but vociferous following at Chapel Hill who knew him affectionately as "Lobo."

The so-called Long Island package of Brown and Heyman wound up wearing opposite shades of blue. As sophomores, the old New York rivals triggered a brawl late in the regionally televised 1961 UNC-Duke game in Durham that, once and for all, elevated basketball over football at the two schools set eight miles apart.

The fight, which lasted ten minutes, involved students and fans from Duke and took a dozen policemen to break up. It was another in a series of controversies that surrounded Frank McGuire and doomed his career as Carolina's head coach only four years after he had won the national championship with an undefeated team. It was also another example of the fierce, even explosive, rivalries of that era.

When McGuire resigned in August of 1961 to take over the Philadelphia Warriors and to coach Wilt Chamberlain, UNC promoted the thirty-year-old Dean Smith to replace him. Larry Brown and Donnie Walsh, who with Heyman had been suspended for the remainder of the 1961 season after the fight at Duke, became the key player links between the McGuire and Smith eras.

Walsh was a rising senior and had little choice but to finish out his career at Carolina, but Brown all but quit when the coach who had recruited him left Chapel Hill. Brown idolized McGuire for his eminence and manner, the way he charmed people, and especially how he dressed.

Once, after the Tar Heels went out to warm up for a game his sophomore year, Brown ran back to the locker room to use the bathroom. McGuire, who never appeared on court until just before tip-off, was dressing for the game and was in his underwear. Brown was stunned by this skeletal, half-naked older man, hardly the charismatic character in those perfectly tailored suits with padded shoulders, French cuffs, and gold cufflinks.

Brown did not let McGuire see him as he slipped in and out of the bathroom. However, he always remembered that revealing moment, which belied McGuire's amazingly manicured style.

Brown really did not want to play for anyone else. Through his own Hall of Fame career as a college and NBA coach, Brown never forgot the man who gave him a scholarship. He continued to honor McGuire's Carolina legacy long after it was overshadowed by Smith's accomplishments.

The bridge needed to carry Larry Brown between McGuire and Smith came very close to never being built. Back in Long Beach for most of the summer of 1961, Brown heard rumors about McGuire possibly leaving UNC, but he chose not to believe them until the official announcement in early August. When it came, he decided not to go back to Carolina for his junior year.

Besides losing their coach, the Tar Heels' 1961–1962 regular-season schedule was being cut in the wake of the point-shaving scandal. Brown's dream of playing in the defunct Dixie Classic was now also gone.

His family rejoiced because it meant their handsome young star would surely stay in New York and transfer to St. John's, NYU, or another local school. Brown himself was resigned to that fate because he could not envision himself playing at UNC for another coach.

"Coach McGuire was bigger than life, and the relationship I had with Dean as an assistant was much different," Brown said. "All of a sudden, Frank was gone and Dean took over. It was like my whole life changed, and I was ready to run."

A week after McGuire resigned, Brown came home from playing in the schoolyard to find Smith and Bob Gersten in his kitchen, talking with Ann Brown and eating pieces of Hittleman's cherry pie. They had come to ask Ann to send Larry back to Chapel Hill and continue his college career with Smith, then an unknown assistant to most of the college basketball world.

"Bobby says you should go back to Carolina and play for Coach Smith," Ann said. "I agree with them, so you're going back."

When Larry protested, saying his various cousins, aunts and uncles, and his grandfather, not to mention his old friends, wanted him to transfer to a school closer to home, Ann was having none of it. She had entrusted her son to Gersten throughout his high school career, and because of him and his relationship with McGuire, Larry landed the full scholarship that most New York college coaches were not prepared to offer him.

On the same trip north, Smith went to Brooklyn to see the parents of incoming freshman Billy Cunningham, who was McGuire's last great recruit at Carolina. One of McGuire's sisters had known the Cunningham family, which had sent their son to play for the man they trusted to take care of him.

"My father said I was going to Catholic school or to play for Coach McGuire," Cunningham said. "I never visited another school, never thought about one."

Fortunately, Cunningham decided to enroll at Carolina. Imagine if McGuire had never gone to Chapel Hill, or if he had not hired Smith, or if UNC had not promoted the unheard-of assistant coach? Even though all of that happened, Brown and Cunningham's decision to stick with Carolina was the key. They in turn later helped lure Bobby Lewis and Larry Miller, Smith's first two great recruits, when they visited Carolina over the next two years.

That linkage has been a hallmark of Carolina Basketball for

the last half century. It was a key ingredient to Smith's survival and eventual success and the critical crossroad in the history of the Carolina blue ascendancy.

A point guard himself in college, Smith bonded with Brown in a way that made Larry soon want to learn more from his new coach. They toughed out their two years together. It didn't hurt when they accidentally invented the Four Corners one day in practice during the 1963 season when Brown mistakenly drove the ball against zone and found an open man cutting to the basket.

Cunningham became Smith's first All-American and the indispensable star who played in the shadow of Art Heyman and the great Duke teams of the mid-1960s. Without Cunningham, Smith's chances of keeping his job long enough to have some success would have been severely compromised.

In Smith's first season, with Brown and Walsh leading a team depleted by McGuire's departure and his star recruits who never came, Carolina played a regular-season schedule limited to sixteen games by a university bent on cleaning up the mess that had marked McGuire's last years.

The Tar Heels were ending a one-year probation stemming from expenditures the NCAA alleged had been funneled to scouts and recruits. Plus, gamblers had infiltrated college basketball in the South and brought with them a point-shaving scandal like the one that rocked New York City colleges ten years earlier. Carolina wanted to rein in basketball and get it under control.

UNC finished 8-9 in 1962, and only slight unrest followed Smith into his second season, when Cunningham moved up to the varsity and led the ACC in rebounding with more than 16 per game (the next best rebounder averaged only 10).

Brown was the glue of this group, leading the team to ten ACC victories and fifteen overall as a senior. He was now in sync with Smith, respecting him for reasons other than those that attracted him to McGuire. Brown, already a coach in the making, had become a keen student of changing defenses and the tempo offense that Smith was teaching.

Brown now had a trio of mentors, all with Carolina connections. Bob Gersten had introduced him to UNC, McGuire had recruited and coached him for one year, and Smith's resolve during a tough transition endeared him to Brown forever. During two college head-coaching jobs and ten stops in pro basketball, Brown never failed to mention all three men as the guiding influences of his basketball life.

Though he was too small to make one of the nine NBA teams in 1963, Brown wanted to keep playing. With Smith's help, he landed a job with Goodyear and starred for its AAU team in Akron, Ohio.

That earned him an invitation to the 1964 Olympic trials, where Brown went against some of John Wooden's first national champions at UCLA and other players with more size and reputation. Brown played unselfishly throughout the trials in New York City, and Olympic coach Hank Iba selected him to the squad that would represent the United States in Tokyo. Brown was the first of more than a dozen Tar Heels who have played or coached in the Olympic Games since then.

In Long Beach, after he returned from Japan, a parade down Park Avenue was held for Larry Brown—the neighborhood boy and gold medal winner. For Brown, it was more than a brush with fame and it felt good.

Torn between still playing and starting his coaching career, Brown returned to Akron for one more season while staying in contact with Smith and McGuire, who had since gone to South Carolina. He turned down several small college coaching jobs and instead married his college sweetheart, Gayle Venters from Jacksonville, North Carolina. Brown visited Chapel Hill periodically, once in January of 1965 when he heard that students had hanged Smith in effigy after the Tar Heels lost their fourth straight game. He told anyone who would listen how hard Smith had it when he took over and what a great coach Smith would be if given enough time.

Fortunately, the Tar Heels pulled it together to win fifteen games and finish tied for second in the ACC. Smith put the silly lynch mob behind him and, more importantly, dodged fat cat alumni who remembered only the good of the McGuire years.

After the 1965 season, assistant Ken Rosemond accepted the head-coaching job at Georgia, and Smith called Brown in Akron. Within a week, he and Gayle had moved back to Chapel Hill to begin a stretch that Brown always described as "having died and gone to heaven."

Two months later, Smith received approval for a second full-time assistant. He kept it in the extended family by hiring a charming high school coach from New York named John Lotz, the brother of former Frank McGuire player Danny Lotz.

Brown and Lotz helped Smith close on a recruiting class that eventually put the Tar Heels over the top. The grumbling over Carolina basketball hung around like the morning dew before the 1966 season until Smith held a public scrimmage between his varsity and the new freshmen—6'11" Rusty Clark, 6'9" Bill Bunting, 6'5" Joe Brown, 6'3" Jim Bostick, 6'4" Dick Grubar, and 6' Gerald Tuttle.

Brown was their coach and had the so-called dream team fired up to beat the varsity. They did, and Smith called his twenty-six-year-old assistant onto the carpet for the potentially divisive maneuver. A week later, Smith gave the varsity a closed-door rematch. Both squads claimed to have won, but it settled matters internally.

While Carolina struggled to a mediocre 16-11 season, best remembered by the 21-20 slowdown loss to Duke in the semifinals of the 1966 ACC tournament, the attention generated by the freshman team had fans focusing on the future and not as much on the coach. For the next forty years, when Brown's freshmen held occasional reunions, they chortled about how hard he ran them, but they also admitted how well prepared they were for the varsity.

In 1967, Brown became a small part of Carolina history when those super sophs helped the Tar Heels win Smith's first ACC championship and reach his first Final Four. Despite lopsided losses to Dayton and Houston (in the third-place game) in Louisville, Brown was so proud of how far his third mentor had taken the Tar Heels. "People have no idea how hard it was for him," Brown said, "and what he had to survive after Coach McGuire left."

Still only twenty-seven, Brown had not kicked the urge to play. With Smith's blessing and encouragement, he left the staff to join the new American Basketball Association, which was seeking good players from anywhere and everywhere. Brown and former UNC star Doug Moe, who by then was a basketball hero in Italy, signed shaky contracts with the New Orleans Buccaneers and became pioneers in a wild ABA. The league featured a red, white, and blue basketball, a three-point shot, and very little defense.

Brown made the 1968 ABA all-star team, earned the All-Star game MVP, and went on to set assist records for the five years he starred for four different teams in the struggling league. He and Moe, also an ABA all-star, added to a short list of former UNC players in pro basketball. To that point, Cunningham and Lee Shaffer, who quit the NBA after three seasons to enter private business, were the only pro standouts from Carolina.

Knowing since high school that he wanted to coach, Brown got his first head job at Davidson after he and Moe had led the Oakland Oaks to the 1969 ABA championship. The Wildcats had enjoyed a great run with Lefty Driesell, who left for Maryland, and Brown at first thought it was an ideal situation. Right away, though, he second-guessed himself and began looking for ways to get out of his commitment. First, Davidson would not replace the carpet in his office. Then the small school outside of Charlotte did not provide the kind of housing it had promised for Gayle Brown and their infant daughter while Larry went off recruiting during the summer. Finally, his first paycheck came up way short of what he had expected.

He phoned Smith and said he was going to quit.

"Stay there, I'm coming down," Smith ordered him.

By the end of the day, Smith was at Davidson and whisked Brown away for some golf and a heart-to-heart, thinking he had turned around his protégé. But a few weeks later, against Smith's advice that it would hurt his chances of getting another college job, Brown fled Davidson. He returned to the ABA for three more record-breaking seasons before chronic knee and hip ailments forced him into retirement in the summer of 1972. Larry Brown, who had played basketball seemingly forever, was finally finished.

The Carolina Cougars of the ABA, who played their home games in Raleigh, Greensboro, and Charlotte, hired Brown to jump-start a losing franchise that had tried old Bones McKinney as its first coach. By bringing along Moe as his assistant and signing a couple of stars off UNC's 1972 Final Four team, Dennis Wuycik and Steve Previs, Brown hoped his Carolina pedigree would sell more tickets. He and the 6'7" Moe became the Mutt and Jeff, Abbott and

Costello, and yin and yang of the crazy new league, which never approached college basketball in popularity in the Tar Heel State.

While attendance was spotty in the three cities, Brown and Moe led the Cougars to 104 victories and two playoff appearances before the team was sold and moved to St. Louis. During Brown's second season with the Cougars, he met a graduate student at UNC named Roy Williams, who was helping out Dean Smith's program by refereeing scrimmages and keeping stats. Their paths would cross and intertwine repeatedly for the next 30 years.

Brown and Moe followed Cougars general manager Carl Scheer to his new job with the ABA's Denver franchise, staying there for four-plus years, four more playoff runs, and through the team's eventual inclusion in the NBA merger. The only sad side to Brown's early days in Denver was that his marriage ended. Gayle and their two daughters returned to North Carolina and settled in Charlotte.

Brown reenergized the newly renamed Nuggets (formerly Rockets) by installing a wide-open style of play that turned a sleepy franchise into a happening in the Mile High City. The Nuggets sold out the Denver Auditorium for every home game—perfect timing with the opening of McNichols Arena coming the next year—and finished 40-2 at home.

Still only thirty-four, with good looks, and a bachelor again, Brown became a cult figure in the city. He also played the part with bright sweaters and wild outfits like designer jeans and overalls. It was the 1970s, and the Nuggets' coach was indulging in a little self-expression.

"The ABA let you be who you were and wear whatever you wanted," Brown said. "In college I played for a coach, Frank McGuire, who respected the way he dressed and looked, and he wanted me to understand that. So clothes became an important part of who

I am. I got a lot of flak for some of those outfits, but it was fun that the ABA didn't really care what you wore."

Despite winning more than 65 percent of his games and the Nuggets making the playoffs every year, Brown gradually tired of dealing with spoiled and troubled players. He began to believe his rightful place was back in college basketball.

His favorite player at Denver had been former UNC star Bobby Jones, whom Brown helped become an all-star and whom he promoted as the greatest defender in pro basketball. Jones had asthma that worsened in the high altitude, and Brown convinced Scheer to trade him to Philadelphia for George McGinnis. Brown had admired McGinnis from afar but later learned he did not want to work hard in practice.

The drug problems that killed David Thompson's career also devastated Brown, who had recruited the former N.C. State All-American to sign with the Nuggets instead of the NBA's Atlanta Hawks. The Virginia Squires had made Thompson the ABA's top draft pick, then they traded his rights to Denver. At first, Brown refused to believe rumors that, like many NBA players of the day, Thompson used cocaine as a recreational drug and was spending thousands of dollars to support his new habit.

After Moe moved on to coach the San Antonio Spurs and Brown hired Donnie Walsh off McGuire's South Carolina staff to be his chief assistant, Brown's fight-or-flight syndrome grew worse. Spending long nights on the road reminiscing with Walsh about their days at North Carolina, Brown grew even more disillusioned with pro basketball.

Following the 1977 season, which ended with UNC's loss to Marquette in the NCAA tournament championship game, UCLA athletic director J. D. Morgan called Dean Smith and asked him if he wanted to coach the Bruins. John Wooden had been retired for

two years, and his successor, Gene Bartow (despite fifty-two victories and one trip to the Final Four), was resigning to start a new
program at Alabama-Birmingham. Smith, who had divorced Ann
in 1974 and recently married psychiatrist and native Californian
Linnea Weblemoe, turned Morgan down but suggested that
Brown be considered.

Morgan contacted Brown in Denver and said he was offering
the job to former Wooden assistant Gary Cunningham, who he
thought would accept. But Morgan also told Brown he had been
highly recommended by Smith and if the high-profile position ever
came open again he would be the first person called.

Although Cunningham became UCLA's next coach, the epi-
sode further rekindled Brown's fire for college basketball. However, a major stumbling block for Brown was the difference in
coaching salaries: far greater in the pros than in college. Brown's
mentors, McGuire and Smith, had yet to crack the $100,000 an-
nual income level; Brown had two daughters to support from his
first marriage and the adopted daughter of his new second wife.
He spent the summer questioning his resolve to stay with the
Nuggets for another season—discussing it with McGuire when
he attended McGuire's induction into the Basketball Hall of
Fame in May of 1977. McGuire had tried the NBA for one season and gravitated back to his first love, college basketball.

Brown remained with the Nuggets, while in the Appalachian
Mountains, 2,000 miles to the east, a much younger coach was winding down his short high-school coaching career. Even as Brown was
trying to justify coming back to the college ranks, Roy Williams was
trying desperately to get there from a different direction.

Leaving Owen High School in Swannanoa after five years, Williams joined the UNC staff as a part-time assistant. He was ten
years younger than Brown and decades apart in basketball experi-

ence on and off the court. Thus, his own first step toward the pinnacle of the profession began while Brown ended his first stint coaching in the NBA. Williams found a strong connection remained to Brown's era and, even after seventeen years as a head coach, Smith still referred to "how Coach McGuire did it."

Brown walked away from the Denver Nuggets with twenty-nine games left in the 1979 season and, to break the boredom and contemplate what he would do next, began hanging around the University of Colorado team in Boulder. He got to know head coach Bill Blair and assistant Kevin O'Connor and met a tough, young coach named Gregg Popovich. An Air Force graduate, Popovich had served five years' active duty and undergone espionage training before taking over as head coach at Division III Pomona-Pitzer in California.

In April, Brown interviewed at what was then called Memphis State, but it didn't remind him very much of Carolina and Chapel Hill. In May, after Gary Cunningham resigned under pressure at UCLA, Brown got the call from J. D. Morgan that he had been waiting for, and he was named the man in charge at UCLA.

Frank McGuire's last year as a college head coach was Larry Brown's first, and the 1980 season proved as unhappy at South Carolina as it was exciting at UCLA. McGuire and Dean Smith encouraged Brown to coach the Bruins, whose fans had finally learned that the John Wooden days of winning repeated national championships were priceless but not repeatable. The expansion of the NCAA tournament and the seeding of teams that equalized the four regions of the country had made certain of that.

At one point during the season, South Carolina and UCLA had similarly pedestrian records. Testimonials for the retiring McGuire distracted his thirtieth college team, while Brown struggled to re-make the Bruins in his own image. While speculation about Mc-Guire's successor dominated the media in the South, the national press took Brown to task for a transition that *Sports Illustrated* labeled "The Bruins Are in Ruins."

On January 20, 1980, UCLA was 8-6 and in serious jeopardy of missing the NCAA tournament for the first time in fourteen years. This would have been a calamity in Westwood.

However, the toughness Brown took from his first college coach and the patience he learned from his second prevailed when he gave freshmen Rod Foster and Michael Holton bigger roles, and he turned floor leadership of the team over to senior captain Kiki Vandeweghe. Dubbed "Kiki and the Kids" by a local writer, the Bruins went on a roll and earned an at-large entry and eighth seed in the NCAA West Regional. Brown had his players believing the old McGuire mantra of "Us Against the World," but he also knew they had jelled into a pretty good ball club. After UCLA stunned top seed and No. 1–ranked DePaul and upset Ohio State, the Bruins beat Clemson to find themselves in the 1980 Final Four.

The retiring Frank McGuire and the aspiring Dean Smith were in Indianapolis to see UCLA and their protégé compete for the national title, which McGuire had won twenty-three years earlier and Smith had never won. The Bruins defeated Purdue in the semi-finals, then came within one missed shot by Vandeweghe of perhaps beating Louisville.

Heading for Market Square Arena and the championship game against Louisville, Brown had been a mixed bag of emotions. He fretted over how his freshman-laden team would handle the ultimate spotlight in college basketball. Another thought was: "Would it really be fair for me to win this in my first season when it took Coach McGuire ten years to do it and Coach Smith hasn't won one yet?"

After the five-point loss to Louisville, Brown did not have to worry about apologizing to his two mentors. In any case, he had a better team returning the next season, even though Kiki was leaving the Kids.

Brown could not know as he left Indianapolis that his UCLA world was ready to fall apart. Illness forced J. D. Morgan into retirement, and those now running the school's athletic department were irritated by Brown's constant complaining about the need to upgrade the facilities at Pauley Pavilion and the salaries of the coaching staff. After all, *Wooden won* all those national championships with similar resources.

NCAA investigators were also hovering over UCLA, questioning Brown about some minor recruiting violations and digging far deeper into serious transgressions around the Bruins' football and basketball teams during the past ten years. With Wooden retired, officials were finally scrutinizing the association with prominent alumnus and godfather to the players Sam "Papa Bear" Gilbert. Before it was over, UCLA would be placed on probation and Gilbert banned from any future contact with the basketball program.

Although wildly popular among UCLA fans and students, and on the way to a 20-7 record and No. 3 seed in the 1981 NCAA East Regional, Brown negotiated with the NBA's New Jersey Nets. The forthcoming offer would turn his $50,000 college salary into $250,000. He was too embarrassed to tell close friends, who were shocked to learn right after the Bruins lost to BYU in the regional that he had accepted.

Brown had consulted with Smith, who advised him to stay at UCLA and keep asking for more support, but Brown decided to go back east because he and his second wife, Barbara, and stepdaughter could not afford to live in Los Angeles in the fashion they wanted. He took the bigger money and ran, insisting all the way across the country that he really loved UCLA and was more cut out to be a college coach than a professional baby-sitter. It was clearly a conflict between money and love of the college game.

Late in his first season with the Nets, Brown joined McGuire at the Superdome in New Orleans on March 29, 1982, to witness Smith's first NCAA title and UNC's first since 1957. In turn, the following May, McGuire and Brown were in Springfield, Massachusetts, to see Smith's induction into the Basketball Hall of Fame.

Brown's coaching brilliance turned around a moribund Nets franchise, bringing fans back to the Meadowlands and earning the team's first playoff berth in three years. But he confided to Smith and McGuire that he wanted back into college coaching some day soon.

The opportunity to bolt came late in his second season at New Jersey after the Nets had traded former UNC star Phil Ford, who was losing his battle with alcohol and drug addiction. Brown was too embarrassed to tell Smith about the Ford trade before it was announced.

When Ted Owens retired at Kansas after nineteen years (with a 348-182 record and .657 winning percentage), KU athletic director Monte Johnson called the school's most famous coaching alumnus and asked Dean Smith if he wanted to come home. Almost certainly knowing the answer, Johnson also asked for recommendations. Smith said Larry Brown was sorry he left UCLA and really wanted back in the college game.

"He won't stay forever," Smith said, "but while he's there he'll win and do a tremendous job developing players." Johnson expressed concern over the UCLA probation, which had been linked in part to Brown's two years with the Bruins. Smith assured him that Brown's role was minor and related to helping one recruit with a ride home and another with a hotel room for his brother.

Brown accepted the Kansas job and expected to finish out the 1983 season with the Nets, who had won forty-seven games, when owner Joe Taub learned he was losing his coach. Recently, Ray Perkins had resigned as coach of the New York (football) Giants to go to Alabama, and the local media squawked about it. Taub didn't want the same problem, so he suspended Brown and promoted his assistant and old friend Bill Blair.

Another of these Carolina basketball symmetries formed when Kansas introduced Brown as its new coach in April of 1983. He had played for Smith and McGuire, who had long ago been linked to the Jayhawks since his St. John's team lost to them in the 1952 NCAA title game and his undefeated Tar Heels beat Wilt Chamberlain's KU team in the 1957 triple-overtime classic at Kansas City.

As was his habit when he landed in yet another location, Brown professed respect for the Kansas basketball tradition, pledged undying love, and thus generated huge excitement all over the state. He also agreed to the first Midnight Madness at KU, a tradition that grew steadily from its premiere.

Lefty Driesell had started Midnight Madness at Maryland in 1970, when he opened a team scrimmage to the public at 12:01 A.M. on the NCAA-mandated first day of practice. The publicity gimmick caught on with several schools and became a staple of college basketball after ESPN showed up in the early 1980s.

When Brown settled at Kansas, he agreed to host this event, stealing the name from David Letterman. The first "Late Night with Larry" drew a surprising crowd of 6,000 fans to Allen Fieldhouse. The tradition grew from there and carried over to Brown's successors.

The crowd doubled the second year when Letterman foil Larry "Bud" Melman appeared and told a few jokes before introducing Brown and the Jayhawks. The entertainment was so popular that

Late Night became more of a talent show than a scrimmage. In Brown's last season, the players began lip-synching songs and performing skits before midnight, when they were allowed to use a real basketball on the court.

During his second year at KU, Brown lost some support among Tar Heel fans when he recruited Greensboro high school star Danny Manning away from Smith and UNC. Brown hired Manning's father Ed, a former teammate in the ABA and an out-of-work truck driver, as his assistant coach. Although Smith said Brown had every right to recruit anyone he wanted, several members of his coaching staff regarded the maneuver as an affront to the Carolina Basketball Family.

In Manning's sophomore season, the second-ranked Jayhawks won the Big Eight regular-season and tournament titles and reached the 1986 Final Four, where they lost a close game to Duke (which went on to lose to Louisville for the national title). After barely making the tournament as a sixth seed in 1988, Kansas played Duke again in the national semifinals at Kansas City.

Smith and McGuire were honored at the fiftieth Final Four anniversary lunch before Saturday's doubleheader. After Kansas broke out to a big lead and held on to beat Duke, they remained for Monday night's championship game. The Jayhawks were led by All-American Manning and dubbed Danny and the Miracles. In the final, they played fourth-ranked and heavily favored Oklahoma, which carried a 35-3 record into the game.

Brown's brilliant preparation had KU ready for Billy Tubbs' high-scoring Sooners. The Jayhawks managed a 50-50 tie at halftime. The pace slowed in the second half. Kansas wound up shooting 64 percent for the game and made four of its six three-pointers while frustrating free-shooting Oklahoma, which fired up twenty-four three-pointers and barely shot 40 percent. Manning's spectacular 31 points and 18 rebounds earned him the Final Four most outstanding player award.

After the amazing 83-79 upset, the seventy-three-year-old McGuire and fifty-seven-year-old Smith greeted Brown outside the jubilant Jayhawks locker room. The champions from three generations shared a warm embrace.

Soon, though, Brown would be gone, jumping back to the NBA for San Antonio after first flirting with a return to UCLA. His disdain for what he considered petty NCAA rules had also left Kansas under investigation, just as UCLA had been when he coached the Bruins.

In the case of Kansas, Brown had been misled by recruit Vincent Askew, who asked him for money to fly home to visit his "sick grandmother." Brown committed a few other careless violations that, regardless of their gravity, damaged both Brown and the Kansas program.

Smith was asked again to help find a coach for his alma mater, someone who could withstand the short-term fallout from the NCAA probe and continue the Jayhawks' long tradition of dominating the old Big Eight Conference. This time Smith told KU athletic director Bob Frederick that Roy Williams was ready to become a head coach after ten years on the Carolina staff, the last two as a full-time recruiting assistant. Williams had replaced Eddie Fogler in the role when Fogler departed for Wichita State.

Frederick demurred, saying that with his school coming off a national championship, he needed to hire a current head coach with a bigger name. He promised, however, to keep Smith's suggestion in mind.

When Smith walked down the hall of his office in May of 1988, and stopped at Williams' door, he had a stunning little secret for his then-thirty-seven-year-old assistant. "Don't do anything or say anything, but you might have a chance at the Kansas job," Smith said. He privately believed that Kansas would have a harder time landing an established coach than expected.

"Well, now I thought he had really lost it," Williams said of Smith. "There was no way in hell I was going to be the next Kansas coach."

With probation rumors swirling around KU, and at least two head coaches turning down the job, Williams suddenly became a viable candidate. It did not matter that he was a North Carolina product, just like the coach who had left Kansas with some problems.

Williams met with Frederick in the Delta lounge at the Atlanta Airport on the way to Bermuda—his first vacation alone with his wife, Wanda, in four years. He then cut the trip short when Frederick asked him to fly out to Lawrence. He interviewed with the search committee, which included several longtime friends of Smith.

At one point, Williams grew teary-eyed while recounting his life in western North Carolina, growing up in the mountains where he and his wife were born and bred, and how they pulled a U-Haul down to Chapel Hill, leaving a $30,000 household income behind to take a part-time college coaching job with the Tar Heels and follow his fantasy.

"Chapel Hill has been a dream place for me," Williams started slowly, his voice cracking. "Everything I wanted my dream to be started and happened there. I am coaching college basketball at North Carolina."

That deep, abiding love for his home state, along with almost paralyzing fear of coaching a storied program like Kansas, was on his mind. Soon, he thought, the interview would be over and he could go home.

"Folks, I'm not trying to upset you or anything," Williams said. "But I've got this little voice in the back of my head saying, 'Boy, why don't you tell these people thank you and apologize for wasting their time and get your tail back to North Carolina.' That's what I've got to fight, my love for North Carolina and leaving there."

His eyes puffy, Williams looked across the room to see teary-eyed Galen Fiss, one of Dean Smith's roommates at KU and a former linebacker with the Cleveland Browns. Fiss wiped his cheek and addressed Williams. "Roy, I want you to know this doesn't make me think any less of you at all," he said. "It makes me think more of you. Nobody can love Kansas any more than I do, and I know you could love it like that, too. I want that kind of person as our coach."

Williams was a few weeks from his thirty-eighth birthday but still had not seen much of the country and the world. Fiss' raw feelings for Kansas touched Williams and allowed him to think he just might like Kansas, too. After a brief recess, the committee called him back in.

"If this job was offered to you, would you accept?" he was asked. Williams swallowed hard and said yes.

Frederick's wife called him crazy and warned he was going to get fired for hiring this "no-name assistant from North Carolina . . . The alumni are going to kill you." One prominent KU alum told the Dallas *Morning News* it was a worse decision than Notre Dame's hiring of Gerry Faust, the former high school football coach who lasted five unhappy seasons with the Irish.

Nevertheless, on July 8, 1988, Kansas introduced Williams as the seventh coach of the Jayhawks. More than a few KU fans figured Doctors James Naismith and Phog Allen were turning in their graves right there in Lawrence.

Aware of the doubters, Williams also knew he would not fail

from a lack of effort. He had the Carolina basketball example to draw from, along with an unrelenting work ethic from his mother. His fear of failure kept his motor running all the time.

Roy Who? remained the big question beyond the summer of 1988. Even Williams could not be sure he was properly prepared to succeed under the glare of Middle America's marquee college basketball name. It may be that only Dean Smith knew for sure.

The NCAA did put Kansas on probation for one year, taking away three scholarships and banning the Jayhawks from defending their NCAA championship. This effectively gave the rookie coach a grace period.

Williams understood that his new school was very similar to UNC in resources and tradition. He set out to follow Smith's model: Sign his share of the good players that KU (like UNC) would inevitably have a chance to get and then coach them pretty much the way Smith would.

"We always talked about North Carolina-type basketball, about trying to get the high-percentage shot and pushing the basketball up the floor," he said of his early days at Kansas. "Everything we did was modeled on Carolina, from how we ran the office, to how we organized practice, to how the players dressed on the road and how we traveled."

From day one, Williams appeared to know his stuff, embracing the opportunity in a humble way. His skill and folksy charm made most fans, including Frederick's wife, cautiously optimistic. When high school star Adonis Jordan honored his commitment to Kansas (after Thomas Hill opted out for Duke), the new coach showed he could recruit. After all, he had done it at North Carolina.

The optimism turned to euphoria when Williams proved he could coach, as well. He continued to rely on the meticulous preparation that he learned from those years of observing and working for Smith. And he worked almost all the time when he wasn't sleeping.

KU's eight remaining scholarship players and five walk-ons began the 1988–1989 season by going 13-1, a spectacular start for the rookie head coach. The doubters then had something to work with, as Kansas went 3-10 in its next thirteen games, losing eight straight during one three-week stretch.

After rebounding to close the regular season with three consecutive victories, Williams' team lost his first Big Eight tournament game to Kansas State. But the Jayhawks weren't going anywhere anyway due to the NCAA probation, and by then the love affair with "good ole' Roy" was in full bloom.

The year before, Williams' last as an assistant at UNC, Duke had rallied to beat the Tar Heels in the 1988 ACC championship game. A perturbed Dean Smith made his team stay on the court as the Blue Devils celebrated, and Williams slumped on the bench dejectedly.

When his own season was over a year later, Williams watched the 1989 ACC final against Duke in Atlanta at his home in Lawrence. He relished Carolina's dramatic 77-74 win, its first ACC championship since 1982. The victory also halted what some perceived as a slow skid for the Tar Heels and his mentor.

Despite losing to eventual national champion Michigan in the Sweet Sixteen, while Duke went back to the Final Four for the third time under Mike Krzyzewski, bringing home the ACC title revitalized Carolina. This set the stage for Smith's charge over the next decade.

He had beaten Krzyzewski two out of three that season and swept both games in 1990 by allowing his guards to dribble penetrate against Duke's overplaying defense. It was one of several philosophical adjustments Smith made that led to four more trips to the Final Four and a second national championship before he retired.

At the same time, Larry Brown's nomadic coaching career continued. Now divorced twice, Brown stayed in San Antonio for four-and-a-half turbulent years, was fired midway through the 1992 season, and immediately got hired by the Los Angeles Clippers.

Brown was happy to be back in California, where he reconnected with old friends from UCLA. While looking for the house on the beach that he finally could afford, Brown met the woman who became his third wife, Shelly, a high-end real estate agent.

A continent away, Brown's first college coach and boyhood idol was in a passage of his own. Frank McGuire had suffered a serious stroke and would be confined to a wheelchair for the rest of his life. Sorrowful, Brown felt like it was time to get grounded again.

He and Shelly were married a year later in a small ceremony attended only by their closest friends and family. Popovich, his assistant with the Spurs, who had taken a job at Golden State, served as his best man.

By the end of Brown's second season with the Clippers, he had led them into the NBA playoffs twice and turned a laughingstock franchise into serious competition for the cross-town Lakers. His next move was a return to his roots, reuniting with former UNC teammate Donnie Walsh, the general manager of the Indiana Pacers, who hired Brown as his next coach after the 1993 season.

In Kansas, Brown was already old news. Williams had led KU to thirty more wins in 1990, and back to the NCAA tournament and into the Final Four two of the next three years. He also continued "Late Night with Roy," and in his younger, more experimental days went with all kinds of suggestions that eventually led to the formula he kept for the rest of his stay at Lawrence and after he returned to Chapel Hill.

One year, Kansas charged $5 admission to pay for two rock bands that entertained the crowd before the scrimmage. The ensuing controversy convinced Williams to make it free from that point on. He moved Late Night from the official first day of practice (October 15) to the weekend, so students wouldn't have to get up for class the next morning. He allowed fans to participate in a dunking contest with his players, and once used sports icons and off-season golf buddies George Brett and Tom Watson as honorary coaches in the scrimmage.

In 1996, Williams called a young woman named Mindy Camp, the girlfriend of Jayhawk star Scot Pollard, down to the court from the stands. He handed the microphone to his player.

"Mindy, will you marry me?" Pollard said, holding up an engagement ring.

"Yes!" she said as Allen Fieldhouse erupted.

The annual senior ceremony after the last home game—something Williams invented and had not been done at Carolina—was just as emotional. All graduating players took the mike at a still-full field house and professed their love for Kansas and gratitude to Williams. Anyone witnessing one of those stirring scenes could only imagine how difficult it would be for Williams to ever leave the school that had given him his career break.

Back in North Carolina, Williams had become somewhat of a folk hero from afar, as word filtered back of the new basketball family he was building in Kansas. It gave rise to the first speculation that he would leave Kansas some day to succeed Smith. The undercurrent added to a surreal setting when both teams advanced to the 1991 Final Four in Indianapolis and squared off in the first semifinal.

After his team held on to win an ugly game between two teams that knew too much about each other, Williams' joy over the victory was tempered by his feelings for Smith, who had been ejected in the last minute with his second technical foul. Smith had stopped to shake his protégé's hand on his long walk off the playing floor.

The underdog Jayhawks had most of Tar Heel Nation rooting for them two nights later when they met Duke for the national championship at the Hoosier Dome. The strange juxtaposition of Carolina's biggest rival beating Williams for its first national title just added fuel to the fire. Maybe, thought more and more Tar Heel faithful, Williams was the logical choice to follow Dean Smith.

Larry Brown's nomadic coaching career that began in the old ABA took him out of the running in the eyes of most Carolina fans. In the process, however, he presided over a UNC farm system of sorts. With the help of pro coaches and front office executives like Brown, Doug Moe, Billy Cunningham, Donnie Walsh, and Mitch Kupchak, dozens of former Tar Heel players had shined in both leagues, giving Smith the longest line of pro players and coaches in history.

While Brown's strange journey among teams and places was curious, it proved beyond doubt that his coaching genius was in demand. Brown's mantra of playing basketball "the right way" became closely associated with his training under Carolina coaching legend Smith and, for those who still remembered, Frank McGuire.

8

Living Legacies, Family Ties

FAMILIES grow up, sometimes split apart, and always the under-lings go off on their own. Marriages and births are cherished be-cause they welcome new family members. Eventually, young men become old men who cannot believe—or really understand—where the time has gone.

When Dean Smith went after his second NCAA title in New Orleans, disabled Frank McGuire watched from home in South Carolina. Fifty-three-year-old Larry Brown was watching from Los Angeles, where he was guiding the once-comical Clippers into the NBA playoffs for the second straight year.

Both mentor and protégé celebrated Smith's second Final Four in three years, and indeed the 1993 trip seemed almost trium-phant. In 1991, there was more relief than anything else because, after a nine-year absence, some people thought Smith would never get back there again.

Bound to a wheelchair, McGuire was certainly alert enough mentally to relish Smith's renewed success. Brown also reveled in seeing his second mentor catch a second wind in his four-decade coaching career.

Since the late 1980s, Smith had been upstaged by Duke and Krzyzewski. Carolina went seven years without winning an ACC title, and making at least the Sweet Sixteen of the NCAA tournament each season meant little if it did not culminate at the Final Four. That ended after the Tar Heels blew out the Blue Devils to win the 1991 ACC championship and advanced to Indianapolis. Their triumphant return to the national semifinals, however, was sullied by their loss to Kansas, Smith's ejection late in the game, and Duke shocking top-ranked UNLV on the way to its first national championship.

Krzyzewski became the fresh face of college basketball when Duke won its second straight national championship in 1992 while UNC fell to a forgotten third place in the ACC and was way overshadowed by the media frenzy following the back-to-back Blue Devils. Tar Heel Nation grew sick of it.

That had been a particularly tough year for the Carolina family. Besides McGuire's stroke, Roy Williams lost his mother, Mimmie, after a long battle with cancer, and Smith's parents, both in their nineties and living in a Raleigh retirement home, died within nine months of each other.

On the court, Smith's mistake-prone Tar Heels had been wiped out by Duke in the 1992 ACC championship game and made only a mild NCAA run before losing to Ohio State in the Sweet Sixteen. It looked like Carolina had fallen a step behind, maybe for good.

Harkening back to McGuire's tough love, Smith ordered off-season scrimmages to be half court, four on four, rather than 94-foot dunking contests with little or no defense. He challenged his players to work on the weakest parts of their games and tried some Final Four visualization by placing a picture of the Superdome in each of their lockers. They were 17-1 after rallying from 22 points behind at home against Florida State. When they beat the No. 6 Seminoles in the brutal road rematch, they earned UNC's first No. 1 ranking in five years and were poised to answer Duke.

So when Smith took a solid team that collectively proved better than its individual parts to the 1993 Final Four, while the Dukies missed for the first time in six seasons, the Tar Heels had a chance for oneupmanship. And they did it the hard way after beginning their NCAA quest with leader and point guard Derrick Phelps nursing a serious back injury suffered in the ACC tournament.

Phelps returned to full strength for the Sweet Sixteen at the Meadowlands, where the Tar Heels defeated 12th-ranked Arkansas and then faced No. 7 Cincinnati for a second trip to the Final Four in three years.

Carolina trailed the Bearcats by a point at halftime, largely because of six three-pointers thrown in by loquacious left-hander Nick Van Exel. He had angered the Tar Heels before the game by saying Smith should have won more than one national championship "with all his talent."

That's when Smith used a tried and true Frank McGuire technique. He asked Phelps, UNC's best on-the-ball defender, if he thought he could shadow Van Exel during the second half. Without saying the exact words, it was Smith's way of employing McGuire's old challenge, *You can do it; why do you think I recruited you?*

Phelps spent the rest of halftime walking around the locker room saying, "He's mine now. He's mine now."

Van Exel scored only two points in the second half. Carolina needed every defensive stop to survive in overtime and return to the site of Smith's first national championship eleven years earlier.

Kansas and Roy Williams were waiting in New Orleans, a national semifinals rematch of the 1991 game won by the Jayhawks at Indianapolis. This time, there was a whole different feel.

The intense desire by UNC alumni for Smith to win another NCAA title outweighed any sentiment for Williams. Two years before, some Carolina fans may have found solace in losing to one of their own, but that would not wash this time. There was a mission to be accomplished; winning Smith's second championship was the consuming goal because only a final victory would keep UNC Basketball on pace with Duke in what was clearly the twilight of Smith's career.

On Friday, the day before the game, Carolina assistant coach Bill Guthridge underscored the difference between 1991 and 1993 by refusing to meet Williams for a run the morning of the game. "We ran together two years ago in Indianapolis, and you beat us, so this time we're not going with you," Guthridge said, only half kidding. When the teams came out late that afternoon, the coaching staffs had a good laugh about it in front of the scorer's table.

Junior center Eric Montross and senior captain George Lynch bolstered perhaps Smith's best *team* ever, combining for more than 30 points and 17 rebounds a game. They were just under those marks against Kansas, mostly because Donald Williams lit it up from outside with 25 points on 5-for-7 three-point shooting.

The Tar Heels won impressively, 78-68, advancing to the championship game against Michigan's Fab Five. They were a win away from answering Duke's two straight titles with one of their own.

The next morning, another link was made between Frank Mc-Guire and Carolina when Vanderbilt coach Eddie Fogler, a former UNC player and assistant, accepted the head-coaching job at South Carolina. In the thirteen years since McGuire's forced retirement, the Gamecocks had reached the NCAA tournament only once and needed to restore respectability. Bobby Cremins wanted the job badly when he was at Appalachian State, but he had since gone to Georgia Tech and won three ACC championships.

Cremins, as all South Carolina fans remember with unease, took the Gamecocks job only to renege forty-eight hours later. Some USC fanatics put up a billboard with a line through Cremins' picture, and McGuire plaintively wanted to know if authorities ever caught the "assholes" who made a mockery of one of his players.

On Monday night, a record crowd of 64,151 began filling the Superdome, while a pep rally at the UNC team hotel was just ending. There, a rumor finally lost steam.

Jean Durham, wife of longtime radio voice of the Tar Heels Woody Durham, heard it first. Apparently, Dean Smith had delayed the taping of his radio interview for an hour so that he could meet with the team at the pregame meal. That was not part of his routine leading up to tip-off.

Michael Jordan, so the rumor went, had flown into town on his private jet. On the way, he first went to the West Coast to pick up James Worthy and Sam Perkins. Upon arriving in New Orleans, they joined Jimmy Black, who was on the Notre Dame staff and attending the annual coaches' convention, and Kansas assistant Matt Doherty, who stayed in town after the semifinals loss to watch the championship game.

Jordan, Worthy, Perkins, Black, and Doherty—the five starters on Carolina's 1982 NCAA championship team—were said to be having a pregame meal with the current Tar Heels, reminding them of their own Superdome experience and triumph. That all sounded at least plausible, given the tradition of the Tar Heels and the bond that existed among members of their fabled family.

It was fantasy. Although Black and Doherty were indeed there, sitting with a pompon-waving Roy Williams in the UNC section, the three NBA stars watched the game from their respective living rooms in Chicago, Los Angeles, and Seattle. Jordan had already begun his run of world championships with the Bulls and, as one Carolina official put it, would have "caused a riot" had he shown up in New Orleans that night.

In any case, stealing some thunder from Duke was probably all the inspiration the Tar Heels needed in New Orleans. The UNC players had overdosed on fans and media members who treated their neighbors from Durham like rock stars in the state *they* were supposed to own. They gave the back-to-back NCAA titlist Blue Devils credit in public, but privately admitted tiring of America's fawning love affair with them. Duke and Carolina shared the same press corps, and when one team's season ended the coverage just doubled on the other still in contention.

After the Tar Heels took a six-point halftime lead, Michigan rallied late to go ahead. However, Donald Williams was duplicating his performance against Kansas, nailing another five shots from behind the arc and finishing with 25 points for the second straight game. His four free throws preserved the 77-71 victory after Chris Webber's infamous technical foul in the last minute, which came after Webber called a timeout his team did not have.

Together with the panicky pass and turnover by Georgetown's Fred Brown that secured UNC's title in 1982, Smith had now won two NCAA tournaments with at least some help from freakish plays in the final seconds. "OK, call us lucky," Smith said after again trimming the Superdome nets, "but also call us national champions."

While the parties went deep into the night on both Bourbon and Franklin streets, the sixty-two-year-old Smith resisted a big celebration. He dined quietly with his family and a few friends. Early the next morning, he boarded a plane for Philadelphia and a recruiting visit to the home of high-school star Rasheed Wallace. He had learned long ago from Frank McGuire to leverage every advantage.

That evening, fewer than twenty-four hours after they had seen him on national TV, Rasheed and his mother, Jackie Wallace, fixed dinner for Smith and assistant coach Phil Ford. Not surprisingly, the 6'10" and immensely talented Wallace soon signed with the Tar Heels and joined Jerry Stackhouse and late commitment Jeff McInnis in a freshman class that made Carolina a strong favorite to repeat in 1994.

Smith was perhaps prouder of his over-achieving 1993 team than any of its predecessors. And after kidding with President Bill Clinton during the Tar Heels' visit to the White House, he was pressed into another protective role that he never envisioned. In July, James Jordan was murdered while sleeping in his car on the side of Route 74 in rural North Carolina.

Michael Jordan had become the most famous athlete in the world, having a month before led the Chicago Bulls to a third straight NBA championship. But he quickly returned a call from his college coach, and three days later Smith was at the private Wilmington airport to embrace Jordan when he arrived for the funeral.

"When my father was killed, Coach Smith and the rest of the Carolina family was there for me, my mother, brothers and sister," Jordan said. "I had been okay until I saw him. When I hugged him, I couldn't contain myself anymore." Michael broke down and wept on Smith's shoulder. From then on, he always included Smith in any statement about the most influential people in his life, as if Smith had assumed a surrogate father's role. On Smith's urging, Jordan did not skip their annual late-summer golf outing with other members of the Carolina inner circle. By then Smith was comfortable with being openly affectionate toward many of his former players and not only the stars.

The signing of Wallace, Stackhouse, and McInnis marked another philosophical shift for Smith. He made the subtle adjustment toward aggressively going after more great athletes whose stated goals were to reach the NBA as soon as possible. Though the change turned recruiting into more of a sweepstakes than a science, Smith's stature and UNC's exposure still made them hard to beat on players who would keep Carolina among the college basketball elite throughout the 1990s.

Nonetheless, a funny thing happened on the way to a repeat for the Tar Heels in 1994. Led by Montross, now a senior All-American, this was a team that had lost only one starter, Lynch, and was two deep at every position. It had outstanding experience and freshmen capable of superstardom. Yet it never came close to forming the chemistry that made the 1993 champs so special. It began with expectation, so often the root cause of trouble. Since preseason, when Stackhouse, Wallace, and McInnis had wowed fans at open pickup games at the Smith Center, speculation swirled that the freshmen were better than senior incumbents Kevin Salvadori, Brian Reese, and Phelps.

This chafed Smith because he lived by his loyalty and would never bench seniors who had led Carolina to a national championship. He could say "the best players will play" till the cows came home, but there had to be overpowering evidence and a spot open for a freshman to leapfrog a senior. He always came up with a reason, such as defensive fundamentals, to support a senior starter. He had done that for years, since 1981, when journeyman senior Pete Budko started over freshman star Sam Perkins for much of the season.

When the supposedly unbeatable 1994 Tar Heels lost a November game to 18th-ranked Massachusetts at Madison Square Garden, grumbling began inside and outside of the program. With Smith standing by his seniors, they won ten straight games and returned to No. 1 in the polls.

Then, they lost by 20 points at Georgia Tech, when Donald Williams came back from missing three games with a separated shoulder and went 0-for-8 from the field. That began a dismal stretch for the Most Outstanding Player of the 1993 Final Four in which he sat out six more games with injuries and his outside shooting dropped eight percentage points.

Carolina held the No. 1 ranking for one more week in the regular season and gave it up by losing again to Georgia Tech, this time at home. Tech was unranked, finished 7-9 in the ACC, and did not make the NCAA tournament. This deep-and-talented UNC team lost five ACC games and seemed especially motivated only when it saw Duke royal blue. The Tar Heels beat the Blue Devils twice, ruining Grant Hill's last home game in a dramatic 87-77 victory sealed by Wallace's flying monster dunk that shut down the Cameron Crazies for the night.

Smith became the second major college coach to reach 800 victories in a rare season when his coaching brilliance and recruiting success clashed. The No. 800 milestone came in the semifinals of the 1994 ACC tournament in Charlotte, when the Tar Heels tied Wake Forest on a last-second shot by sophomore Dante Calabria and then hung on to win in overtime. Carolina then captured

Smith's twelfth ACC title by beating Virginia, which had upset Duke in the semifinals, but the mood in the postgame locker room was not exactly joyous. The long season of infighting had tested Smith's patience as a coach and teacher.

"What do we have here?" he said one afternoon, sighing. "A group of young people all trying to do the best they can."

At one point, Smith checked in with Jane McGuire after her husband had suffered another stroke. When she said Frank could not speak but still understood what people told him, Smith joked, "Tell him I know what he went through after 1957." With three starters back from the national championship team and sophomore star Lee Shaffer, McGuire's 1958 Tar Heels lost six of their last fourteen games.

Carolina's confounding 1994 season continued with a win over little Liberty University in the first round of the NCAA tournament at Landover, Maryland. That was followed by a second-round battle against unranked-but-rugged Boston College.

The Tar Heels, now ranked No. 1 again, found a rallying point against the Eagles of the Big East, when BC's Danya Abrams knocked Phelps out of the game with a tomahawk foul midway through the second half. They fed off of their anger and rallied from 10 points down to tie the score on two clutch Montross free throws, but without Phelps they could not hang on and lost 75-72. Their shot at going back-to-back like Duke ended with a 28-7 record and snapped Smith's string of reaching consecutive Sweet Sixteens at thirteen.

Early in their second season together with the Indiana Pacers, Larry Brown and Donnie Walsh flew to Columbia, South Carolina, to attend the funeral and memorial service for McGuire, who passed away quietly on October 14, 1994, a month after turning eighty. They were surprised and renewed by the outpouring of love and praise for McGuire from former players and protégés and friends and, especially, the media.

They arrived from New York, North Carolina, and across the country. Every pew was filled, the mourners 500 strong.

From New York came Lou Carnesecca, who played baseball for McGuire at St. John's and later coached the Redmen to 526 victories; Al and Dick McGuire, the brothers unrelated to McGuire who both played for their namesake; and his former Xavier stars who became high school coaches and fed his recruiting pipeline, like Jack Curran and Dan Buckley.

From North Carolina came Dean Smith, Lee Shaffer, Billy Cunningham, York Larese, and all five starters from the 1957 team, who owed McGuire for their lives in the sport. Starting point guard Tommy Kearns had been on a business trip to Ireland when Jane McGuire called his hotel to tell him it was only a matter of days. Kearns left his traveling party and flew home.

From Philadelphia came Al Attles, Guy Rodgers, Tom Gola, and Wilt "the Stilt" Chamberlain, who "jumped" against the 5'11" Kearns to start the 1957 national championship game and scored 100 points in a 1962 NBA game—both memorable moments that McGuire engineered.

From South Carolina, McGuire's final stop, came Bobby Cremins and a dozen more of his ardent ex-players, including his first African-American recruits, Casey Manning and Alex English; other friends who knew him; and people who wished they had. The dignitaries on hand included two governors, fourteen years after McGuire had coached his last game in their state.

Sportswriters around the nation penned columns about the man who earned 549 victories at three schools, taking two to the national title game and all three to the No. 1 ranking in college basketball. Their words gave pause to people who remembered him.

"They must be careful when they lay Frank McGuire's body out for burial," wrote Ron Green Sr. of the *Charlotte Observer*, "that the lapels of his suit lie just right. The neck tie is expensive and has a perfect knot.

"And the hair must be combed just so. Otherwise, it won't look like him. Frank McGuire always looked like a million bucks."

Green was one of many great scribes who waxed eloquently about how McGuire "cursed refs with clenched teeth so that he looked to the fans like he was smiling." He used his "Irish blarney and soul of a New York street cop to produce some wonderful teams and helped make basketball what it is in the Carolinas."

Thirty-seven years had passed since McGuire's Miracle, but those who lived through it called the 32-0 season the singular most important sports accomplishment in the history of a state and region. This changed not only the way North Carolinians regarded basketball but created a story stranger than fiction. "To complete an undefeated season and win the national championship in triple overtime against Wilt Chamberlain—no game ever played in the Carolinas had more of a lasting impact, a lasting glow," Green wrote.

Danny Lotz, one of the native New Yorkers who settled in Raleigh after graduation and married the Reverend Billy Graham's daughter, said McGuire was a life-changer for many long before Carolina won those thirty-two games, *the last two in six overtimes*.

"He brought us to North Carolina and the South, so far away from home," Lotz said. "But Coach, and his wife, Pat, gave us so much support. We were over at their house often. I'll never forget the days playing with his dog, a boxer he called Rebound. They made us feel we had a home."

To hear McGuire's former players talk, they regarded him as the ultimate father figure who began the tradition of the Carolina Basketball Family. "He just made you want to play for him," Rosenbluth said. "He did so much for all of us, you never wanted to let him down."

Smith, the pupil who was just four days from beginning his thirty-fourth season as McGuire's successor, served as one of his pallbearers. "I learned so many things from him, it's hard to pick out one," he said. "I learned about dealing with people by just watching him in his office, at games, in everyday situations. He was a great psychologist and a great leader who would have been a great football coach, a good president of a company. The people who worked under him—assistants, players, secretaries, janitors, everyone—all wanted to please him."

Smith has long pondered what path he might have followed without McGuire's influence. "I wouldn't be in North Carolina, except for Frank asking me to come as his assistant," Smith said. "I had intended to be an assistant at Kansas after the Air Force. I am grateful to him for that as well as the many things he taught me as a coach and about life. I was most lucky to be one of his dear friends for these thirty-six years. Anything I am or hope to be, I owe to him."

Through McGuire's actions more than his words, Smith learned that coaching was overrated without good players. With assistant Smith available to write practice plans and run drills, McGuire rarely missed a chance to take off and recruit for a day or two. The message was clear to Smith that organization, discipline, and strategy were important, but not as much as having more talent than the other team.

Smith recalled how McGuire played that card with every kid he had, bolstering his confidence by asking, "Why do you think I recruited you?" That also became the underpinning of Smith's philosophy: Successful recruiting is the foundation of any sustained program.

On the day McGuire was buried, Smith said, "There's a great deal of sadness. He was a dear friend, very loyal. Loyalty is a great trait, but with Frank it was number one."

From his childhood days when "policemen and longshoremen stuck up for each other," McGuire tried to develop a feeling of group loyalty within every team he coached and every organization for which he worked. It became the air he breathed.

He passed it on to Smith, who had a different background but similar standards. Eventually, Roy Williams lived and worked by the same credos.

Loyalty, in fact, has been the adhesive holding the Carolina Basketball Family together for more than fifty years. The careers of caretakers McGuire, Smith, Guthridge, and Williams, plus honored members like Larry Brown, have this commonality: *Sometimes the subject of controversy over style of play and claims they underachieved with overwhelming talent, all remained fiercely loyal to each other and nurtured those who wanted to begin or maintain careers in the game.*

From McGuire, Smith passed on to his disciples the practices of protecting and advancing family members. He helped some outsiders but always took care of his own first.

Smith labored to land part-time and summer jobs for his players so they could stay in Chapel Hill and remain on pace for graduation while bonding with their teammates. His program made millions to justify chartered jets for road trips and the finest hotels. He chose the jets so his players could get back to school the next day, and he chose five-star hotels because he wanted to indulge them. All of the perks helped recruiting and made positive impressions on young men. If their eyes were open, they saw the world they would enter after graduation.

A believer in tough love, Smith made sure they all studied and went to class and occasionally suspended someone who did not. Two other ways to make him angry were not hustling and being late to practices and appointments. He was known for honesty and integrity. He believed there was always a right way and preached that there were no shortcuts to success.

These were often the principles behind his Thought of the Day, with which he opened every practice and made every player remember and recite at a later time. It might have been a famous quote, a bit of ancient philosophy, or something from the national news he wanted his team to know—and think—about.

Highly compassionate, Smith lamented injuries that cost his players time on the court. He was known to don a surgical gown and mask to observe serious procedures.

After graduation, former Tar Heels remained in the fold and continued to rely on their coach for recommendations, even those who did not have a chance to play professionally. Smith kept track of them all and seemed to know whenever illness struck or some misfortune befell their families. In one such example, Smith years ago assured John Stokes, who filmed UNC games and practices, that his job was safe after Stokes lost a hand in a home accident.

He tried to move his assistant coaches along in the profession, but not until he found them what he thought to be the right jobs. After Larry Brown left to play pro basketball in 1967, John Lotz stayed for six years (before going to Florida), Eddie Fogler for thirteen (Wichita State) and Roy Williams for ten. Bill Guthridge turned down at least three head-coaching offers and remained until Smith himself retired, timing it to allow only Guthridge the chance to succeed him. A much longer list of former players benefited from Smith's valuable references and went on to coach at the high school and small college levels.

All of them used something they learned from Smith. During his third year at Kansas, Roy Williams once left star guard Adonis Jordan back in Lawrence because he missed the team bus to the airport. The Jayhawks lost the game but used the incident to rededicate themselves and reach the Final Four. The Adonis story became so famous that future players always showed up ten to fifteen minutes early before any bus departure.

Besides the emphasis on punctuality, many of Smith's ideas and innovations were copied by other coaches and spread nationally. He was the first to start his seniors, whether walk-on or star, in their last home games on Senior Day. Every stall or spread tactic became a "version of the Four Corners," according to telecasters.

Smith's players began the method of back-tapping missed free throws, and his defenders trapped the ball handler to the baseline and corner instead of the longtime tenet of "forcing to the sideline." You still see both NBA and college players pointing to the passer as credit for the assist. Off the court, Smith pushed the coaches association and NCAA to recognize graduation rates, and eventually those schools that ignored academics risked losing scholarships.

For an icon who seemed always in the public eye, Smith protected his privacy fiercely. Married twice and the father of five, he managed to keep his family members and their personal lives out of the press. He lived in the same home on the southwest side of Chapel Hill for more than thirty years, but few people knew its location. Though sometimes as candid as Smith was cautious, Roy Williams has steadfastly refused to tell television networks where his wife, Wanda, sits at games so they would not put her on camera.

This great contradiction of publicity and privacy left Carolina Basketball somewhat insulated for almost fifty years. McGuire, Smith, Guthridge, and even the ebullient Williams were never glad-handers, backslappers, or partygoers. Their small cliques and golf foursomes were proud to be buddies and confidants but never spoke of these times together. Smith's main foursome, for example, resulted in a very private, forty-year friendship between Smith, his psychiatrist friend Earl Somers, one-time UNC chancellor Chris Fordham, and Simon Terrell, the husband of his first secretary.

Williams' ultra-tight inner circle has not changed much in years, expanding only guardedly, from Carolina to Kansas. He had native Tar Heels on his original staff at Kansas, helped find college and NBA jobs for former UNC and Kansas players, and brought all of his KU-connected coaches with him to Chapel Hill in 2003.

This importing of Kansans only strengthened an undeniable bond between two states and state universities that began more than a half century before when McGuire left New York for North Carolina a month after his St. John's team beat the Jayhawks and reserved Smith for the national championship.

Like Williams, Larry Brown's devotees have grown beyond native Carolinians, and his link to players, coaches, and administrators on almost every NBA team numbered into the dozens. UNC brethren have always topped his protected list—from Doug Moe and Donnie Walsh in the early years to helping save the modest coaching careers of John Kuester, Phil Ford, Dave Hanners, and Pat Sullivan in more recent times. Kuester got his chance to be an NBA head coach with the Detroit Pistons in the summer of 2009.

After losing four seniors off of the loaded 1994 team, Smith played three guards and no true center, rarely substituted, and shielded his starters with a clever zone defense more predicated on guarding the basket than stealing the ball. The tight-knit team would have made McGuire proud because it was undersized and overmatched against more than half the schedule. However, it had the confidence and killer instinct to win twenty-one of its thirty-four games by 9 points or more.

Led by Calabria, who shot 50 percent from three-point range all season, the 1995 Tar Heels were as fun to coach and watch as the 1994 team had not been. They finished in a four-way tie for first place and lost in the ACC tournament final to Wake Forest in overtime after Rasheed Wallace went down with a sprained ankle. Then, they played one of the most brilliant games of Smith's career in the NCAA South Regional championship at Birmingham, Alabama.

An underdog to bigger and deeper Kentucky, Carolina stood up to Rick Pitino's Wildcats from the opening tip—with Wallace and UK's Walter McCarty nearly tangling at one point—and broke open a close game by executing a superb spread offense.

The 74-61 victory was as much a testament to everything Smith learned from McGuire as any game he ever coached. Without toughness, tenacity, and teaching, the Tar Heels could not have won. The outcome also ruined the victory party the cocksure Pitino had already planned for a downtown Birmingham restaurant.

With Duke's Krzyzewski sitting out the season under doctor's orders, Smith regained the mantle as America's leading coach by taking this talented-but-threadbare team all the way to his third Final Four of the 1990s. Pundits automatically installed the Tar Heels as the favorite to win another NCAA title, but their lack of depth showed against defending champion Arkansas in the semifinals. Jerry Stackhouse suffered a bruised thigh on the opening tip and Calabria missed all seven of his three-pointers, which dropped his season percentage under fifty. The Hogs won 75-68 at the Kingdome in Seattle, with President Bill Clinton, an Arkansas native and the self-proclaimed "Head Hog," watching from a suite.

The loss did little to diminish what might have been Smith's best coaching job to date, producing a 28-6 record and showcasing Stackhouse and Wallace so well that they were the first Carolina players to leave UNC for the NBA after their sophomore seasons. Stackhouse went third overall to Philadelphia followed by Wallace to Washington in the draft, giving Smith twenty-four of his eventual twenty-seven first-round selections.

The early departures left the 1996 Tar Heels too young to challenge Wake Forest in Tim Duncan's junior season and Georgia Tech in Stephon Marbury's one-and-done. With Carolina's first-round loss to Clemson in the ACC tournament and another second-round NCAA ouster (to Texas Tech) came the inevitable questions about the sixty-five-year-old Smith's longevity.

Complicating matters was the chase to break Adolph Rupp's record for the most coaching victories in college basketball history. As he closed to within fifty of Rupp's 876, Smith claimed the milestone meant only that he had coached at Carolina for thirty-five years. He once blurted out that he would quit before ever getting a chance to pass Rupp, prompting many former players to ask him *not* to retire.

It looked like the 1997 season was in serious jeopardy when the Tar Heels lost their first three ACC games for the first time ever and fell to No. 22 in the national polls. They should have been playing better, and Smith knew it. Sophomores Antawn Jamison, Vince Carter, and Ademola Okulaja, junior Shammond

271

Williams, and senior center Serge Zwikker added up to one of the best lineups in the league, if not the country.

Smith showed remarkable patience with the team, which had to rally at home from nine points down with two minutes to play against N.C. State to avoid losing its fourth straight ACC game. Keeping slick freshman point guard Ed Cota on the bench and by his side to observe the game's first few minutes, Smith gradually molded the Tar Heels into perhaps his most efficient offensive team. They wound up shooting 50 percent or better for 15 out of 16 games, won 16 straight (including the ACC tournament and NCAA East Regional) on the way to Smith's fourth Final Four in seven years and his eleventh overall.

By then, of course, Smith had caught and passed Rupp as the major college coach with the most career victories. After the Tar Heels defeated Colorado in the second round of the NCAA East Regional in Winston-Salem, for his 877th career win, dozens of former players and their families surprised Smith outside the UNC locker room at the Lawrence Joel Coliseum in an emotional re-union that touched the teary-eyed coach.

When too many shots finally stopped falling, Carolina's 28-7 season ended with a loss to Arizona in the national semifinals at Indianapolis. And, although the basketball world did not know it yet, so had Smith's career.

Larry Brown was in the RCA Dome that evening, winding down his fourth season with the Indiana Pacers after twice lead-ing the team and Reggie Miller into the NBA Eastern finals, but giving no hint that he was about ready to move on again. After the Pacers missed the playoffs in 1997, Brown said he had taken the franchise as far as he could and left to coach at Philadelphia. His new challenge was to convert Allen Iverson from a ball hog into a team player. To succeed, he would need all of McGuire's guile and Smith's fatherly touch.

As he had for four years at Indiana, Brown held his first Sixers' preseason training camp in Chapel Hill. He and Smith visited often and talked basketball, doodling plays on sheets of paper and restaurant napkins. Smith always marveled at Brown's boundless enthusiasm during the morning and evening workouts and never let on that he was having trouble working up much enthusiasm about another season at UNC.

With Brown in town and staying with his team at the Omni Hotel, Smith pulled his famous October surprise on the basketball world. A week before practice began for the 1997–1998 season—which would have been his thirty-seventh as coach of the Tar Heels—he announced the end of his Hall of Fame career. Smith retired with 879 victories, thirty assorted ACC titles, two national championships, one NIT crown, and an Olympic gold medal. He posted twenty-two seasons with at least twenty-five victories and made thirteen consecutive trips to the NCAA tournament Sweet Sixteen (1981–1993), both NCAA records when he retired.

Maybe the most telling statistic of Smith's success, and indicative of the dynasty he built, was Carolina's road rage in the ACC over his last thirty-one seasons—going 139-76, winning 65 percent of its games in hostile settings. Duke, for example, went 89-125 over that same span, including four straight seasons in the 1970s without winning an ACC road game.

Records and statistics do no justice to Smith's off-the-court contributions and the lives he touched. His dedication to racial equality spanned his career, from helping to desegregate a Chapel Hill restaurant in the 1950s, to breaking UNC's color line for athletics in the '60s, to the full integration of his program in the '70s, to his controversial defense of what he considered a racial slur against his black players ("J. R. Can't Reid") in the '80s. He cared not what the critics said about his sometimes over-the-top reactions, only that the public might recognize bigotry in a different light.

Brown called an old friend in a daze the night the news leaked out. "I'm sick to my stomach," Brown said. "I can't imagine college basketball without him. He's meant so much to the game. You can talk about [John] Wooden, [Frank] Leahy, [Vince] Lombardi, but he has to be the greatest team sport coach of all time. I'm happy for him, but I feel bad for the game of basketball."

Brown accompanied Smith into his farewell news conference, fit for a president or governor. It attracted a throng of one hundred reporters and film crews while hundreds more waited outside. Until his voice cracked at the end as he talked about his players, Smith was the most composed person in the room. He had thought about his decision for weeks and did not waver as the new season approached. He was asked how he would like to be remembered. Smiling at the start and biting his lip as he went on, Smith gave it a shot: "He knew a little basketball, did a good job, loved all of his players and received great loyalty in return."

Smith anointed as head coach his longtime assistant Bill Guthridge, the ice-chewing and competent second banana who helped define the program for three decades. Then Smith said modestly and somewhat amusingly that, aside from him not being on the bench and at practices, nothing about Carolina basketball would change.

Displaying the loyalty by which he led his life, Smith bequeathed to Guthridge a loaded team with juniors Jamison and Carter captaining the preseason No. 1 pick. Had Smith stayed one more year, he could have tied John Wooden's record for twelve

Final Fours and Bob Knight's for twenty-eight NCAA Tournament appearances, but that meant nothing to him. He was tired of what coaching at Carolina had become—a monster of media requests, personal appearances, and other off-court demands on his time. If he could have just stayed in the Smith Center and taught the game, he might have coached a few more seasons.

The move also allowed him to dictate Carolina's succession plan, providing Guthridge with a serious increase in salary, added retirement benefits, and a substantial stipend for weekly radio and TV shows, plus the lion's share of what Nike paid UNC's primary head coaches. However long Guthridge stayed, four assistant coaches and an office staff would all have their jobs. If the Heels kept winning, who could argue with Smith's thinking?

As expected, Carolina got off to another great start with Guthridge regularly referring to his first squad as "Dean's Team." Fine and good, but Guthridge was hugely responsible for holding together thirty of Smith's teams. He was the glue, an organizational master offsetting Smith's occasional moodiness and creative swings.

The 1998 Tar Heels held the No. 1 ranking three different times on the way to another ACC championship and No. 1 seed in the NCAA tournament, where they survived three tough games to reach San Antonio. It was Carolina's fifth Final Four of the 1990s, a sure sign that Smith had left the program on solid footing.

But they again shot miserably in the national semifinals, losing by six points to seventh-ranked Utah. Smith agonized from the CBS broadcast platform at the Alamodome, where he served as a decidedly uncomfortable analyst. After the game that ended Carolina's season at 34-4, Jamison kissed the NCAA logo on the floor. Two weeks later, he and Carter exercised their rite of passage at UNC and gave up their last season of eligibility. They became two more of Smith's first-round NBA picks.

Guthridge, who was consensus national coach of the year in 1998, lost to Duke three times in his second season and finished six games behind the Blue Devils (who were the first to go undefeated against a sixteen-game ACC schedule). Still, fifty-eight victories in his first two seasons set an NCAA record.

Insisting he would stay all five years of his contract and "might even ask for a few more," Guthridge clearly was battling an uncertain future. Joseph Forte was Carolina's only five-star recruit since Smith retired, while Duke continued landing its fair share of high school All-Americans.

Out in Lawrence, Kansas, Roy Williams was having more trouble than usual convincing prospects he would coach them all four years. Reports continued to surface that Williams soon would succeed Guthridge, and the fact that he showed up at Carolina home games fueled the speculation. The rumormongers dismissed the truth. Williams was in fact there to see his son, Scott, a walk-on guard for Guthridge, and his daughter, Kimberly, a member of the UNC dance team.

Larry Brown had put up only his third losing record in 1998 before introducing Iverson to team play and turning the Sixers into a playoff contender in the strike-shortened 1999 NBA season. Forever fighting the off-court controversy that engulfed Iverson, Brown's first love remained Carolina and college basketball. He had long harbored a dream of some day coaching the Tar Heels.

He could not escape that Carolina connection, even if he had wanted to. In September of 1999, for example, Brown, Smith, and virtually the entire 1957 team attended the first Frank McGuire Awards, which honored high-school coaches in metropolitan New York. Brown had been recruited by McGuire, played for Smith, and through his various coaching stops knew virtually every person in the large banquet room at the New York Athletic Club. Naturally, curiosity abounded over the future of UNC Basketball.

Guthridge retired on the last day of June 2000 after rallying his Carolina team that was unranked in February and March to his second Final Four in his first three seasons, one of only two coaches to do that (Ohio State's Fred Taylor was the other). The 2000 Tar Heels won four straight NCAA tournament games before losing the national semifinals to Florida at Indianapolis, and finished 22-14.

Roy Williams, who in twelve seasons had already earned more than 300 victories, elected to stay at Kansas because he had promised to coach his latest class of recruits for all four years. He still felt, ten years later, that he had betrayed the kids he left behind at Owen High School.

The decision shocked Carolina fans and much of college basketball, since Williams had been expected to come back whenever summoned. After all, it was home and an even better job than Kansas. The Tar Heels' tradition and their exposure of playing virtually every game on television with more than twenty each season shown nationally made it so.

What can be best described as a big misunderstanding—everyone in the Carolina camp assumed Williams was returning while he has always insisted there was no guarantee—created something of a vacuum. UNC was left with no discernible second choice to become head coach at the university.

Brown, meanwhile, told Smith he would take a $4 million pay cut from the NBA and move to Chapel Hill. Despite the probations he had incurred at UCLA and Kansas, Brown owned a .744 winning percentage in seven college seasons and clearly wanted to try again. But due to those two controversial coaching stints,

UNC never officially offered him the job. Instead, the university turned to Matt Doherty, the former Tar Heel who had just finished his first season as head coach at Notre Dame.

In an ironic twist of irony, UNC hired Doherty for his own connection to the Carolina Basketball Family, only to be disappointed with Doherty's apparent insensitivity to many of the family's members. He did not retain any assistant coaches and made some sudden changes in office personnel. There was anxiety in the air almost from the beginning.

In 2001, Doherty led his inherited Heels to eighteen straight victories and a No. 1 national ranking, but his impetuosity and temper were sowing the seeds of bigger trouble. From the start, Doherty did his imported assistants (none of whom had any ties to UNC) a disservice by not finding them less-pressurized positions elsewhere and keeping a Carolina coach or two.

However, Doherty maintained the Tar Heels' fifty-year linkage by recruiting and signing three players who would be at the core of their next national championship team. Raymond Felton, Sean May, and Rashad McCants were bound for Chapel Hill regardless of the head coach, but they became part of Doherty's legacy when they signed in the fall of 2001 before the start of Carolina's first losing season in 40 years. If they had waited until after the 8-20 disaster, one of them or all of them might have gone somewhere else.

The same season, Brown won his 750th professional game and led the Sixers (who were basically Iverson and a bunch of role players) to a 56-26 record and into the NBA Finals, where they lost to the defending champion Los Angeles Lakers in five games. He won the NBA coach of the year award in a landslide.

Brown's star-crossed career continued through his induction into the Basketball Hall of Fame in 2002, handling the mercurial Iverson for six seasons, and his ill-fated appointment as coach of the USA men's team for the 2004 Olympic Games in Athens. And what was to be his last year in Philly coincided with unprecedented controversy at his alma mater, putting Brown's name in the sports headlines again.

Doherty resigned under pressure in March of 2003, following only twenty-seven victories in his last two seasons and the snapping of three sacred Dean Smith streaks. Gone were unbroken strings of NCAA bids, top-three finishes in the ACC, and twenty-win seasons. Brown was again briefly rumored for the Carolina coaching job, but Roy Williams remained UNC's first choice.

This time, Williams made the agonizing decision. He left Kansas with 418 career victories and an .805 winning percentage and returned home.

The Tar Heels actually were lucky that KU athletic director and Williams mentor Bob Frederick had been forced into retirement, leading to a series of controversial changes at the school. Suddenly, Williams' dream job seemed more like a nightmare. Kansas had hired egotistical Al Bohl as its new athletic director, and Williams began reconsidering his commitment to stay at Kansas through retirement. When Carolina called again after the Jayhawks lost the 2003 national championship game to Syracuse, even some of Williams' assistant coaches and support staff with Kansas roots urged him to make a fresh start at Carolina.

"The family business needed me," he said upon arriving in Chapel Hill, wearing a Kansas tie at his welcome-home press conference. He promised the distraught players he inherited that if they listened to him they would be as successful as the Jayhawks had been under his lead.

A month later, Philadelphia lost to Detroit in the semifinals of the 2003 Eastern Conference playoffs. Brown resigned abruptly and then agreed to coach none other than the same Pistons.

Brown already had tapped Williams as one of his assistants for the Olympic team. On Memorial Day weekend they both left their new workplaces for San Juan, Puerto Rico, and the FIBA Americas Olympic qualifying tournament.

They never had worked together, since Brown was long gone from Chapel Hill before Williams arrived as a UNC student. They met when Brown coached the Carolina Cougars, and Williams followed his career closely from there. Even before Williams succeeded Brown at Kansas, they spent time at Dean Smith's annual alumni coaching clinic, when Carolina guys congregated each summer for basketball chalk talk, a round of golf, and dinners over a few days.

Their players on the 2003 Olympic qualifying team—mostly veteran NBA all-stars with size and outside shooting—swept through ten games in Puerto Rico by an average of 31 points, making them eligible for pool play in Athens the following summer.

At the time, Brown seemed likely to receive the same kind of accolades that eventually went to Mike Krzyzewski in 2008. As an Olympic player and coach of various USA teams, Brown had a 43-3 international record heading into the 2004 Summer Games. With his pro pedigree, he looked like the perfect coach to bring home the gold from Greece.

After Puerto Rico, both Williams and Brown returned to their new teams. Williams was eager to turn around the struggling Tar Heels, and Brown was excited about taking over likely the most talented group of players he had seen in eight professional stops.

Carolina's returnees often had been portrayed as malcontents who deserved some blame for Matt Doherty's debacle. Although several players were unhappy with Doherty, and might have transferred had he stayed, Williams found them all to be quality people. He believed he could help them understand that achieving as a group was better for each individual in the long run.

Force-feeding defense while trying to gain the new players' respect and confidence, Williams experienced the most difficult season of his coaching career. Before Valentine's Day 2004, the Tar Heels had lost three of their last four games, were 14-7, were ranked 14th in the country, and were on the bubble for an NCAA tournament bid.

"It was very hard to get everyone at the university, including the former players, pointing in the same direction," said Williams. He had scheduled an alumni reunion in the middle of the season and was doing all he could to soften the hard feelings caused by the Doherty implosion. He was also fighting off his own anxiety over the broken link with the Kansas program he had loved and left after fifteen years.

"Like some Carolina fans were mad at me when I didn't come back in 2000, a lot of people I thought were my friends from Kansas were mad at me when I left there," he said. "But I came back with the goal of doing the best job possible here. So we had to focus on one thing, moving ahead."

During the 2003–2004 season, Carolina never won more than two straight ACC games, lost narrowly to Duke twice, and finished fifth in a league that had only one great team (Krzyzewski's Blue Devils at 31-6). But eighteen victories and having Williams on the bench were enough to earn UNC's first trip to the NCAA tournament in three years as an eighth seed. The Tar Heels fell to Texas in the second round at Denver and ended up 19-11—only the second time that Williams had not won twenty games as a college coach, falling one victory short in his first years at Kansas and Carolina.

The most painful season of Williams' coaching career had one more kick in the gut to it. In May 2004, his father Babe died after a prolonged illness, during which Roy saw him a dozen times and made peace with the alcoholic father who long ago left his family impoverished. They shared one last cathartic exchange when father congratulated son for all he had accomplished.

"I learned a lot from you," Roy said, smiling.

"I didn't teach you one god-damned thing," Babe snorted back.

"Yeah, I just saw what you did, and I did the opposite," Roy said.

They laughed about it and when Babe died Roy at least felt they had reached some sort of closure. He went back to basketball less angry in that corner of his heart.

Meanwhile, Larry Brown had relied on Dean Smith's positive recommendation of the volatile Rasheed Wallace to complete the trade that turned Detroit into a serious contender for the NBA title. Smith assured Brown that Wallace practiced hard and wanted to win. He also suggested looking beyond Wallace's on-court outbursts, saying he was a vocal leader and would not hurt team chemistry. The Pistons suddenly were the new beast of the NBA East heading into the playoffs.

They rolled unselfishly through the Eastern Conference tournament and shocked the Lakers in five games of the 2004 NBA Finals. Brown became the only coach to ever win NCAA and NBA championships. His happiness was sobered by the knowledge that his Olympic team had fallen apart and he would have precious little practice time to train another.

The fact that his squad had *already* eroded went largely unnoticed. Brown, over the next three months, went from winning the NBA crown by "playing the right way" to becoming the scapegoat of his Olympic team's collapse in Athens. This failure gave Krzyzewski almost single-handed control over USA Basketball in the future.

What happened in Greece hardly repudiated the Carolina

system Brown used in the NBA, no matter what may have been written and said in the media. Brown's peripatetic past overshadowed the facts.

His original Olympic roster had an average age of more than twenty-five, and among them were some of the biggest NBA names. Of the twelve players he had in San Juan, nine decided to leave the team for reasons ranging from nagging injuries to fear of terrorism.

Only Iverson, with whom Brown had a workable relationship, Tim Duncan, and Richard Jefferson stuck it out. Gone were outside shooters Ray Allen, Vince Carter, and Tracy McGrady; established inside scorers Jermaine O'Neal, Elton Brand, and Kenyon Martin; and experienced leaders Jason Kidd and Mike Bibby. Nick Collison, an NBA rookie and Kansas All-American forward who Williams had coached for four years, also quit.

The hastily reconfigured team now averaged only twenty-three years of age and included iffy replacements such as the selfish Stephon Marbury and teenage NBA rookies LeBron James and Carmelo Anthony. The latter two had become superstars in America but were not prepared to be role players across the globe.

The 2004 Olympic effort from America included a strong NBA influence. Commissioner David Stern wanted his fresh faces—James and Anthony—on the team for the international experience and publicity. Brown had only marginal input on the replacement players.

With barely two weeks of practice and only six exhibition games, the revamped and weakened USA team badly needed another qualifying tournament. The Americans wound up a disjointed and dispirited bunch. Brown clashed with players like Marbury and the immature James and Anthony. The rookies did not want to work as hard as the veterans because they figured they were not going to play as many minutes.

Brown no longer had seasoned vets accepting supporting roles, like Brand, who shot 60 percent coming off the bench in Puerto Rico. The team would have been far better off filling in with lesser-known NBA reserves than spoiled superstars who had never been out of the spotlight.

In 1976, critics piled on Dean Smith for putting four UNC and seven ACC players on the USA squad. But those were collegians who knew and respected him and would not dare squawk about anything. Working hard on the way to the gold medal was a foregone conclusion. But had the Americans not survived a couple of close games in Montreal, Smith would have come home a failure and perhaps never lived down his 1976 Olympic experience.

Brown had precious little time to get the reconstructed 2004 Olympic team ready. In San Juan, "we beat Argentina by 33 points, and it wasn't even that close," Roy Williams said. "We had the best players and the best character guys, and we won easily. In 2004, the NBA put a couple of kids on the team who weren't ready. LeBron was a year out of high school, and Carmelo didn't want to be a role player. We traded Jason Kidd for Stephon Marbury. The negative things being said about Larry just weren't fair."

Brown could not get his Olympians to "play the right way" or any way together, and they lost three games in Athens. Two of the defeats came at the hands of Puerto Rico and Argentina, countries his original team had thumped four times in 2003 by a combined 83 points. Brown returned from Greece despondent and furious that his dream had turned into a disaster of petulant players and red, white, and blue red tape.

The downfall led USA Basketball to reorganize and put veteran NBA owner and general manager Jerry Colangelo solely in charge for the next go-around. Colangelo's pick as head coach was Krzyzewski, who was given almost single-handed control of an interchangeable NBA all-star squad for three years leading up to the Beijing Olympics in 2008.

The Olympic controversy made Williams very happy to be back on American soil, coaching his own team again. He had his top seven players back and added freshman forward Marvin Williams. Under his tutelage for a full year, the talented and tougher Tar Heels got better and better as the 2005 season progressed—especially on defense—and they made history.

Playing without McCants, their second-leading scorer, they rallied to beat Duke (with a closing 11-0 run) in the finale to win UNC's first outright ACC regular-season championship since 1993. Williams brought out a ladder and had the team cut down the Smith Center nets.

The win also secured a No. 1 seed in the NCAA East Regional. There, Carolina ran through Oakland and Iowa State at the Charlotte Coliseum and then survived Villanova and Wisconsin at the Carrier Dome in Syracuse to reach the 2005 Final Four at the Edward Jones Dome in St. Louis.

After his team rallied from a poor first half against Michigan State, Roy Williams also joined Frank McGuire (St. John's and UNC) and Larry Brown (UCLA and Kansas) as the only coaches to take two different teams to the NCAA championship game. Then he returned glory to Carolina basketball by capturing his school's fourth NCAA championship, and his first, when the Tar Heels held off Illinois—disappointing 30,000 orange-clad Illini fans, many of whom had crossed the Mississippi River into Missouri.

The Tar Heels cavorted on the podium, stripped the nets and watched "One Shining Moment." They were joined in their victorious locker room by Carolina icons Dean Smith and Michael Jordan, who alternately hugged and shook hands with every player and coach who had helped restore their legacy.

"That team had in mind two things, winning a national championship and several of them getting to the NBA," Williams said. "With those two goals together, they figured out, 'For me to reach the second one, I have the best chance if we do the first one.' As the season went along, those kids believed it more and more."

Final Four Most Outstanding Player Sean May's big bear hug with Williams as the 75-70 victory over Illinois ended was as much in relief as jubilation. He and his teammates had endured far more than three or four years of college, and carpe diem became their motto. The three juniors decided to get out on top, refusing to risk another fall from grace, and who could blame them? Nobody did.

Williams had now returned North Carolina to the blue chip status it enjoyed during most of the last fifty years with McGuire, Smith, and Guthridge. The Tar Heels also were inching closer to Duke, which had controlled the famous rivalry for ten years by beating Carolina in fifteen of the last eighteen meetings.

By contrast, Brown's post-Olympic gloom continued. He coached the Pistons to the seventh game of the 2005 NBA Finals before losing to San Antonio and his close friend Gregg Popovich. Then he spent one disastrous season with the New York Knicks, going 23-59 and settling his $50 million contract while taking a year off from coaching for the first time in his career.

The failure wasn't much fun for a native New Yorker like Brown. He was especially humiliated because James Dolan, owner of Cablevision, the Knicks, New York Rangers, and Madison Square Garden, sided with general manager Isiah Thomas over the Hall of Fame coach. Thomas's tenure turned out to be even more of a disaster.

Jordan, who had become Charlotte Bobcats managing partner,

spoke with Smith regularly and tried to bring Brown in midway through the 2007 season to replace retiring coach Bernie Bickerstaff. However, Brown had just moved his family from New York to Philadelphia and gone to work in the Sixers' front office. Jordan instead hired former NBA assistant Sam Vincent, then fired him after Charlotte finished 32-50 in 2007–2008 and ranked twenty-fourth among thirty NBA teams in home attendance.

Of course, Jordan knew college basketball was still king in his home state. Nothing short of an NBA contender would change that for Charlotte. What other choice did he have for a pro franchise hemorrhaging millions and in jeopardy of failing in the Queen City for a second time in the decade? He tabbed Brown as his head coach. The Bobcats were scrambling to revive interest in the NBA since divisive owner George Shinn moved the Hornets to New Orleans in 2002.

Now Brown would be challenged to rebuild the Bobcats roster, stabilize the team's psyche, and restore some goodwill in the Charlotte region. The move also was personal for the sixty-eight-year-old Brown.

After playing for Frank McGuire and Dean Smith at UNC, and being succeeded by Roy Williams at Kansas, what looked like his last stop closed the circle on his honored-if-controversial career. Coming in a state where he landed his first coaching job forty years earlier, Brown found himself surrounded by blood—as well as basketball—family.

Smith, Williams, and Chapel Hill were only two hours down the road. Brown's two daughters were raising his five grandchildren in Charlotte, and his one-hundred-and-two-year-old mother, Ann, lived there in a retirement home.

The Bobcats front office also included Jordan's old Carolina teammate and roommate Buzz Peterson, the director of player personnel, and president Fred Whitfield, another UNC alum. Alongside Brown on the bench were Smith disciples Phil Ford and Dave Hanners. On the court were Williams' former star players Ray Felton and Sean May.

After more than forty-five years crisscrossing the country, Larry Brown was back where he started. Through turmoil and triumph, his Tar Heel bonds had not been broken.

9

The Recruiting Game

FOR years, the *coaching* of Carolina's head coach has been open to debate. After all, second-guessing is considered a God-given right among most basketball fans.

Frank McGuire admittedly wasn't much of an X-and-O guy; in fact, he did not bother with many details. He left most of that to Buck Freeman at first and then Dean Smith while he went recruiting. The Irishman believed that coaching was overrated without talent.

Smith, some said, tinkered too much with the game and its nuances. But once he got his program rolling, he had the players to experiment all he wanted. Former N.C. State coach Norman Sloan put it bluntly one day when asked about his adversary twenty-five miles down Tobacco Road. "Dean Smith is a great recruiter," he said, "period."

Roy Williams fuels his own argument by saying he'll never be another Dean Smith. He owes "ninety-five percent" of what he knows to Smith, yet Williams admits he's too stubborn to try a lot that hasn't already worked for one of his own teams.

There was no doubt, however, that Williams could bring in the players—with even more success than Smith and perhaps more than McGuire, one of the game's greatest recruiters. Having talent remains the single strongest plank in the Carolina foundation.

McGuire taught Smith, who in turn showed Williams how to recruit strategically and eventually more effectively than his mentor. All three devoted themselves to a system of scouting good high school players and targeting those they wanted. Some people called it a selection process, rather than recruiting, in deference to UNC's national reputation.

Long before recruiting received much publicity, McGuire was the most masterful salesman the college game had ever known, using the power of his persuasion and guile. He had scouts all over New York identifying the best players. When McGuire walked into a high-school gym, he couldn't care less about the game that was going on. He was there to see if a certain young man measured up to his two standards: talent and toughness.

After he left St. John's, McGuire's special brand of magic lured Catholic kids from New York to the South in the 1950s, and he did it by winning over parents of the teenagers. Sometimes, he brought along a parish priest when he visited Catholic families to assure them that attending Sunday Mass would be required, even five hundred miles away from home.

McGuire's main recruiting turf was New York because he had grown up there and was so well connected. He also favored the style of freelance offense and zone defense New York high schools liked to play.

When McGuire zeroed in on a youngster, he had little trouble finding someone familiar with the targeted family. Certainly they all knew of *his* name and reputation.

"McGuire was a giant figure in New York," Lennie Rosenbluth said. "He either liked you or you were the enemy. If he liked you, he'd do anything in the world for you. If he didn't like you, forget about it."

When he decided which players he wanted to recruit, McGuire made visits to their homes like they were royalty. He treated the parents with utmost respect and expected them to have complete faith that he would take care of their sons because that is what he promised.

Paying homage for raising such a fine young man, McGuire often spent more time with the mother in the kitchen or the father on the porch. In an era when parents had more control over their children, McGuire's methods resulted in a top-down decision on which college to attend.

When he first arrived at UNC from the Air Force Academy, Smith had almost no recruiting experience. McGuire did most of that in person or through his people in New York. Smith sometimes accompanied his boss to observe players, and the shy Kansan learned how to "move around the city." When he took over at UNC, Smith drew from McGuire's lessons and also watched how young Duke coach Vic Bubas, who had been Everett Case's chief recruiter at N.C. State for years, went after high school stars.

Smith inherited McGuire's longtime friends from New York and made them his contacts, too. Although Smith wanted to recruit throughout the East, what he learned from McGuire about the hurried and sometimes nasty Northeast allowed him to continue North Carolina's success there.

Through McGuire, Smith developed his own network of coaches

and contacts, which eventually helped him sign key players from New York City, although not exclusively. Smith quickly learned that McGuire was more comfortable coaching city kids who had already been recruited to play for prep schools in the rugged Catholic leagues, which had the best competition and were akin to today's AAU teams. They came to Carolina from schools like All Hallows, Christ the King, and Archbishop Molloy, where players had great coaching and were tough beyond their years.

"I liked the New York City talent because they had a head start in my system of play," McGuire once said, a system predicated on physical toughness. "We got most of the rebounds in games; Bobby Cunningham would always get an important rebound. Kearns could also rebound for his size. Rosenbluth knew how to block out and was called 'Goose' because he got that one hand up there. Quigg and Brennan had a lot of experience in New York rebounding in traffic on those small courts."

Smith was to take a slightly different route. Unlike McGuire, he thought he needed some North Carolina stars on his roster. Smith decided to go after a mix of the best players anywhere who were good students, and he later presided over one of the great national recruiting machines in college sports.

Smith embraced the McGuire way, began recruiting regionally and added academics to the sales pitch. Phil Ford always remembered that, in Smith's first visit to his home, there was virtually no talk of basketball. While other coaches guaranteed Ford a starting position as a freshman, Smith's only promise to Phil Sr. and Mabel Ford was that their son would be the first from their family to graduate from college. That set Smith apart from the other coaches and made Carolina the winner.

In McGuire's nine years at UNC, he signed nearly three dozen players from the New York area. Smith brought in far fewer in his thirty-six seasons, but most of his players from New York and New Jersey were stars like Dick Grubar, Charlie Scott, Bill Chamberlain, Mitch Kupchak, Mike O'Koren, Sam Perkins, Kenny Smith, Derrick Phelps, and Ed Cota, or key role players like John O'Donnell, Jimmy Black, Matt Doherty, King Rice, Pat Sullivan, and Brian Reese.

Whereas McGuire surrounded himself with New York players, Smith wanted only the best of them and signed other quality recruits from North Carolina to California. He attracted some great homegrown talent (Ford, Worthy, Jordan), but Smith liked filling his bench with well-rounded student-athletes from almost anywhere. "Coach Smith and Coach McGuire had different approaches, but they had a lot of similarities as well, which is why Carolina has been so successful," said Larry Brown, who played for both men.

Smith ranked the players he recruited by position and told them all where they stood, hoping those rated second and third would still come if Smith lost out on his top choice. He disdained how other coaches told all of their recruits the same story, trying to get away with it.

His candor worked most often, especially before scouting services and ratings popped up in newspapers and on the Internet. Smith got burned in 1988 when he asked New Jersey point guard Bobby Hurley to wait for New York City star Kenny Anderson to make his decision. Hurley, who had grown up a Carolina fan, instead signed with Duke. Anderson then went to Georgia Tech, leaving Smith with neither of his top two choices, but still insisting his honesty was the best policy.

One earlier case had some history attached to it. Back in 1956, McGuire had signed a guard from New Jersey named John Crotty, who was unhappy with his playing time in his last two seasons, during which Smith was an assistant coach. Twenty-five years later, Smith recruited John Crotty Jr. but wanted to sign more than one point guard. Crotty's father feared the same thing that happened to him would befall his son. So John Jr. went to Virginia, where he was a two-time All-ACC point guard. King Rice, from upstate New York, began at UNC the same year, played behind Jeff Lebo his first two seasons, and won the starting position as a junior.

Eventually, Smith relied more on assistant coaches Bill Guthridge and Eddie Fogler, who were savvy talent evaluators, as his lead scouts. He saw fewer high school games and, once he decided on his top targets, used the entire UNC experience to close the deal. A recruit spent most of his campus visit with the Carolina team, which had to sign off before Smith offered him a scholarship. Smith usually made his final pitch at a home visit with his two assistant coaches, strategically scheduling it a few days after the recruit had been to another school he was seriously considering.

Like Smith, Roy Williams has fixated on the character of young men, and he has either cut recruiting visits short or never scheduled them if he thought there was as much bad temperament as talent in the offing. He once visited a recruit who showed up late for the appointment, walked right past Williams, and grabbed something from the fridge, then came back to chow down in front of the bemused coach. When the mother tried to intervene, and the youngster treated her rudely, Williams told the onetime recruit two things as he got up to leave: Don't treat your mom that way, and pick another school.

Williams said he nearly accepted an offer to coach in the NBA during his last few years at Kansas, when he grew disillusioned with recruiting and how some high-school stars had become influenced by AAU coaches, shoe company shills, and others not interested in just their welfare. Then Williams signed Nick Collison, Drew Gooden, and Kirk Hinrich, whom he called "great players, great kids from great families" and who eventually led the Jayhawks to consecutive Final Fours.

Being clear about character became so important to Williams that he logged thousands of miles to see a prospect play a second and third time, often the only college coach left at a high school tournament game that went on until midnight. He kept going even after the recruit signed because he wanted to demonstrate that the relationship was just beginning as the courtship was ending. Williams has had capable assistants at both Kansas and Carolina and relied on them for many recruiting duties, but he has done more in-person visiting and phone calling than most head coaches.

Like McGuire and Smith, who didn't use the typewriter or email, Williams is surprisingly low tech, but remains remarkably relevant to the younger set. He uses his cell phone for convenience on the road but does not carry it everywhere he goes. He does not text, or tweet, and he has barely heard of Facebook, despite several home pages of the social networking Internet site being started under his name. His secretary prints out emails to him and responds after showing them to the coach. Williams' biggest need is to have private planes at his disposal so he can recruit more efficiently. At Carolina, one of three small jets can be ready within an hour.

Williams has cast a wider net than either McGuire or Smith, sometimes recruiting as many as seven or eight players from one high-school class and ranking them by position similar to the way Smith did it. He will never lie to a player from the moment he meets him. He is plain honest, and he has seen other coaches burned by making promises they could not keep.

A perfect example was a recent one. Unsure whether Sean May and Marvin Williams would be back for the 2006 season, he assured Tyler Hansbrough and the other five players he was recruiting only that they could "help the team in some way" their first year in school.

The selectivity of Carolina coaches over the last fifty years has created a Catch-22 of sorts. The Tar Heels were always expected to recruit and sign the most talented players, but style of play (McGuire), academic promise (Smith), and good character (Williams) have often narrowed the pool of prospects. The head coaches were unwilling to exchange problems during the regular season to bolster their chances for a run in the NCAA tournament. This is the reason Smith and Williams have talked so much about not dwelling on the destination but enjoying the journey.

By the time Williams returned to Chapel Hill, so many local, regional, and cable networks had begun carrying college hoops that the Tar Heels now played every game on television. TV had become their most important recruiting tool.

Once the umbilical cord for Carolina fans, radio was left to a still-sizable audience that could not get in front of a TV set or the loyal fans who still turned off the TV sound and tuned into the longtime Voice of the Tar Heels, Woody Durham. Fifty years earlier, before Durham took over, listeners hung on the words of raspy Ray Reeve and Mouth of the South Bill Currie to follow just about every game.

Smith came to rely on radio during his early recruiting days because WBT-AM in Charlotte had such a strong north-south signal that high-school players, their families, and coaches as far north as New York City could hear the Carolina games on a clear night. Some even went on to rooftops to tune in the Tar Heels.

Radio became less important to Smith, obviously, when more games went on national and cable TV.

Actually, the television era of college basketball began in Chapel Hill even before pioneer producer C. D. Chesley transmitted a grainy black-and-white picture of Carolina's 1957 Final Four games from Kansas City. As early as 1955, UNC-TV (the state's educational television network) carried the Carolina–Wake Forest game from Woollen Gym without sound. One camera at the corner of the court followed the action, and a hand-operated wooden scoreboard at the end of the UNC bench at the opposite corner allowed viewers to keep track of the score if they weren't paying attention to the radio play-by-play broadcast.

UNC-TV carried three more games in 1956 over what became known as Broadvision, which attracted a relatively small audience and, for the most part, was considered a fad. That all changed during the season of McGuire's Miracle.

The February 9, 1957, game between Carolina and Duke in Chapel Hill sold out quickly, and thousands of fans clamored to see if the Tar Heels could keep their unbeaten season alive. With the game set for Broadvision, UNC officials wanted to improve the quality of the telecast that was going to stations in Raleigh, Greensboro, and Charlotte.

William Friday, president of the Consolidated University of North Carolina, and chief financial officer Billy Carmichael Jr. directed that a sledgehammer and pick be used to cut a round hole in the cinder-block wall at midcourt above and behind the bleachers at Woollen Gym.

Workers built a platform for the TV camera on the other side of the wall and pushed the lens through the hole. An estimated 50,000 people watched the Tar Heels win their eighteenth straight game and preserve the No. 1 ranking they had taken away from Kansas three weeks earlier.

The response was so overwhelming that, after witnessing Carolina survive the ACC tournament, Chesley decided to televise the national semifinals and championship game back to North Carolina the same way. When the Tar Heels defeated Michigan State and Kansas on consecutive nights—both in triple overtime—more than 100,000 people watched the picture with no sound while listening to the radio call of Jim Reid and Bill Jackson.

Because the games began after 10 o'clock eastern time both nights, Chesley wasn't sure how many people would stay up to watch. "They were renting TV sets for hospital rooms," he said. "It was the damnedest thing you ever heard of. I knew right there that ACC basketball could be as popular as anything shown on TV in North Carolina."

Chesley, who had already offered the ACC $75,000 to televise three regular-season football games, sold the conference on a twelve-game basketball schedule for the 1958 season. He drove from South Carolina to Maryland, signing stations and securing sponsors like Pilot Life Insurance Company. The eight schools agreed to split Chesley's small rights fee and other profits equally, and ACC basketball on TV was born. Chesley started a company and hired announcers to call the games.

Television almost immediately began changing the face of the game in the ACC, presaging its dominant role a half century later. The Duke-Carolina rivalry took a quantum leap after the fight that erupted late in their February 4, 1961, game at Durham was seen by thousands of viewers trapped in their homes by a snowstorm. Chesley's ACC regional network, highlighted by the famous "Sail with the Pilot" jingle, spread between Pennsylvania and South Carolina, allowing high-school players and their families to *actually watch* the teams that were recruiting them.

In 1964, Chesley convinced the conference to televise the ACC tournament championship game. The starting time was moved twice to accommodate other programming on the network of stations, and the first game-time complaints were heard from fans. Today, NCAA tournament regional games start as late as 10:00 P.M.

Carolina's powerhouse teams of the late 1960s appeared regularly on Saturday afternoon telecasts, and by then Chesley was showing the ACC tournament semifinals as well. Dean Smith, the shy Kansan who would have been happy coaching in an empty gym, became famous and recognized on most streets along the East Coast.

The Tar Heels were on the tube throughout the first weekend in March by reaching the 1967–1969 ACC tournament championship games. After winning all three years, they advanced to the NCAA East Regional on network television and then on to the Final Four in prime time on national TV the following Friday and Saturday nights. UNC's Charlie Scott was the only black star from the South in those days, and his example prompted Michael Jordan to call him the "Jackie Robinson of college basketball" years later.

The Tar Heels made so many appearances on television during the 1970s and early 1980s that their fan base grew exponentially across the state, regionally and nationally. With stars like Phil Ford, James Worthy, and Jordan, their following compounded almost daily. Smith once told a sportswriter who wanted to interview him, "We don't need any more promotion."

Baby blue became the color of choice for many, and when UNC began collecting royalties on officially licensed products after the 1982 season, the take grew from $6,000 the first year into millions that supported need-based academic scholarships at the university.

Roy Williams entered college basketball coaching in the very season it exploded in popularity. The 1979 NCAA championship game at Salt Lake City featured Michigan State and Magic Johnson against undefeated-but-underdog Indiana State and Larry Bird. The NBC telecast beat the ratings of every prior title game, including those with the UCLA dynasty. That two schools from within a few hundred miles apart could capture America's imagination said as much for college basketball as it did for the two stars who continued their individual rivalry into the NBA for another twelve years.

Williams worked for Smith during the 1980s, when UNC played in back-to-back Final Fours and won more games than any other college program in the decade. By the time he went to Kansas in 1988, Williams was used to the glare of the TV lights that carried Big Eight conference games. But the league Williams left behind was about to experience a brand new level of exposure, spreading Tar Heel Nation like wildfire.

Raycom Sports, which was owned and operated by UNC alumnus Rick Ray, agreed to pay the ACC $8 million a year in 1981 to televise about forty conference games and the ACC tournament to the five-state footprint. Ten years earlier, Chesley was paying $500,000 for the TV rights.

On top of that, the ACC gave national networks CBS, ABC, and NBC first priority to pay separately for marquee matchups such as Carolina-Duke. Plus, ESPN cable could pay the ACC even more to carry other games nationally, some in prime time, and to pick up Raycom regional games and show them to the rest of country.

The UNC-Duke game on February 3, 1993, televised by Raycom and ESPN, set a record for total viewers (five million–plus) that stood for fifteen years. It prompted ESPN to launch its second cable network, forcing viewers outside the ACC to subscribe in order to watch the Tar Heels play the Blue Devils in their first regular-season game each year. Little wonder that, in 1994, the ACC signed the richest TV contract of any conference in history, granting Raycom all of its TV rights including syndication to the national networks. That contract has since grown to $30 million a year for the ACC.

Williams returned to UNC as a household name after taking his last two KU teams to the Final Four. The Jayhawks were the most popular college basketball team in the Midwest, but Williams came back to coach an even bigger program. Since his second season, most Carolina games have been on national television, helping him recruit across the country. Winning, and winning on TV, has everything to do with UNC's ability to stay atop the popularity polls, collect more licensing royalties than any other school in the last ten years, and drive its athletic profitability.

One national poll from EA Sports, makers of licensed college basketball video games that add to UNC's royalties, rated the Smith Center the toughest place to play for visiting teams, even though the great majority of voters had never been in the building. Such a result only came from having so many victories at the Dean Dome seen on television.

Like any hardcore Yankee who comes to the South, Frank McGuire rubbed some people the wrong way. He was a charismatic charmer early on, relishing his role as a carpetbagger hired to end the dominance of N.C. State and Everett Case. Once he signed up the players making up a championship team, the Tar Heels played with an attitude that came from their coach. The more they won and were beloved by Carolina fans, the more resentment grew among opposing schools. McGuire's style of dress, his cool demeanor, and the arrogance his teams demonstrated on the court were part of a colorful era that featured regular confrontations and occasional fisticuffs.

He angered his own fans when he asked them to treat the visiting teams with respect, especially considering how the Tar Heels were received on the road. A fierce competitor, McGuire still believed in proper sportsmanship. As McGuire's successor, Dean Smith made that a priority. For years, Smith mirrored McGuire's philosophy by asking fans sitting behind the basket to stop waving their arms while an opponent shot free throws. (Eventually, Smith gave up after such distractions became common at arenas all over the country.)

When McGuire claimed the NCAA was out to get him in 1961, he stonewalled the Infractions Committee and pulled his team out of the ACC tournament after it was banned from accepting an NCAA bid. He resigned with his program on probation and under university sanctions, but his 1957 team has remained the greatest sports story in the history of his adopted state. Except for winning another national championship, McGuire repeated much of the same pattern when he resurfaced at South Carolina in 1964.

Smith had little trouble staying in McGuire's shadow after he took over in 1961. But that was OK with him, since his mandate was to bring the basketball program's profile down a notch. He was told that graduating his players and keeping them out of trouble on and off the court were more important than victories. He still had to win to keep his job, and he couldn't avoid the controversy that surrounded his efforts to rebuild. There was his hanging in effigy in 1965, his slowdown game against Duke in 1966, and, finally, a championship team for which some fans refused to give him enough credit.

He became an icon by fulfilling, and exceeding, his job description. He recruited well-mannered players who tried hard, were good students, and eventually won most of their games. Instead of breaking the rules as McGuire did on occasion, Smith used them to his advantage by devising a clever offense—the Four Corners—that became fodder for a national debate.

Smith spoke out only occasionally, but when he did all hell seemed to break loose, like the time he criticized Virginia for its rough play underneath and drew a public rebuke from Cavaliers coach Terry Holland. Smith was apolitical in public, but most people still knew he was a liberal who fought against racial injustice and, later, the death penalty.

Roy Williams' candor can sometimes be his own worst enemy. Unlike Smith, who always measured what he said, Williams has little filter between his mind and his mouth. Among the most popular coaches in the profession, he gets in trouble on occasion with his homespun slang such as "Dad gum it" and a variety of synonyms that sound like the "f word." When he slipped during a press conference and used the real thing, the faux pas was front-page news the next day and the subject of talk shows for a week.

Williams no longer agrees to give on-camera interviews when he leaves the court at halftime because he might be too irritated from the last few plays of the first half. He will always speak with a TV reporter before the second half begins, off camera; by then he's had a chance to calm down and be more objective about his team's performance.

Smith learned a similar lesson early in his career when after a loss at Vanderbilt he criticized a player in the locker room. Upon watching the film the next day, Smith realized he had chewed out the wrong culprit. Win or lose from that point on, he always waited until he was calmer and had reviewed the game film before addressing the team.

Each of the three Carolina coaching legends openly criticized the ACC tournament for its inflated importance in their respective eras. McGuire hated that it was played on N.C. State's home court, Reynolds Coliseum, and that it determined the ACC's only bid to the NCAA tournament. He called it Russian roulette because one loss and the season was over. McGuire thought what a team did over the prior three months should be regarded more heavily. Since then, that "body of work" has become more important than the conference tourney.

Smith agreed with McGuire, and after his first five years as head coach the ACC tournament was moved to a neutral site in 1967. Even after winning four titles in six years, Smith still campaigned for the regular-season champion to get an at-large NCAA bid if it did not win the ACC tournament. When that finally happened, beginning in 1975, Smith began focusing more on the NCAA tournament. He returned to more emphasis on the ACC tournament in 1988 after the Tar Heels went five years without winning it, and he wound up with four more titles (for a total of thirteen) before he retired.

Williams said during one press conference that playing three ACC tournament games in three days might earn a trophy, but it did not help teams that had already secured NCAA bids. He called it a "social event" and a "big cocktail party" and pointed out that none of his Final Four teams at Kansas had won the Big Eight or Big 12 tournament. That did not please some fans and members of the Rams Club, the booster organization that used UNC season tickets and priority seating for the ACC tournament as golden carrots to raise money for athletic scholarships at Carolina.

Adored by thousands, and later hundreds of thousands, Tar Heel basketball players and coaches developed habits and rituals that became well known and, at times, mimicked by their growing fan base. Their most fervent followers learned the team's regular schedule, like eating the pregame meal four hours before tip-off and arriving at Carmichael Auditorium and later the Smith Center ninety minutes before home games. Old-timers looked for Dean Smith to subtly shake the hands of his assistant coaches when he believed a victory had been secured, a private version of Red Auerbach's victory cigar.

Since freshmen became eligible for the varsity in 1973, Tar Heel lore has included stories about even the most ballyhooed recruits chasing the loose balls in practice, lugging the heavy equipment on road trips, and getting the worst seats on planes. All three coaching eras placed a high priority on seniority and earning everything from playing time to freedom from mandatory study halls.

Imitating UNC players was the highest form of flattery, if not hero worship. In the 1960s, knee socks were the rage after Smith's Tar Heels broke them out, followed by Carolina blue Converse sneakers, the first basketball shoes ever made that were not either white or black. George Karl's floppy socks and hair of the early 1970s changed the look again.

Clotheshorse coaches McGuire, then Smith, and now Roy Williams have been de facto fashion models for fans who emulated their styles and, in turn, did some business for designers like Alexander Julian, who in 1990 at Smith's request remade the once-stylish, v-neck UNC uniforms with a more contemporary argyle trim. When the university signed its multi-million-dollar contract with Nike in 1993, replica basketball jerseys became one of the fastest-growing items in the sale of officially licensed products.

McGuire turned the dramatic entrance before games into something akin to Elvis entering the building. He never appeared with his team during warm-ups, dressing and primping alone in the locker room as his assistant coaches went out. Then, after leading the players in the Lord's prayer, McGuire sent his team out and let all eyes in the arena focus on the runway before he emerged as the pregame clock went to double-zero. It was a tour de force that other coaches like Jim Valvano and Mike Krzyzewski embellished with an entourage of staff that likened them to entertainers taking the stage.

Smith began his career by holding back, as well, but that was because he could have a last cigarette or two before tip-off. Unlike McGuire, he came to the arena dressed ready for the game and walked out with his team but stood in the hallway watching warm-ups as he puffed away. Writers who knew this routine sometimes went back to visit with him. After Smith won his two-hundredth game in 1972, *Daily Tar Heel* sports editor Mark Whicker gave him a carton of unfiltered Kents (Smith's smoke of choice), which contained ten packs of twenty cigarettes each. After Smith quit smoking in 1988, he came out with his team when official warm-ups began.

Williams has never smoked and followed Smith's later routine, adding his own touch that he began at Kansas after one of his assistants told him they had T-shirts left over from their first midnight madness practice. He emerged with a few rolled-up shirts and tossed them to students as he walked by. It became such a hit that, before every game since at Kansas and Carolina, a manager has handed Williams four T-shirts that he stops and throws out, two lobbed to kids close by and two heaved with an outfielder's arm toward the back of the student section.

Carolina's first-class label did not stem from appearance alone. McGuire really began the Carolina Family when he made a commitment to the youngsters he convinced to leave their comfort zone in the Northeast for the radically different South. How he and his wife, Pat, opened their home to their players and took care of them on campus and around Chapel Hill created a legendary tradition of loyalty. It was more than fifty years and four head coaches ago, but McGuire's boys have remained honored and esteemed alumni of UNC and Tar Heel basketball. In many ways, they were pioneers just like Charlie Scott.

Smith had rebuilt the Carolina program and already developed his own loyal legions when he signed Scott as the first black scholarship athlete at UNC. A few letters from bigoted alumni arrived at the basketball office, but Smith wanted to break the color barrier at Carolina because it was the right thing to do for the university as well as his basketball team.

Just as McGuire's early recruits had to be happy in order for him to continue running the Underground Railroad from New York, Scott had to succeed to help Smith bring other great black players into his program. It was also more than skin deep. Smith treated Scott differently because he was sensitive to his plight. Nothing was more important than having all of his players leave the program happy. Different but equal became part of Smith's brilliant stewardship.

Carolina has been criticized as boringly consistent. That is the foundation begun by McGuire, built by Smith, and nurtured by Bill Guthridge and Roy Williams. The consistency is authentic;

otherwise, over fifty years, contradictory stories would have sur-
faced from disgruntled members of the family who were not
treated fairly and accordingly. They cannot all get the same playing time—and star status—but almost everything else is equal.
Off the court, they share the experiences, from chartered jets to
the best hotels available to five-star restaurants.

They are the privileged characters of a profitable enterprise.
Forbes magazine has ranked UNC the "most valuable" college
basketball team in the country in 2008 and 2009, generating more
than $16 million in operating income and having a value of just
under $26 million based on what it gives back to the university
and the community. Duke, by contrast, was ranked No. 8 in the
country and produced only $6.6 million in operating income.

Smith, who occasionally mentioned how much money his program made for the athletic department, was more corporate than
McGuire, always accessible but keeping arm's length with his
players until they graduated. The 1967 Tar Heels lifted Smith on
their shoulders after his first ACC championship, but such public
celebrations did not happen often, if ever, after that. Smith held
back, hoping his team would get the credit.

Tar Heel Nation knew what to expect, too. There were players
thrusting a fist toward the bench as a tired signal; pointing to the
passer who made the assist; huddling at the foul line to spring a
surprise defense like the run-and-jump; timeouts after baskets during a late rally; substitutes standing when a player leaves the game,
with Guthridge tapping each one on the back as he walked by.

There was no question as to who got the best tickets closest
to the court, and it was not the head coach's wife and kids as at
most schools. They went to the players' parents and their families.
Smith made it clear that former players were always welcomed
back; and the closer seats went to the older alumni, not necessar-

ily the better players. Like Smith, Williams always sets aside time the day before a game to personally handle the hundreds of ticket requests and pretty much knows where every person is sitting.

Many college athletic programs have great coaching staffs that lead and teach their players to compete hard and handle themselves with both pride and dignity. Some even have a bond that has lasted through generations. Carolina basketball is always in such a discussion, because the Tar Heels have done it that way for so long. Under the constant gaze of public scrutiny and a mass media that, seemingly, has new methods of transmitting information every day, that kind of track record is not only genuine, it is genuinely amazing.

The grand result is not just an adoring alumni and fan base. It is articles from the *New York Times* to the *Wall Street Journal* to *USA Today* that put the Tar Heels at or near the top of profitability, popularity, and position in their genre. Developing that presence translated into successful recruiting.

UNC have long owned most of the media coverage in North Carolina, losing its favor briefly when N.C. State's Valvano won a national championship in 1983 and Duke's Krzyzewski went back-to-back in 1991 and 1992. Since the day swashbuckling Frank McGuire moved to Chapel Hill in 1952, the Tar Heels have been the story.

Most of McGuire's practices were open to the press, and he often humored reporters while his team scrimmaged. He was a captivating interview—candid and rarely contrite about any shortcoming, real or perceived. From his early days in New York, when he learned how to manipulate sportswriters, McGuire had most of them hanging on his every word. McGuire's postgame press conferences were of so much interest to fans that the local radio station began covering them live.

When he arrived in Chapel Hill, Smith marveled at how Carolina had so many supporters among the media covering the team. While rivals claimed UNC turned out partisan journalism students in droves, McGuire was largely responsible for the favoritism that came to exist among many writers and broadcasters in the state.

McGuire cultivated relations easily in North Carolina after learning how to maneuver around the world's toughest writers in New York City. He usually schmoozed sportswriters, but as his aura grew he could get the same positive results by snubbing someone he thought had wronged him or his team. The miscreant often grew paranoid and sought to win back McGuire's approval with a complimentary story.

Smith rarely tried that approach, but he developed longtime friendships with young writers in each major market who were still growing up when they covered him. Smith honored and respected the old dogs getting ready to retire, but the amazing consistency of Carolina's treatment by the press stemmed from his early ties with writers like Ron Green Sr. in Charlotte, Irwin Smallwood and Smitty Barrier in Greensboro, and Dick Herbert in Raleigh. Most of the young guys coming up fell in line, more or less.

However, the more Smith tried to stay in the background, and the longer he coached at the state university after succeeding McGuire, the more the spotlight followed him and his nationally ranked team.

In time, Smith learned to regard press conferences as a necessary evil. He began to hold them regularly during the ACC season to reduce the number of requests for one-on-one interviews. Smith used his stature and credibility to be the single source of information about his program, angling to educate sportswriters or shape their opinions. He almost always had his own agendas, such as promoting underrated members of his team, campaigning for the game to be officiated more closely, or incessantly praising upcoming opponents so his players would not get overconfident. As media coverage expanded, though, Smith inevitably lost control of it.

Although he was once an overwhelming favorite of writers, Smith's penchant for giving them only what he wanted became passé. Young gun coaches like Valvano and Krzyzewski won over media members with their candor, occasionally poking fun at Smith and Carolina. Valvano mocked the pirouetting post moves of UNC's big men, and Krzyzewski occasionally cracked on Smith's chain-smoking before the Carolina coach quit.

Smith hated what the invasion of TV media meant for his players and for him. He rued the day that he capitulated to ESPN and scheduled his first practice of the 1992–1993 season at midnight so it could be televised. There was never another "Late Night with Dean" as long as he was in charge. He almost never let the TV people into his practices because he worried his team would lose concentration and play to the cameras. Once, during an open NCAA tournament shoot-around, he blew his whistle and pulled everyone in tight so he could criticize a player without anyone else seeing or hearing him do it.

In his later years, after Valvano left coaching and Krzyzewski's success made him less accessible, Smith regained favor with the media as an elder statesman. He enjoyed jousting with writers during press conferences and allowed that the TV overkill may well have helped recruiting. Smith never had the time to fully understand the Internet, which came in as he went out. When the mother of recruit Jason Collier told him that the website Inside Carolina said Smith and Carolina weren't interested in her son, Smith replied, "I don't know what Inside Carolina is, but let me be the source on how we feel about Jason." Perhaps unfairly influenced, Collier eventually signed with Georgia Tech. An unwillingness to continue dealing with the changing recruiting landscape hastened Smith's retirement.

Roy Williams was almost the polar opposite personality from Smith in public from the day he returned to UNC as an assistant coach and eagerly followed Fogler and Guthridge around to learn the recruiting ropes. Williams knew his junior place on the staff but meshed easily with the media and other coaches, loving to tell funny stories.

Although the restricted-earnings assistant could not recruit off campus, Williams served as host when prospects and their families visited Chapel Hill. He grew so close with Michael Jordan's father, James, that Williams built a deluxe woodstove for the Jordans' new home in Wilmington.

Williams was far from the introvert he had been as a boy in the mountains by the time he took the head coaching job at Kansas. Williams became a media favorite in the Midwest and, as his program grew, across the nation. Sometimes he said a little too much, but he always did it to deflect criticism from his players onto his shoulders. When he returned to Carolina, he had long ago learned the value of using the media in recruiting, and almost everything he says contains at least some underlying message about him and his program designed for the consumption of high-school athletes, their parents, and coaches. At the same time, all of it comes naturally to him.

Williams engendered such loyalty and respect from his players that he could poke fun at them in public, saying he wanted to strangle one of them for taking that shot, or another player made a stupid pass, or still a third could not jump higher than the thickness of a piece of paper. In most cases, it's to promote the family atmosphere that surrounds him because, in today's college basketball, everything relates to recruiting.

Williams dances with his team at "Late Night with Roy" and

talks about jumping into the locker room "mosh pit" of players after significant victories. Practices are as organized down to the minute as Smith's were, but Williams generally opens them to the public on Thursdays. Spectators sit halfway up in the lower arena but close enough to notice an upbeat atmosphere that is occasionally splintered by banter between the coaches and players. None of the private, real important conversations leave the locker room, and the players ignore what Williams says in public because they get the real story from him face to face.

"With Coach Williams, like with Coach Smith, all of the players know where they stand," said Steve Kirschner, UNC's long-time sports information director. "They know he's trying to make them better players." Like Williams, all of Carolina's legendary coaches have used the media to promote or protect their team members.

McGuire made sure the "Four Catholics" on his championship team were not overshadowed by the coverage of All-American and national player of the year Lennie Rosenbluth. Smith harped on selfless acts such as assists and defense for unsung players like Steve Previs, and Williams spent much of Tyler Hansbrough's career pointing out how much physical contact he endured, often without hearing a whistle from the officials.

They all wanted to set their version of the record straight.

Frank McGuire coached his team, cajoled the media, and intimidated the refs to gain an advantage, but the Irishman admitted none of that was worth a cheap suit without *players*. UNC basketball's ultimate edge over the last fifty years has been in recruiting, and the periodic challengers to the Tar Heels' throne fell back because they could not consistently sign star players or keep coaches who could.

Duke dropped off the radar in the early 1970s after Vic Bubas retired and the Blue Devils suffered some serious attrition. Maryland and N. C. State climbed to the top of the conference behind All-Americans Tom McMillen, Len Elmore, and John Lucas for the Terrapins and David Thompson, Tom Burleson, and Monte Towe for the Wolfpack. Both of those schools slipped back to the middle of the league in the late seventies, while Duke coach Bill Foster brought in Mike Gminski and Gene Banks to contest the Tar Heels.

Following Foster's departure and during Mike Krzyzewski's rebuilding project, Virginia reached its zenith by signing Ralph Sampson and keeping him for four years. Duke and Carolina have dominated the ACC since.

Between 1986 and 2009, Duke finished at the top of the ACC standings eleven times and won ten tournament championships. Carolina was first for ten seasons and won seven tourney titles. During those twenty-four years, the schools only eight miles apart combined for nineteen trips to the NCAA Final Four and won six national championships.

The two college basketball bluebloods remain atop the nation's elite programs and in a class by themselves in the ACC for one reason: Behind those sterling team records are dozens of all-conference and All-American players, two and three times as many as any other school in their own league.

Hansbrough left Carolina as the most decorated Tar Heel in history and the all-time leading scorer in the ACC. Yes, he got great coaching, dominated the headlines, and went to the foul line an NCAA record 1,241 times. He also set the unofficial standard for signing his name to everything from the bare skin of the fans who watched him play to pieces of the floor on which his team won the 2009 NCAA championship.

But his most important signature at North Carolina remains the first one: his letter of intent to play for the Tar Heels.

10

Great Expectations

NOT since the Duke team of 1992 defended its national championship and, two years later, the 1994 Tar Heels began their pur-
suit of back-to-back titles had there been such an overwhelming
favorite. It reminded old-timers of the UCLA dynasty under John
Wooden, who for a dozen years relegated everyone else to competing for second place.

"Anointed before we ever played a game," Roy Williams said
of the enormous expectations that came close to suffocating
North Carolina's 2008–2009 season. The hype can be traced back
four years, when the untested leftovers from UNC's last national
championship team and five newcomers began the true rebirth of
Carolina basketball.

When Williams put the house back in order only two years after his return to UNC, he insisted there would be "no difference"

between winning the 2005 NCAA championship with mostly Matt Doherty–recruited players and one with those he had signed. Many fans and followers of America's most popular college program, though, saw a difference.

Williams had reason to believe that Raymond Felton, Sean May, and Rashad McCants went to Carolina in spite of Doherty rather than because of him. Each recruit had his own affinity for the program that had little to do with who was in charge at that particular time. Felton and McCants both grew up in the Carolinas as Tar Heel fans. May could not go to the school (Indiana) that fired his father's old coach, Bob Knight, and did not want to go to Knight's new school (Texas Tech). Carolina was the compromise choice.

Like an adoptive father, Williams gave them a place and a purpose. They rewarded him and Tar Heel Nation with a two-year climb to the top of the ACC and ultimately the school's fourth NCAA championship. Williams dogged them about playing defense and channeled their innate toughness into the disposition of a title contender. The veterans who cut down the nets in St. Louis were a combination of street savvy, textbook teaching, and a deadly determination to rewrite their own history.

When Williams sat in the green room at Madison Square Garden the following June and watched Felton, May, and McCants follow freshman Marvin Williams in the first fourteen NBA draft picks, he was happy for them but anxious for his alma mater. Carolina was virtually starting over. His incoming recruiting class centered around 6'9" Tyler Hansbrough, but it was not celebrated enough to land the 2006 Tar Heels in most preseason national polls. They were picked to finish sixth in the ACC. A rebuilding year, most pundits called it.

In that regard, Roy Williams was the perfect foreman for a proud program he had followed since walking on to the UNC freshman team in 1968. He had an emotional parting with Kansas, and a heartfelt homecoming back to his roots.

Williams did not have to feign endearing affection for his school, as many new coaches and administrators do in their first years on the job. He had learned of the tradition Frank McGuire began in the 1950s, loved it as a student in the 1960s, and lived it as Dean Smith's assistant in the 1970s and 1980s. Relying on everything he had soaked up from Smith, Williams grew into a great coach during his fifteen seasons at Kansas.

Perhaps the combination of restored coaching excellence and a winning tradition should have taken the surprise out of UNC's 2006 season. Williams liked being a rare underdog as much as Frank McGuire and Dean Smith relished similar roles early in their Carolina careers.

McGuire stunned Everett Case's heavily favored Wolfpack three times in his first four seasons—twice at Reynolds Coliseum—and gave notice that his program had arrived by crushing fifth-ranked Alabama at Woollen Gym in December of 1955. His Cinderella 1957 national champions were not always favored on the road and faced the ultimate underdog scenario against Wilt Chamberlain and Kansas in the NCAA championship game at Kansas City.

Smith expanded on McGuire's penchant for pulling upsets by adding surprise strategies against heavily favored opponents. His 1963 squad shocked Kentucky at Lexington with a spread offense, the early version of the Four Corners he used in a victory at Ohio State in December of 1965 and to frustrate McGuire's second-ranked South Carolina team in 1971.

Whenever the Tar Heels had a daunting challenge, their legions always believed Smith would "come up with something" to help them pull it off. It became an article of faith among Carolina fans.

Due to the amazing road record Smith posted in his thirty-six seasons—Carolina was the only ACC team to win more away league games than it lost—the Tar Heels were never an obvious underdog. But, in truth, they weren't always favored in places like College Park, Charlottesville, Durham, Raleigh, and Winston-Salem; they just won more often on those hostile courts and were known for their poise, confidence, and ability to come back.

Williams instilled the upset tradition from the start at Kansas, which was picked dead last before his first season in the old Big Eight conference. The Jayhawks won at Texas Tech, Kansas State, Colorado, and Oklahoma State and finished 6-8 in the league and 19-12 overall in 1989, the one time Williams did not win at least twenty games at KU. Mirroring Smith's success, he was the only Big Eight/Big 12 coach to have a winning road record in his tenure.

Williams was prepared to carry on that tradition at Carolina, returning to find the cauldron at Cameron and the crowds at Wake Forest and Clemson no worse than the mayhem at Missouri and Manhattan, Kansas, and one particular surprise at Stillwater.

"The first time we played at Oklahoma State and Pistol Pete shot off that gun behind our bench, it about scared me to death," he recalled.

Tyler Hansbrough was ticketed for Kansas when Williams started recruiting him as a high-school sophomore from Poplar Bluff, Missouri. That's where the prep All-American would have gone had Williams stayed at KU. Painfully shy, 6'9" kids from small towns who love their families usually go six hours down the interstate rather than make two plane changes to North Carolina. Having signed with UNC in November of 2004, Hansbrough called Williams from the locker room moments after his high-school team won the Missouri state championship the following March.

When May and Marvin Williams entered the NBA draft after the 2005 season, Hansbrough had the Carolina frontcourt, and the team, to himself. Not only did he become an instant star, three others in his class also made an immediate impact. Illinois guard Bobby Frasor, a coach's son, had in savvy what he lacked in speed. New York forward Danny Green was unpredictable, but that included his offensive explosions off the bench. Swingman Marcus Ginyard, from Virginia, gave Williams leadership and a willingness to set the defensive tone from day one. Along with one experienced returning senior, David Noel, who had averaged five points a game for his college career, the new recruits were eager to prove they could contribute.

The 2005–2006 Tar Heels lost their fourth game, a rematch with Illinois in the annual ACC–Big Ten Challenge, but they impressed fans by how hard they played. Hansbrough's work ethic behind the scenes was already rubbing off on his teammates.

They beat an overrated Kentucky team, and the victory in Lexington gave them confidence on the road they never lost. After splitting their first six ACC games, this remarkable young team led by the newly nicknamed Psycho T (for Tyler) won ten of its next eleven regular-season starts and steadily rose in the conference standings and the polls.

Hansbrough won nine ACC rookie of the week awards, and fellow frosh regulars Ginyard, Green, and Frasor provided pluck and fortitude far beyond their years. Noel was their leader, but the heartbeat was that of youngsters getting stronger by the day.

"The most fun year I ever had coaching in my life," Williams has said. "Very seldom have we been the underdog, very seldom have I had a leader any better than David Noel, and very seldom have we had freshmen who were tough enough to say we're going to be freaking good."

They had battled Boston College for second place in the ACC and went to league-leader Duke with a feeling they could win the regular-season finale and avenge a February home loss. Williams told them they were the only team in the country that could win in such a setting, noting their seven road victories to date. He loved to point out that their national champion predecessors had won only seven games on enemy courts!

By the time they stunned the top-ranked Blue Devils and ruined J. J. Redick's last home game for their twenty-first victory of the season, the Tar Heels were the new darlings of the ACC. In the process of becoming the league's second-best player, Hansbrough took over for Redick as the most newsworthy, as well. His three-pointer from the top of the key nailed down the 83-76 victory— only Carolina's second at Cameron Indoor Stadium in the last ten years—and cinched his place as the first freshman voted unanimously to the All-ACC team.

The initial postseason experience for the Tar Heel freshmen was not a good one, as ramped-up defenses closed down their inside game and forced them to shoot too much from outside. They lost the hard-fought ACC semifinal game to a physical BC team and an NCAA second-round shocker to Final Four–bound George Mason.

The body of work, though, could not be denied. Williams had taken Carolina to the Big Dance three times in three seasons and made his seventeenth consecutive appearance overall. The surprise second-place finish in America's best college basketball league gave him a second straight national coach of the year award. (He was a landslide winner in the ACC voting.)

To make matters worse for the Anyone-But-Carolina crowd, Williams was bringing in one of the nation's top recruiting classes the next season. Before practice started in November of 2005, Williams had received commitments from mercurial Maryland mini-guard Ty Lawson, silky smooth Philly sharpshooter Wayne Ellington, California post men Alex Stepheson and Deon Thompson, and talented 6'8" forward Thaddeus Young from Memphis.

Then Williams received a call that left him almost speechless. Brandan Wright, a long-armed 6'9" forward from Nashville, Tennessee, who the Carolina coaches were sure was going to Duke, said he wanted to come, too. Williams had told Young his first choice was Wright and pulled back the scholarship offer. Young signed with Georgia Tech instead.

Williams' newest recruiting class made the 2007 Tar Heels more potent on both ends of the court. They shot just under 50 percent from the field (a rarity in the three-point era) and improved their rebounding differential and assist-turnover ratio from the year before. They lost an early game to Gonzaga, but came back to beat Tennessee, Ohio State (without freshman star Greg Oden), and Kentucky on the way to twelve consecutive victories and Carolina's first No. 1 ranking since a two-week stretch in 2001, Matt Doherty's maiden season.

That was hardly uncharted territory for Roy Williams, who had now reached 500 career wins in fewer seasons than any other college coach. His teams had been ranked No. 1 or No. 2 at some point during all but four of his fifteen seasons at Kansas. Thanks to so much balance in the ACC and Duke's drop to sixth place after losing Redick and Shelden Williams, Carolina hovered around first place despite five league losses and two to upstart Virginia Tech. The second came three days after the Tar Heels' biggest ACC blowout of the season, a 37-point pasting of the late Skip Prosser's last Wake Forest team the weekend of the anniversary celebration for UNC's 1957 and 1982 national championship teams.

The regular-season finale against Duke seemed like the most

uneventful game of the rivalry in years—until the last minute of play when Hansbrough took a flagrant elbow across the nose from Blue Devil freshman Gerald Henderson. The story of Hansbrough's bloody and unnecessary injury pushed two key achievements to the second page of the sports sections—that Williams had swept Duke for the first time since his return and notched his one hundredth victory as Carolina's head coach.

With cotton stuffed up his nostrils, Hansbrough looked in the mirror and was so amused by his blood-spattered jersey that he asked a photographer to take a picture. The photo quickly became a Carolina classic.

Henderson drew a suspension for one game of the ACC tournament—which Duke lost, ending its incredible run of ten straight years as regular-season or tourney champion—while Hansbrough adjusted to playing with a plastic mask that made him more of a cult hero among Tar Heel fans. Replica masks started selling over the Internet like the "Make It Wayne" T-shirts that popped up in Wayne Ellington's honor the next season.

As Hansbrough struggled with the face mask all weekend in Tampa, his young mates took over to win UNC's sixteenth ACC tournament title, but the first in nine years. Carolina had last cut down the ACC nets in 1998, three head coaches ago.

Freshmen starters Ty Lawson, Wayne Ellington, and Brandan Wright made the all-tournament team. Wright joined Bob McAdoo (1972), Phil Ford (1975), Sam Perkins (1981), Jerry Stackhouse (1994), and Duke's Jason Williams (2000) as the only first-year players to win the Everett Case MVP award.

Hansbrough played the entire ACC tournament and a first-round NCAA victory over Eastern Kentucky with the mask, then ripped it off during an early timeout against Michigan State. He went on to score a season-high 33 points, the most by a Tar Heel in an NCAA tournament game since Al Wood's legendary 39 versus Virginia in the 1981 Final Four.

Carolina looked even tougher six days later while scorching Southern Cal in the second half of their Sweet Sixteen match at the Meadowlands despite a season-low five points from Hansbrough. By now a sophomore consensus All-American, Hansbrough came back with 26 points and 11 rebounds as his team held a 10-point lead over Georgetown and stood six minutes from reaching the 2007 Final Four in Atlanta.

Danny Green's missed 20-footer from in front of the UNC bench barely ten seconds into the shot clock began a rash of quick misses that, coupled with poor defense, allowed the Hoyas to tie the game on Jonathan Wallace's late three-pointer. Regulation ended with the Georgetown zone surrounding Hansbrough and another wayward jumper from Ellington. The outcome already blown, the stunned Tar Heels were outscored 15-3 in overtime.

"I was dumbfounded the way my team played for a four- or five-minute stretch, and regardless of what I said and did I couldn't reel them back in," Williams said. "Took bad shots, took hurried shots, couldn't get the basketball inside, and got out of character more than any team I've ever had. That team got tighter with every possession."

The shocking collapse was part of a tragic weekend for Carolina. Cheerleading mascot Jason Ray was struck from behind by a vehicle while he walked along the shoulder of Route 4 in nearby Fort Lee, New Jersey, and he died the morning after the team's loss.

Then, a week or so later, projected lottery pick Brandan Wright declared for the NBA draft. He eventually went as the No. 8 pick to the Charlotte Bobcats, who then traded him to Golden State. Thaddeus Young, whose scholarship Wright had taken at Carolina, went four slots later in the first round after leaving Georgia Tech.

Williams' spirits were raised from that painful post-season with his election to the Naismith Basketball Hall of Fame in Springfield, Massachusetts. During his moving induction speech the following September, which Williams proudly composed by longhand, Hall of Famers Dean Smith and Larry Brown stood off to the side beaming.

Later, Williams said that he would have gladly postponed any Hall of Fame glory if one more jump shot versus Georgetown had gone in, and that he wanted to work even harder to prove he deserved the honor. The pledge also proved a foreshadowing of the next two seasons.

Even with Brandan Wright gone after one season, Carolina faced great expectations in 2008. Part of the reason was the postseason schedule: The Tar Heels could qualify for the Final Four without leaving their home state. First- and second-round games were slated for the RBC Center in Raleigh, and the East Regional was set for the same Charlotte Bobcats Arena that also hosted the ACC tournament two weeks earlier.

But two important starters were gone, which left holes not easily filled. Reyshawn Terry, the lone incoming freshman Williams had inherited from Matt Doherty four years earlier, was a fine defender and a streak scorer with the best three-point percentage on the team. When Wright left for the NBA lottery, however, Carolina lost its only real shot blocker and a second inside scoring threat who could not be immediately replaced.

Williams tried to warn the local media and fawning fans that the Tar Heels were less than a lock to win their second straight ACC championship. Among the other competition, Duke was angrily coming off a relatively bad season for the Blue Devils. The national media, at least, should have known better than to hand Carolina a crown in the preseason.

Take *Sports Illustrated* and Kansas, for example. *SI* had tabbed the Jayhawks to win it all in 2007, with Carolina picked third. Kansas, which wound up losing in the Elite Eight to a UCLA team headed to its second of three straight Final Fours, returned four starters and added sophomore Darrell Arthur, whom the magazine called a "capable replacement" for the fifth starter (Julian Wright, who turned pro early).

Yet when the 2008 preseason issue hit the stands, Kansas was picked only sixth. The Tar Heels were the new No. 1, even though they had more attrition. Other national analysts, such as ESPN's Dick Vitale, followed suit and called Carolina king.

"Reyshawn was at times the best defensive player I ever coached, and Brandan could erase a lot of mistakes and block shots," Williams said. "You don't lose a guy who was the number-eight pick in the draft and not lose something."

That comment was buried in the fifth paragraph of the season outlook in the UNC media guide. If Williams repeated it to reporters, they never took him seriously or they considered it "coachspeak" from someone who held weekly press conferences and had become the most engaging local sports celebrity.

When the Tar Heels won their first eighteen games, challenged only in a comeback win at Clemson and in a one-point victory at Georgia Tech, they appeared to be living up to the hype. With Deon Thompson and Marcus Ginyard moving into the starting lineup, they actually raised the fast pace Williams wanted a notch higher and held their own on defense. Better pressure on the perimeter made it harder for opponents to get the ball inside, where Brandan Wright had been a neutralizer.

They were upset at home by faster-breaking Maryland for their first defeat and lost again at the Smith Center to Duke without Ty Lawson, who had suffered a high ankle sprain at Florida State on Super Bowl Sunday. Lawson sat out six games before returning with a gimpy leg at Boston College, where Carolina rallied from 18 points behind in the second half to win its twenty-seventh game despite 46 points by Tyrese Rice.

First place in the ACC, and the 2008 NCAA tournament seed that would keep the winner closer to home, came down to the regular-season closer in Durham. Perspectives on the game, though, were changed by the murder three days earlier of UNC student body president Eve Carson at the hands of gang thugs in Chapel Hill. Carson was a Morehead Scholar, exemplary student and, by all accounts, an amazing young woman in every way.

Williams and his players, some of whom knew Carson personally, attended one of the on-campus vigils that drew more than 10,000 mourners. From that point forward, Chancellor James Moeser and his successor, Holden Thorp, called Carson "our own angel."

The Duke and UNC communities bonded beforehand to honor Carson. Carolina coaches put on light blue ribbons, and each Tar Heel player wore a black patch with the white letters "EVE" on his uniform for the remainder of the season. (Thousands of Carolina fans wore "EVE" stickers, as well.) Both teams came together at midcourt for a prayer that momentarily silenced an otherwise raucous Cameron Indoor Stadium. Still, the game had to go on.

After a typical fast start by the home team, junior Danny Green came off the bench and blocked seven shots, grabbed eight rebounds, and scored 18 points—two on a flying facial slam over Duke's Greg Paulus that became a YouTube favorite. The Tar Heels won for the third straight season at Cameron to finish first in the

ACC. They secured a record twelfth No. 1 seed in the NCAA tournament, their second in a row and third in the last four years.

Having lost his first three games to Duke since returning, Williams had now evened his UNC record against Krzyzewski at 5-5, symbolic that his Carolina program had regained equal footing with the Blue Devils. In reality, though, another passage was occurring that would be completed the following season with two more victories over Duke.

With placement in the NCAA East Region almost assured, the 2008 Tar Heels survived scares from Virginia Tech and the Clemson team that they needed three overtimes to sweep during the regular season, and won a second consecutive ACC tournament championship which marked a conference high of seventeen for UNC. The players cut down only one of the nets in Charlotte and seemed relatively quiet on the court and in the locker room after the game.

Someone suggested they were copying the 1982 Tar Heels, who left the nets hanging at Reynolds Coliseum after winning the East Regional. That was two years before the oldest of these players was born, though. This was *their* turn.

Hansbrough, who added the ACC tournament MVP trophy to his conference player of the year award and third straight unanimous selection to the All-ACC team, called it only "good preparation" for the NCAA tournament. "These teams played us really aggressively, and that's the type of atmosphere we'll face in the tournament," he said stoically.

Not in the first two rounds, as it turned out. With a one-sided, sellout crowd roaring for them in Raleigh, the Tar Heels blew out sixteenth-seeded Mount St. Mary's and No. 9 Arkansas by a combined score of 221-151, the first time a team had scored more than

100 points in its first- and second-round NCAA games. Almost un-noticed, Hansbrough set the ACC career record for free throws made, passing Christian Laettner's four-year mark before his junior season ended. It was the first of numerous league and national records for Hansbrough.

Going back to Charlotte for the Sweet Sixteen, the Heels were considered a shoo-in for San Antonio, where Carolina had played in the Final Four ten years earlier. Things were certainly falling into place. Fourth-seeded and deliberate Washington State lacked the personnel to pull off an upset in what was essentially a road game. The Tar Heels pulled away and won, 68-47.

But they had to exorcise the ghosts of Georgetown in the regional championship game against 13th-ranked Louisville, which had routed favored Tennessee in the other regional semifinal. The Cardinals' twenty-three-year-old senior center, David Padgett, had been part of Roy Williams' last recruiting class at Kansas and wasn't happy when the coach who had signed him left for North Carolina. Padgett played one season for Bill Self at KU, then transferred to Louisville.

A McDonald's All-American and once as touted as Hans-brough, Padgett had hoped for the kind of career that the Tar Heel star was enjoying. Instead, Padgett became a great-passing post player and modest scorer who, after missing almost half of the season with a broken kneecap, was almost the forgotten man in the younger Louisville lineup. This was his chance to break Hans-brough's heart, and to help eliminate Carolina in the Elite Eight for the second straight year. Instead, his career ended at the hands of Hansbrough.

On the verge of blowing another lead in another Elite Eight game, Carolina nailed three big outside shots to stave off the Cards' comeback. Lawson hit the first from the corner near the

UNC bench. The next two were atypically taken, and made, by Psycho T from the left elbow. Both face-up jumpers were in the face of Padgett, who had his typical game—6 points, 6 assists, and 8 rebounds.

Hansbrough turned in a spectacular 28-point, 13-rebound performance—his nineteenth double-double of the season. The 83-73 victory not only sent Carolina off to San Antonio, it set off wild parties from Charlotte to Chapel Hill.

The Tar Heels celebrated in earnest after they joined UCLA as the second team to qualify for the 2008 Final Four. It would be Sunday before they knew their opponent in the national semifinals the following weekend. It would either be the team they beat in an unexpectedly tough season opener five months earlier, Cinderella Davidson, or the last team in the world they would have chosen to play, the Kansas Jayhawks.

San Antonio, the southern Texas cow town famous as the home of Davey Crockett's last stand, might be the best site of all for the Final Four. The guaranteed great weather, the raucously fun Riverwalk, and the relatively good sight-lines for a football stadium at the Alamodome could make the city favored if the NCAA ever held a vote for where to permanently stage college basketball's crown jewel.

The Carolina contingent might give it a thunderous thumbs down, however. The Tar Heels were easily the best team in the field on their prior trip to San Antonio and endured one of the most embarrassing weekends in their glorious history. The dismal dome shooting that had plagued them twice in Indianapolis (1991 and 1997) and Seattle (1995) followed them to Texas in the 1998 national semis against third-seeded Utah. They fell way behind in the first few minutes and, despite an admirable comeback in the second half, went down to the Utes coached by the rotund Rick Majerus.

Ardent Carolina fans also remembered San Antonio from 2004, when Duke somehow blew the second semifinal to UConn in the last three minutes. Had the Blue Devils hung on, they would likely have cruised to their fourth national championship two nights later against a Georgia Tech team they had already beaten twice that season.

Roy Williams had his own bad memory of San Antonio, a 16-point drubbing at the hands of top-seeded Illinois in the 2001 Midwest Regional semifinals. That was when he was rebuilding Kansas into the team that reached consecutive Final Fours the next two years. This time, he was *playing* Kansas in a game he would never schedule.

Although the Kansas athletic director and much of his staff, plus the players and most of the people Williams worked with at KU, were all gone, the game remained a little too close for comfort. During Final Four week, Williams was peppered with questions about his fifteen seasons in Lawrence, beginning in Chapel Hill and escalating once the teams arrived in San Antonio.

In fact, the Kansas connection had become such a sideshow that Williams called Kansas coach Bill Self earlier in the week to see if they could agree to "handle this the right way." Self, who had first been hired as a graduate assistant by former Kansas coach Larry Brown, found a mixed Williams legacy when he returned after the 2003 season. Beloved by most, but blasted by some, Williams' emotional departure had almost torn apart the university and athletic department. The new athletic director, Lew Perkins, wanted to turn the page and, where he could, erase references of Williams from the Jayhawks' past—until he publicly entangled the

Carolina coach in an NCAA reprimand that KU received in 2005 for various minor violations.

Kansas had just missed the Final Four in Self's first season, but then suffered embarrassing first-round losses to Bucknell and Bradley the next two years. The rabid KU fan base had finally embraced Self after the Jayhawks survived Davidson for their first regional championship since Williams had left.

"I've always handled this the right way," Self responded to Williams' comment and cut the phone call short. Williams denied being concerned with the issue in public and tried to hide it from his team, but the whole Kansas scenario might have literally made him sick.

Williams caught the flu two days before the game and woke up on the morning of the Saturday semifinals feeling terrible. The shoot-around and team meetings went well, and Williams has since insisted that when his team left the locker room after the UCLA-Memphis semifinal he thought the Tar Heels would play great.

"We prepared exactly the same way we had for the ACC tournament and the first four NCAA games," he said later. "The team showed me so much confidence looking me in my eye . . . I was shocked we didn't play great."

Carolina had been ranked No. 1 for all but six weeks of the 2008 season and was favored to win the national championship, even though all the No. 1 seeds had reached the Final Four for the first time. Now, it was pretty much a crapshoot.

The Jayhawks were clearly more focused than the Tar Heels. Williams later characterized his team as "so excited to be there we were looking around when Kansas hit us in the mouth . . . like a boxer who gets hit and takes two or three rounds to clear his head."

Then, too, Carolina was mismatched for the first time all season by bigger, stronger forwards and guards. The hype that has always surrounded Carolina basketball hid the real truth this time—that the *favored* team was in over its head.

Four of KU's starters—Darrell Arthur, Darnell Jackson, Mario Chalmers, and Brandon Rush—were in the NBA a year later, and reserves Sherron Collins and Cole Aldrich were upcoming stars. The six combined for 73 points, 35 rebounds, 13 assists, 9 blocked shots, and 7 steals. Together, the ten Carolina players who made the stat sheet fell short in each category.

The game was lost early when Kansas leapfrogged its lead from 5 points to 13 before a media break and then all the way to 38-12 before Williams called a timeout with 7:32 left in the first half. Much has been made of the way Carolina cut the deficit to 17 at halftime and all the way down to 4 points midway through the second half. And, indeed, if Danny Green's long shot that went halfway in had stayed down the Tar Heels might have pulled off the greatest comeback in NCAA tournament history. However, they expended so much energy getting back into the game, they could not stop the next Kansas run.

"We'd played so well, sometimes you fail to see the other team is pretty damned good," Williams said. "The last month of the season, Kansas was playing better basketball than anybody, and I thought they were the best team. But people failed to give them the credit because of Roy Williams and his background."

Williams heard the charges that he felt guilty about beating Kansas after leaving there, causing the Tar Heels to come out with less than a killer instinct. "Biggest bunch of B.S. I've ever heard," he said.

Williams did allow that, for some reason he still can't explain, the Tar Heels ignored his weeklong instructions not to split double-teams by the Kansas guards or dribble more than once in the post because the Jayhawks were too quick and would take the ball away. "There were seven timeouts in the first half and we went over all that each time," Williams said. "They looked at me like I was speaking a foreign language, and all of those things we told them not to do, we did and they resulted in turnovers."

The eventual 84-66 loss tore up Williams and his team. After the season, he held individual and group meetings with his players and coaching staff to find out if anyone could tell him what happened. No one could, or would.

The reality was that if the Jayhawks felt anything from the Williams-KU controversy, it was that they wanted to whip Carolina's ass. By comparison, the Tar Heels were still very young—three sophomores and two juniors in the starting lineup and little bench strength behind Green. Several of them were eventually heading for the NBA, but not for another year.

Williams was still reeling from the loss when he decided to attend the championship game and cheer for his old Jayhawks against Memphis. Two of his former players were on the Kansas staff, and many more of his KU alums were there, some even with mixed emotions involving Williams. Now, with Carolina gone, they could all root together with a clear conscience.

Ryan Robertson, who played for Williams in 1996–1999, stopped and hugged his old coach as he walked to his seat in the Carolina section, and Robertson handed him a Jayhawks sticker. Thinking nothing about it, other than that if his team couldn't win the national championship he wanted Kansas to do it, Williams slapped it on his chest.

When the CBS cameras caught him wearing it during the game, all hell broke loose from San Antonio to Chapel Hill. Williams was even asked about it during a national television interview at halftime, and he said that, with the season over for everyone else, his heart was with the Jayhawks.

"I have nineteen former players at the game," Williams said later. "I'm supposed to look down there and see Jacques Vaughn cheering for Kansas, and I'm not supposed to cheer for them? I'm about people, not buildings. . . . I was doing what I was taught to do by Coach Smith, supporting my former players." Williams carried the bitter feelings from that controversy into the off-season and through the summer, responding to one question in the privacy of his office: Given what you now know about the reaction, would you put on that sticker again?

"I didn't plan it and didn't even think about it when they handed it to me," he said. "Now that I've had a chance to think about it, I'd wear twelve of those suckers the next time." When the official 2009 NCAA Men's Final Four record book came out, it included a picture of Williams wearing the Kansas sticker on page five.

All of Williams' players who explored the NBA came back the next season, and his 2009 Carolina team was an overwhelming preseason No. 1, a lock to secure Williams' twentieth consecutive NCAA tournament bid and leave him three short of the standing record shared by his mentor, Smith, and Lute Olson. That just added some anxiety to the excitement of Tyler Hansbrough's senior year in college. In fact, many UNC fans feared the pressure those expectations would create.

At least as important was the health of the Tar Heels, who began practice as the deepest team Williams had ever coached and perhaps one of the deepest in the history of college basketball. When, if ever in recent years, did the national player of the year return as a senior, and how often in this NBA one-and-done or two-and-through era are there two seniors and three juniors in the starting lineup of a top-five team?

Once Ellington, Lawson, and Green withdrew their names from the NBA draft list at the last minute, Williams called them in to make sure everyone was on the same page.

"If you are coming back to enhance your own situation, we have a problem," he told the talented trio. "You are back here to win basketball games, period."

The players were insulted and let their coach know it. Williams liked that and figured these guys would adopt the same philosophy as the leaders of his 2005 national champions: What was best for the team was also best for their chances to enter pro basketball as high draft choices. The idea worked nicely for Raymond Felton, Sean May, and Rashad McCants.

Lawson and Ellington were already stars on the rise. Also, Marcus Ginyard's off-season ankle surgery gave sixth-man Green an opportunity to become a star.

Before dunking over Paulus, Green was almost more famous for his pre-game dance routine at the Smith Center than for what he did on the court. His flirtation with the NBA might have been more for his father, a former physical education teacher who had been released after two years in jail on drug charges and was looking for a job. So Green's chance to share the spotlight seemed almost ordained.

Williams said that, all season, he felt the pressure of playing or practicing guys who might reinjure themselves and compromise the team's season, along with their pro careers. It was one pressure he never anticipated and certainly one that most other coaches would dismiss. After all, few have as much talent or resources as Williams and the Tar Heels.

However, pressure could have been Roy Williams' middle name from birth. Maybe the poor kid from the mountains of North Carolina still runs scared that he might lose his job or the security he has faithfully provided for his family. He has not only become a famous coach, making almost $3 million a year and on a first-name basis with pro athletes, entertainment artists, and bestselling authors, he is a cottage industry.

He has assisted collegiate careers for people he knew and trusted—from his old Asheville buddy, Jerry Green, to former high school coach Joe Holladay, who helped him during his ten years as a UNC assistant. Williams hired an aspiring head coach like Matt Doherty and rehired a veteran like Steve Robinson. He is a leader for his former players Jerod Haase and C. B. McGrath, capable aides in Chapel Hill whom he tries to help reach their life goals.

They have all hitched their wagons to Roy Williams' horse, and many more times than not have joined him in the winner's circle. Even after losing seven seniors and their top four scorers, the Tar Heels saddled up again with the highest-rated recruiting class in the country entering for the 2009–2010 season, UNC's one-hundredth anniversary of playing basketball.

By winning 70 games the prior two seasons, Carolina (1,984) climbed back to within four of Kentucky (1,988) in all-time victories and added two more names to the list of iconic characters that have helped make its basketball program famous over the last half-century—Frank McGuire, Lennie Rosenbluth, Dean Smith, Phil Ford, Michael Jordan, and now Tyler Hansbrough and Roy Williams.

Echoing Dean Smith and Frank McGuire during their days in Chapel Hill, Williams loves to say, "I am lucky to be the coach at North Carolina."

Like McGuire, the man who put Carolina basketball on the map and gave it panache, and Smith, whose brilliance, loyalty, and longevity took the Tar Heels to their greatest heights during thirty-six seasons, Roy Williams has joined their elite class of coaches. He has a formula that is tough to beat: a great recruiter at a perennial national basketball power, selling a fast break style of play that is showcased on television from late fall through early spring, all the while developing complete players who become first-round NBA draft picks. Also, seemingly, he does it every season.

In June 2009, he was profoundly saddened by the accidental cycling death of his close friend and former Kansas athletic director Bob Frederick, whose hiring gamble in 1988 gave Williams the chance that eventually allowed him to return to North Carolina as one of the most successful coaches in the history of college basketball.

Williams now presides over Carolina's Light Blue Reign of the last fifty years, his own ties to UNC reaching back more than half of that time. His one remaining great expectation rests only in this question: How long can he keep it going?

FOR THE RECORD

UNC Statistics Through 2009 Season

Carolina's Record Since 1953 (Frank McGuire's First Season)
- 1,352-420 (.763 winning percentage), 57 seasons

Carolina's Best 50 Seasons Since 1953
- 1,268-331 (.793 winning percentage)

Frank McGuire (1953–1961, Nine Seasons)
- Overall UNC record: 164-58 (.739 winning percentage)
- At home: 60-12 (.833)
- On road: 48-22 (.686)
- Neutral: 56-24 (.700)
- Vs. Clemson: 21-0
- Vs. Duke: 15-11
- Vs. Kentucky: 0-2
- Vs. Maryland: 12-6
- Vs. N.C. State: 14-11
- Vs. South Carolina: 15-2
- Vs. Virginia: 15-3
- Vs. Wake Forest: 16-7
- ACC regular-season championships: 5
- ACC tournament championships: 1
- NCAA Final Four berths: 1
- NCAA championships: 1

Dean Smith (1962–1997, 36 Seasons)
- Overall record: 879-254 (.776)
- At home: 323-45 (.878)
- On road: 216-116 (.651)
- Neutral: 340-93 (.785)
- Vs. Boston College: 2-1
- Vs. Clemson: 68-13
- Vs. Duke: 59-35
- Vs. Florida State: 20-5
- Vs. Georgia Tech: 40-13
- Vs. Kentucky: 13-3
- Vs. Maryland: 62-21
- Vs. Miami: 2-0
- Vs. N.C. State: 60-30
- Vs. South Carolina: 20-10
- Vs. Virginia: 66-18

- Vs. Virginia Tech: 15-2
- Vs. Wake Forest: 66-28
- ACC regular-season championships: 17
- ACC tournament championships: 13
- NCAA Final Four berths: 11
- NCAA championships: 2

Bill Guthridge (1998–2000, Three Seasons)

- Overall record: 80-28 (.741)
- At home: 31-8 (.795)
- On road: 21-12 (.636)
- Neutral: 28-8 (.778)
- Vs. Clemson: 5-1
- Vs. Duke: 2-6
- Vs. Florida State: 5-1
- Vs. Georgia Tech: 6-1
- Vs. Maryland: 4-4
- Vs. Miami: 1-0
- Vs. N.C. State: 6-1
- Vs. Virginia: 4-2
- Vs. Virginia Tech: 1-0
- Vs. Wake Forest: 5-2
- ACC regular-season championships: 0
- ACC tournament championships: 1
- NCAA Final Four berths: 2
- NCAA championships: 0

Matt Doherty (2001–2003, Three Seasons)

- Overall UNC record: 53-43 (.552)
- At home: 31-16 (.656)
- On road: 12-21 (.364)
- Neutral: 10-6 (.625)
- Vs. Clemson: 5-2
- Vs. Duke: 2-7
- Vs. Florida State: 5-1
- Vs. Georgia Tech: 5-2
- Vs. Kentucky: 0-3
- Vs. Maryland: 3-4
- Vs. Miami: 1-1
- Vs. N.C. State: 2-4
- Vs. Virginia: 2-4
- Vs. Wake Forest: 2-4
- ACC regular-season championships: 1
- ACC tournament championships: 0
- NCAA Final Four berths: 0
- NCAA championships: 0

Roy Williams (2004–2009, Six Seasons)

- Overall UNC record: 176-37 (.826)
- At home: 84-10 (.894)
- On road: 47-17 (.734)
- Neutral: 45-10
- Vs. Boston College: 4-3
- Vs. Clemson: 10-1
- Vs. Duke: 7-5
- Vs. Florida State: 10-2
- Vs. Georgia Tech: 6-4
- Vs. Kentucky: 5-1
- Vs. Maryland: 6-4
- Vs. Miami: 7-1
- Vs. N.C. State: 12-1
- Vs. Virginia: 9-2
- Vs. Virginia Tech: 6-2
- Vs. Wake Forest: 5-3
- ACC regular-season

championships: 4
- NCAA Final Four berths: 3
- NCAA championships: 2

Top Five in All-Time Victories
- Kentucky: 1,988-635-1
- North Carolina: 1,984-703
- Kansas: 1,970-793
- Duke: 1,876-815
- Syracuse: 1,753-806

North Carolina All-Time Statistics

Team
- NCAA championships: 5
- NCAA Final Four appearances: 18 (record)
- NCAA tournament appearances: 41
- NCAA tournament victories: 102 (record)
- National titles before NCAA

tournament began: 1 (1924, Helms Foundation)
- ACC tournament championships: 17
- ACC regular-season championships: 27
- ACC regular-season record: 575-226 (.718)
- Southern Conference tournament championships: 8
- Southern Conference regular-season championships: 9
- Records in national championship seasons
- 1924: 26-0
- 1957: 32-0
- 1982: 32-2
- 1993: 34-4
- 2005: 33-4
- 2009: 34-4
- Career record of 2009 senior class: 124-22 (.849); a school record for victories by a class

Individual Career Leaders

Most Points

PLAYER	YEARS	TOTAL	AVG.
Tyler Hansbrough	2005–09	2,872*	20.2
Phil Ford	1974–78	2,290	18.6
Sam Perkins	1980–84	2,145	15.9
Lennie Rosenbluth	1954–57	2,045	26.9**

*ACC record
**Highest career average

Most Rebounds

| Tyler Hansbrough | 2005–09 | 1,219 | 8.6 |

Most Assists

| Ed Cota | 1996–00 | 1,030 | 7.5 |

Most Steals

| Derrick Phelps | 1990–94 | 247 | 1.9 |

Most Blocked Shots

| Brendan Haywood | 1997–01 | 304 | 2.2 |

Highest Field Goal Percentage

	YEARS	MADE-ATT.	PCT.
Brendan Haywood	1997–01	541-849	63.7

Highest Free Throw Percentage

| Shammond Williams | 1994–98 | 292-344 | 84.9 |

Highest Three-Point Percentage

| Hubert Davis | 1988–92 | 197-453 | 43.5 |

Coaches to Take Teams from Different Schools to the NCAA Championship Game

- Frank McGuire (St. John's, North Carolina)
- Larry Brown (UCLA, Kansas)
- Roy Williams, (Kansas, North Carolina)

INDEX

INDEX

INDEX

345

INDEX

Taylor, Fred, 194
T. C. Roberson High School (Asheville, N.C.), 45–46, 73–74
Teague, Jeff, 8
television, 115–16, 136, 202, 243–44, 297–301, 311. *See also* media
tennis, xxvi, xxvii, 70
Terrell, Betsy, xvi
Terrell, Simon, 269
Terrill, J. T., 94
Terry, Paul, 33–34, 38
Terry, Reyshawn, 324–25
Texas, University of, 58, 281
Texas A&M University, 87
Texas Tech University, 271, 316, 318
Thomas, Isiah, 211–12, 286
Thomas, Kay, xvi
Thompson, David, 49, 110, 194–97, 237
Thompson, Deon, 6, 321, 325
Thompson, Jack, 175
Thompson, John, 75, 213
Thorp, Holden, 326
ticket prices, 202, 308–9
Tin Can (Indoor Athletic Center), xxiv, xxviii, 48, 102, 112
Tobacco Road teams, 103, 117, 119, 146, 172, 176, 197
Toone, Bernard, 204
track and field, xxvi
Truman Harry S., 63
Tubbs, Billy, 244
Tudor, John, 215
Tulane University, 172
Tunney, Gene, xxv, 28
Turner, Booker, 212
Tuttle, Gerald, 233

UCLA. *See* California, University of, Los Angeles (UCLA)
UNC-TV, 101
United States Air Force Academy (Colorado), 70, 117, 135, 138–41
United States Military Academy (West Point), 71, 183
United States Naval Academy (Annapolis, Maryland), xxx, 59, 70, 94, 126, 148
USA Today (newspaper), 309
Utah, University of, 108, 275

Vacendak, Steve, 168
Valvano, Jim, 216, 306, 311
Vance, Dazzy, 52
Vanderbilt University, 171
Vandeweghe, Kiki, 240–41
Van Exel, Nick, 255–56
Vaughn, Jacques, 334

Vayda, Jerry, 97–98, 103–4
Verga, Bob, 168, 173
Vietnam War, 178, 185–86, 202
Villanova University, 13, 212, 217
Vincent, Sam, 287
Vine, Florence, 168, 199
Vine, Lou, 129, 168, 199
Virginia, University of, 99, 103, 167, 201, 211
Virginia Squires, 237
Virginia Tech University, 11
Vitale, Dick, 325

Wake Forest University, 8, 17, 20, 58, 98, 102–6, 108, 111–12, 114–16, 119–20, 122–26, 146–47, 159, 165–66, 169, 174, 182–83, 196, 199, 270–71, 318, 321
Walker, Solly, 87–89, 152
Wallace, Grady, 107, 125
Wallace, Jackie, 259
Wallace, Jonathan, 323
Wallace, Rasheed, 206, 259–61, 270–71, 282
Wall Street Journal (newspaper), 309
Walsh, Donnie, 159, 190–91, 201, 228, 231, 237, 250, 252, 262–63, 269
Walton, Bill, 21, 194
Walton, Travis, 15
Warren, Add, xxv
Watson, Tom, 251
Watts, Justin, 9
Waugh, Jerry, 65
Weathers, Virgil, xxvi
Weaver, Buck, 38
Webber, Chris, 258
Weber, Bruce, 75
Weblemoe, Linnea (Linnea Weblemoe Smith), 238
Weil, Randy, xvi
West, Jerry, 139
Western Kentucky University, 210
West Virginia, University of, 139
Whicker, Mark, 306
Whisnant, Red, xxv
White, William Allen, 35
Whitehead, Burgess, xxvii
Whitehead, Jerome, 202
"White Phantoms," xxiv
Whitfield, Fred, 288
Whittenburg, Dereck, 214–15
Wichita State University, 245
Wiggins, Ernie, 116, 124
Wilkinson, Bud, 19
William D. Carmichael Jr. Auditorium, 48, 171–72, 178, 190, 210
William & Mary University, 171

INDEX